North Korea Policy

North Korea is regarded as one of the major destabilizing factors in the Asia–Pacific region. The centrality of North Korea has been particularly emphasized by the country's suspected development of nuclear weapons and missiles, and its abduction of Japanese citizens. This comprehensive book analyses North Korea policy coordination in the context of great-power relations in North East Asia, focusing specifically on Japan's policy formation towards the country. It also considers 'the Japan factor' in the policies of South Korea, the USA, China, Russia and the EU; focuses on Japanese participation in multilateral forums; and looks at Pyongyang's images of its neighbouring states.

Drawing on perspectives on the interaction over North Korea from a leading team of international scholars, *North Korea Policy* explores issues that are highly relevant to contemporary Japanese foreign policy, clarifying what is happening in the region right now and charting what policy options are available for the future. Providing a more complete understanding of regional dynamics, this multifaceted approach will appeal to policy makers and scholars of Asian foreign policy and international relations.

Linus Hagström is Research Fellow at the Swedish Institute of International Affairs, Sweden.

Marie Söderberg is Associate Professor at the European Institute of Japanese Studies at Stockholm School of Economics, Sweden.

European Institute of Japanese Studies, East Asian Economics & Business Series

Edited by Marie Söderberg
Stockholm School of Economics, Sweden

THE EUROPEAN INSTITUTE OF
JAPANESE STUDIES
STOCKHOLM SCHOOL OF ECONOMICS

This series presents cutting-edge research on recent developments in business and economics in East Asia. National, regional and international perspectives are employed to examine this dynamic and fast-moving area.

North Korea Policy

Japan and the great powers

**Edited by Linus Hagström
and Marie Söderberg**

Routledge
Taylor & Francis Group

LONDON AND NEW YORK

THE EUROPEAN INSTITUTE OF
JAPANESE STUDIES
STOCKHOLM SCHOOL OF ECONOMICS

First published 2006
by Routledge
2 Park Square, Milton Park, Abingdon, Oxon OX14 4RN

Simultaneously published in the USA and Canada
by Routledge
270 Madison Ave, New York, NY 10016

Routledge is an imprint of the Taylor & Francis Group, an informa business

Transferred to Digital Printing 2009

© 2006 Linus Hagström and Marie Söderberg for selection and editorial matter; individual chapters, their contributions

Typeset in Times New Roman by Keyword Group Ltd

British Library Cataloguing in Publication Data
A catalogue record for this book is available from the British Library

Library of Congress Cataloging in Publication Data
A catalogue record for this book has been requested

ISBN10: 0-415-39916-5 (hbk)
ISBN10: 0-415-54690-7 (pbk)
ISBN10: 0-203-96665-1 (ebk)

ISBN13: 978-0-415-39916-6 (hbk)
ISBN13: 978-0-415-54690-4 (pbk)
ISBN13: 978-0-203-96665-5 (ebk)

Contents

Tables, box and figures

Contributors

Dr Tsuneo Akaha is a Professor and Director at the Center for East Asian Studies at the Monterey Institute of International Studies. He specializes in Japanese foreign and security policy, international relations of the Asia–Pacific, international political economy and international marine affairs. Akaha is the author of *Japan in Global Ocean Politics* (University of Hawaii Press, 1985) and numerous journal articles. He is also the editor/co-editor of several books, among others *The Future of North Korea* (Routledge, 2002).

Dr Rüdiger Frank is currently Professor of East Asian Political Economy at the University of Vienna. He has held teaching and research positions in Berlin, in Duisberg, at Columbia University and at Korea University. Frank specializes in economic and security issues surrounding the Korean Peninsula and is the author or co-author of six monographs and over 50 book chapters and articles.

Dr Linus Hagström is a Research Fellow at the Swedish Institute of International Affairs. His research interests include power analysis, foreign policy analysis, Japanese foreign and domestic policy, and international relations in North-East Asia. Hagström is the author of *Japan's China Policy: A Relational Power Analysis* (Routledge, 2005) and has recently contributed articles to the *European Journal of International Relations*, *The Pacific Review* and the *Japanese Journal of Political Science*.

Dr Christopher W. Hughes is a Senior Research Fellow and Deputy Director at the Centre for the Study of Globalization and Regionalization, University of Warwick. He is the author of *Japan's Economic Power and Security: Japan and North Korea* (Routledge, 1999), *Japan's Security Agenda: The Search for Regional Stability* (Lynne Rienner, 2004) and *Japan's Re-emergence as a 'Normal' Military Power* (OUP/International Institute for Security Studies, 2004), and co-author of *Japan's International Relations: Politics, Economics and Security* (Routledge, 2005). He is joint editor of *The Pacific Review*.

Dr Balbina Y. Hwang is a Visiting Lecturer at Georgetown University and senior policy analyst for North-East Asia in the Asian Studies Center of the Heritage Foundation. She has received several writing awards, including from the International Studies Association and the National Capital Area Political Science Association. Her recent work is published in the *Journal of International Security Affairs* and the *Korea Observer* as well as in several edited volumes.

Dr Han S. Park is a Professor of International Affairs and Director of the Center for the Study of Global Issues (GLOBIS) at the University of Georgia. Park's research interests include human rights, sustainable development and East Asian politics. Included in his extensive list of publications are *Human Needs and Political Development* (Shenkman Books, 1984), *China and North Korea* (co-authored, Asian Research Service, Hong Kong, 1990), *North Korea: Ideology, Politics, Economy* (edited, Prentice Hall, 1996), and *North Korea: The Politics of Unconventional Wisdom* (Lynne Rienner, 2002).

Dr Yoichiro Sato is an Associate Professor at the Asia–Pacific Center for Security Studies (Honolulu, Hawaii) and an expert in Japanese foreign policy. His major works include *Japanese Foreign Policy in Asia and the Pacific* (co-edited with Akitoshi Miyashita, Palgrave/Macmillan, 2001), *Growth and Governance in Asia* (editor, Asia–Pacific Centre for Security Studies, 2004) and *Japan in a Dynamic Asia* (co-edited with Satu Limaye, Rowman & Littlefield, forthcoming).

Dr Marie Söderberg is an Associate Professor at the European Institute of Japanese Studies. Her research interests include Japanese domestic politics, foreign policy, development assistance and relations in North-East Asia. She is the author of *Japan's Military Export Policy* (Stockholm University, Institute of Oriental Languages, 1986) and a contributing editor to *The Business of Japanese Foreign Aid* (Routledge, 1996), *Japanese Influence and Presence in Asia* (with Ian Reader, Curzon Press, 2000) and *Chinese–Japanese Relations in the Twenty-first Century* (Routledge, 2002).

Dr Quansheng Zhao is a Professor, Division Director, and Co-Chair of the American University's Council on Comparative Studies. He is also Associate-in-Research at the Fairbank Center for East Asian Research of Harvard University. A specialist in comparative politics and international relations in East Asia, Zhao is the author of *Interpreting Chinese Foreign Policy* (Oxford University Press, 1996) and *Japanese Policymaking* (Oxford University Press/Praeger, 1993). He also edited *Future Trends in East Asian International Relations* (Frank Cass, 2002).

Dr Alexander Zhebin is the Director of the Center for Korean Studies (CKS) at the Institute of Far Eastern Studies (IFES), Russian Academy of Sciences. Zhebin has been TASS News Agency Bureau Chief in Pyongyang (1978–9, 1983–90), senior researcher at the IFES (1992–8), and senior diplomat at the Russian Embassy in North Korea (1998–2001). His works include *Pyongyang, Seoul, Then Moscow* (Seoul, Ton'a Ilbosa, 1991, in Korean) and *Lustre and Misery of Kim's Empire* (Tokyo, Bungei Shunju, 1992, in Japanese).

Preface

Everyone with an interest in North-East Asia closely follows what course North Korea is taking. Japanese policy makers and public have been particularly concerned not only about the possibility that Pyongyang has developed nuclear weapons, but also about its missile development and the revelation that North Korean agents kidnapped a number of Japanese citizens in the 1970s and 1980s – developments which have been cited in attempts to expand Japan's military capability and roles. North Korea policy could therefore be seen as an appropriate case study to evaluate the relative power or influence of Japanese foreign policy vis-à-vis that of other regional actors.

This is why on 17–19 March 2005 the European Institute of Japanese Studies and the Swedish Institute of International Affairs joined forces to organize a cross-disciplinary international workshop on the theme of 'Japan, East Asia and the Formation of North Korea Policy'. Out of dozens of applicants, 15 scholars from Europe, Asia and North America were invited to present their research. This volume is based on a selection of the papers presented in Stockholm, but they have been thoroughly revised and updated to incorporate comments as well as the most recent developments.

We would like to take this opportunity to acknowledge the generous funding from the Japan Foundation and the Swedish School of Advanced Asia Pacific Studies. Our thanks, moreover, go to all workshop participants and the contributors to this volume in particular, as well as to the four external reviewers for very useful comments. We are also very grateful to the Japanese ambassador to Sweden, H. E. Mr Seiichiro Otsuka, who was kind enough to give a keynote address, and to Dr Hans Blix, former director general of the International Atomic Energy Agency (IAEA), who gracefully shared his experience from North Korea with the workshop participants. We would like to thank Kazune Funato, Linda Karelid and Marie Tsujita for various kinds of administrative support, and finally Eve Johansson for superb proofreading.

Linus Hagström
Swedish Institute of International Affairs
Marie Söderberg
European Institute of Japanese Studies

Acronyms and abbreviations

ACSA	Acquisition and Cross-Servicing Agreement
APEC	Asia–Pacific Economic Forum
ARF	ASEAN Regional Forum
ASEAN	Association of Southeast Asian Nations
BMD	Ballistic missile defence
CVID	Complete, verifiable and irreversible dismantlement
DPRK	Democratic People's Republic of Korea
ECHO	European Community Humanitarian Office
EU	European Union
EUR	Euro
G7	Group of Seven industrialized countries
G8	Group of Eight industrialized countries
GSDF	(Japanese) Ground Self-Defense Forces
HEU	Highly enriched uranium
IAEA	International Atomic Energy Agency
JPY	Japanese yen
KEDO	Korean Peninsula Energy Development Organization
LDP	Liberal Democratic Party (Japan)
LWR	Light-water reactor
MSDF	(Japanese) Maritime Self-Defence Forces
NATO	North Atlantic Treaty Organization
NGO	Non-governmental organization
NPT	Non-proliferation Treaty (Treaty on the Non-proliferation of Nuclear Weapons) (1968)
NSA	Nuclear Safeguards Agreement
OSCE	Organization for Co-operation and Security in Europe
PRC	People's Republic of China
PSI	Proliferation Security Initiative
ROK	Republic of Korea
SDF	(Japanese) Self-Defence Forces
TCOG	Trilateral Coordination and Oversight Group
TMD	Theatre Missile Defense
TPP	Thermal power plant
UK	United Kingdom
UN	United Nations
USD	US dollar
WMD	Weapons of mass destruction

Note on names

Japanese words and names are transcribed using the so-called Hepburn system, but long vowel sounds are not marked. Japanese names are written in the Western fashion, with first name first and surname last. Chinese and Korean names, however, are written with surname first, only with the exception of quotations and when referring to people better known by their names in reverse, Western, order.

Introduction

Japan, the great powers, and the coordination of North Korea policy

Linus Hagström and Marie Söderberg

The primary aim of the book is to use North Korea policy as the subject for a case study to analyse Japanese foreign policy. Has the image of Japan as a curiously (or intelligibly) passive and reactive trading state remained an accurate one in the midst of the turbulent changes, both domestically and internationally, of recent years?[1] And how has the power or influence of Japanese foreign policy evolved relative to that of other important actors in the region during the last decade or so? These questions are examined by asking to what extent Japan was pursuing its North Korea policy autonomously of other involved actors in the early and mid-1990s and to what extent it is doing so in the early and mid-2000s. To what extent were those other regional actors exercising power over Japan in the early and mid-1990s – and to what extent and how was Japan exercising power over them – in the bilateral and multilateral interaction over such policy? Has the situation changed a decade or so later? The chapters of this book tackle these questions not only by examining Japan's North Korea policy (Chapter 1), but also by analysing 'the Japan factor' in the North Korea policy of other great powers (Chapters 3–7) and Japanese participation in multilateral forums (Chapter 8). North Korea (the Democratic People's Republic of Korea, DPRK) is treated here primarily as the focal point for coordination efforts between Japan and other major actors in North-East Asian politics. However, in order not to nurture and reproduce the historical tendency to objectify Korea more than necessary, the book also includes a chapter on North Korea's own policy orientations and images of its neighbouring states (Chapter 2).

While this book is primarily focused on Japanese foreign policy, an ancillary aim is to use North Korea policy as a case study to analyse the overall configuration of international relations in North-East Asia: how has the overall pattern of international behaviour in North-East Asia been affected by the end of the cold war, rapid globalization, and what international relations specialists would depict as a 'changing power structure' in the region?[2] With the long downturn of the Japanese economy, much mainstream scholarship on international affairs has certainly gone from 'Japan-bashing' to 'Japan-passing' and then to 'Japan nothing' – that is, from accusing the country of being a 'free rider'[3] to neglecting it in favour of the People's Republic of China (PRC, China),[4] and then to ignoring it altogether.[5] In general, Japan's role in international relations has been so underrated that one recent textbook devotes half a chapter just to explaining why Japan matters.[6] Yet is Japan nearly as insignificant as commonly believed?[7] The focus on China, by contrast, is growing increasingly intense. Although a politically more assertive Beijing is expected to appear, is China rising as quickly, and with such enormous consequences for the assertiveness of its foreign policy, as is believed or even feared? The US government and public debate, finally, is firmly concentrated on the developments in the Middle East, but as a global player it nonetheless retains interests and troops in North-East Asia. Yet, how decisive is the nature of the US regional engagement at this point in time?

Historically, the Korean Peninsula has been a victim of great-power rivalries. Korea's important geo-strategic position and its relative weakness compared with neighbouring great powers have always made the peninsula a tempting battleground for external powers. This is where the interests of China, Japan, Russia and the USA time and again have intersected and collided, often with dire consequences for the Koreans. The present governments of the same countries plus South Korea (the Republic of Korea, ROK) and to some extent policy makers within the European Union (EU) are all concerned about developments in North Korea. Although none of them miss an opportunity to emphasize the desirability of a nuclear-free North Korea, their interests are not completely interchangeable.

The Japanese government, for one, yielding to domestic opinion, often gives what is known as the 'abduction issue' (*rachi mondai*) precedence over the nuclear problem. As argued below, its North Korea policy is appropriate for a case study just because it is so crucial to Japan. The Japanese government has many reasons to be in command of its own policy towards North Korea, and it has many reasons to try to influence the North Korea policy of other actors. To what extent it succeeds roughly illuminates the regional dynamics of power, and therefore the power or influence of Japanese foreign policy, as conceptualized in this book.

Finally, given the protracted drama on the Korean Peninsula, North Korea policy research is also apt to be read as an interesting and even exciting case to study in itself.

Japan and the great powers

As a whole, this book seeks to answer the question how Japanese foreign policy is to be interpreted. However, why put special focus on Japan? Undoubtedly, most scholars would consider the USA a much more important player in North-East Asia – even the primary determinant of Japanese policy. China, moreover, is commonly seen as having succeeded Japan as the potential challenger and threat to US hegemony in East Asia.[8] The answer lies in the following paradox: just as the idea of Japanese insignificance in international affairs is becoming increasingly well established in International Relations (IR) discourse, Japan is also seen as re-emerging as a 'normal' military power.[9]

Japan's development after World War II has been nothing less than astonishing. The journey from military defeat to economic success took just some 20 years to accomplish. Yet many realist scholars have been rather more astonished by the fact that Japan for so long failed to fulfil the prophecy of their theory, namely that it would develop political and military power commensurate with its renowned economic capability.[10] The country has thus been called a 'structural anomaly',[11] and almost everyone, including non-realist and theoretically indifferent scholars, have tended to reproduce the idea of Japan as an 'economic giant' and 'political pygmy'. In the same vein, scholars of Japanese power or influence have concentrated mainly on economic factors such as foreign aid, investment, production networks and technology, or normative ones such as the provision of an economic model or economic leadership.[12] However, the image of Japan as an 'anomalous' or 'enigmatic' power has met with various kinds of criticism.

Most famously, there are two different arguments, both of which boil down to the idea that Japan is just following a different logic in international politics – one that might actually be a model for other states. On the one hand, liberals like Rosecrance emphasize that Japanese foreign policy behaviour is motivated by commercial interests rather than by security ones. The Yoshida Doctrine of 1954 left all military security concerns to the USA, for the sole reason that this would allow Japan to develop into a 'trading state', or, in Prime Minister Shigeru Yoshida's own terms, a 'merchant nation'. Against that background, Japan's supposedly one-sided possession of 'economic' or 'civilian' power is not anomalous at all – it is simply the result of economic rationality.[13] On the other hand, constructivists like Berger and Katzenstein consider Japan's post-war pacifist foreign policy to be a logical consequence of its national identity, historical experience, and domestic cultural, normative and institutional contexts. The gist of their argument is that after the war Japan established a distinctive, comprehensive and generally non-violent definition of security; it opted out of the violent world of realpolitik by institutionalizing anti-militarist culture and norms. Since such ideational factors be taken to transform very slowly – and since norms and identity are believed to infuse national interests with their content and meaning – constructivists predict little change in Japanese foreign policy.[14]

The constructivist approach in particular has become very popular, although a new generation of realists have responded that it underrates the impact of international influences in shaping Japanese post-war norms, institutions, and 'culture of anti-militarism'. Midford, for instance, insists that the non-conventional Japanese foreign policy stance should rather be understood as reassurance. He argues that the cold-war and post-cold war Japanese grand strategy reflects the fact that Tokyo has rationally recognized that 'normal' great-power behaviour could encourage a spiral of suspicion among its neighbours, producing counter-balancing and an arms race.[15] Lind, moreover, finds that post-war Japanese foreign policy is more consistent with a buck-passing strategy, that is, a rational response to the international environment whereby a state delegates its balancing behaviour to an ally, while itself developing only as much military capability as necessary.[16]

According to another, and completely different, perspective, the idea of Japan as an 'enigmatic power' is itself ambiguous as long as a property concept of power in terms of capability is applied, because for some time already Japan has not only possessed great 'economic' or 'civilian' capability; it has also developed exceptional military and political capabilities.[17] Japan's defence expenditure, for example, has been among the highest in the world for many years, and is presently ranked fourth in the world in US dollar (USD) terms at market exchange rates.[18] With the exception of offensive ground warfare capability, its military capability is likewise world-class in terms of both size and quality.[19] A fair assessment of Japan's military power in terms of capability also cannot be made without reference to the security alliance with the USA and the 'borrowed power' that it implies for the country.[20] On the political side, although it has yet to gain permanent representation on the United Nations Security Council, Japan has been elected a non-permanent member more frequently than other countries. It is also a member of the Group of Seven/Group of Eight industrialized countries (G7/G8) and has officials centrally placed in international and regional organizations, where, moreover, it often controls a large percentage of the votes. Scholars who define power in terms of capability should thus conclude that, in addition to being an 'economic power' or a 'civilian power', Japan is also a 'military power' and a 'political power', or simply that it has reached the rank of 'great power'. The reason why they do not do so is probably that the assumed connection between capability and outcome has been regarded as unclear in Japan's case. In brief, the country has not seemed to *use* its vast policy base as anticipated, that is by being preoccupied with security considerations and war-fighting.[21]

None of these approaches, however, can or even purports to explain the changes towards a more proactive and perhaps even assertive foreign policy position that Tokyo has allegedly been taking in recent years. In reality, not much is even reported about Japan in the international press, although considerable changes are taking place in the country's defence policy. Nor are these changes much discussed domestically. In September 2005, for instance, Prime Minister Junichiro Koizumi managed to secure a landslide victory in elections for the lower house of the Japanese Diet focusing the entire campaign on one single domestic issue, namely privatization of the postal service, without Japanese foreign and security policy even reaching the political agenda.[22]

Yet Japan has passed ten related national emergency bills that establish comprehensively – for the first time in the post-World War II period – how to respond to a direct attack; it has dispatched troops to the Indian Ocean and Iraq – entering hostile territory for the first time since World War II – and it has debated whether to revise the 'peace constitution', acquire a nuclear capability, cut its contributions to the UN unless it is elected a permanent member of the UN Security Council, and become a 'normal state' – symbolizing a country with military power commensurate with its economic strength. These developments are all evidence of a change of posture that is difficult to explain with the help of existing theories.[23] So is the fact that the New National Defense Program Guidelines for 2005 and After and the Midterm Defence Programme Fiscal Year 2005–2009[24] both talk about thorough restructuring of the Self-Defense Forces to enable them to respond effectively and proactively to new threats and contribute to international security. These moves, moreover, would have been considered unthinkable throughout the post-war period and even right after the end of the cold war. During the first Gulf War, for instance, the Japanese government dodged involvement by referring to its 'peace constitution'. The same constitution remains in place, but since the early 1990s attributes indicative of a more independent and proactive foreign policy have clearly started to line up. The question is: do they really represent a more independent, proactive, or even assertive Japanese foreign policy?

North Korea policy

To assess how the power or influence of Japanese foreign policy has evolved relative to that of other important actors in the region during the last decade or so, a case that involves the possibility of both bilateral and multilateral interaction between Japan and those actors must be selected. The coordination of North Korea policy presents exactly this kind of context. There are two further reasons why North Korea policy is selected as the subject for a case study.

First, North Korea figures very highly on the agenda of major actors in North-East Asia and it is regarded as one of the major destabilizing factors in the entire Asia–Pacific region, if not the world.[25] The Japanese government, for one, has long considered the suspected development of nuclear weapons by Pyongyang as a major threat to its own security, and a decade ago Mayer contended that if there were ever an issue with the potential to turn Japan into a 'military power', transcending mere capability, this would be it.[26]

The North Korean nuclear issue dates back to the early 1990s, but it was temporarily resolved in 1994 as a result of the Agreed Framework Between the United States of America and the Democratic People's Republic of Korea, through which the North Korean nuclear programme was frozen in return for crude oil supplies and the construction of two light-water reactors, provided by the Korean Peninsula Energy Development Organization (KEDO).[27] However, the North Korean nuclear threat re-emerged in 2002. In the autumn of 2002, a US delegation visited Pyongyang where it confronted the regime with the suspicion that it had begun a secret nuclear programme using highly enriched uranium (HEU). Such an HEU programme was believed to contradict the Agreed Framework, and the USA and its allies in KEDO (including Japan) retaliated by stopping all oil deliveries to North Korea. Pyongyang's next move was to declare the Agreed Framework dead, and to leave the Non-proliferation Treaty (NPT) and the Nuclear Safeguards Agreement (NSA) with the International Atomic Energy Agency (IAEA) in January 2003. The situation escalated as North Korea also restarted its old nuclear programme, and finally declared itself a nuclear weapons state in February 2005. As a result of the discord, in November 2005 the core members of KEDO decided to scrap the project and demand that North Korea return money disbursed to finance the stalled light-water reactor project.[28]

For the Japanese government and public, however, the North Korea threat involves more than the mere production of nuclear weapons. On the one hand, there is the North Korean development of medium- and long-range ballistic missiles. Japanese-North Korean relations between Japan and North Korea were aggravated by Pyongyang's successful test of a Nodong missile in May 1993. When it fired a Taepodong missile over Japanese territorial waters in August 1998 – or put a satellite in orbit, as it contends – the Japanese government's reaction was harsh. It responded by suspending its 1 billion USD contribution to KEDO. In addition, it stopped all its humanitarian aid, withdrew an offer to resume normalization talks, banned all chartered flights between the countries and allegedly agreed on further defence cooperation with South Korea. Since North Korean missiles were believed to be pointed at Japanese territory, Tokyo shifted to a position of increasing military containment of the North, primarily through its decision in August 1999 to begin joint research with Washington into ballistic missile defence (BMD) – a new defence system by which ballistic missiles can be shot down before they reach their target. On the other hand, there is the abduction issue – the long-suspected kidnapping of Japanese citizens from locations in Japan and Europe in the 1970s and 1980s.[29] Prior to the unprecedented meeting between Japanese Prime Minister Koizumi and North Korean leader Kim Jong-Il in Pyongyang in September 2002, Pyongyang denied all allegations, but at the summit meeting Kim suddenly admitted and apologized for 12 abductions and agreed to let five surviving abductees return to Japan. However, if Kim and Koizumi had calculated that Kim's revelation would put an end to the abduction issue, they were gravely mistaken, because it rather made the North Korean regime look even more evil in the eyes of the Japanese people. The Japanese public was enraged by the fact that more than half of the abductees were reported as dead and that the information revealed about their deaths seemed inaccurate.[30] The issue has since received almost hysterical treatment in the media.[31]

Second, North Korea has yet to be integrated with the world economy. Multinational companies are practically non-existent there and flows of goods and capital into and out of the country are insignificant. This situation provides a unique chance to isolate political initiatives from business ones. This possibility is especially important when analysing Japan's role, because business interests have at times been considered substantial in Japanese foreign policy.[32] In the case of North Korea there might be aspirations for closer economic ties in the future, but despite reports of Japanese business surveys having been conducted in the country no vital Japanese private business interests are at stake at the moment. From the North Korean side, however, there are great expectations of Japanese foreign aid, since it has been widely distributed elsewhere in Asia.[33] Hence, for scholars who believe that Japanese foreign policy behaviour is motivated by commercial interests rather than security ones, the North Korea case could give food for new thought.

To assess how the power or influence of Japanese foreign policy has evolved relative to that of other important actors in North-East Asia, two similar instances of international interaction in regard to North Korea should be compared. Using John Stuart Mill's 'method of difference',[34] two similar instances of international interaction stand out as appropriate objects of comparison: first, the international coordination process, roughly between 1993 and 1995, that resulted in the Agreed Framework and the setting up of KEDO; and, second, the present coordination process from 2002 onwards, since 2003 in the shape of Six-Party Talks, again centring on the suspicion that North Korea is developing nuclear weapons. The objects of comparison are similar to the extent that, apart from Tokyo and Pyongyang, they also involve the governments of China, Russia, South Korea and the USA, and to some extent even the EU – all of whom have coordinated with the Japanese government both bilaterally and multilaterally. Moreover, they converge to the extent that in both cases international concerns about the North Korean development of nuclear weapons intersected with bilateral talks with Japan on the normalization of diplomatic relations. Hence, they vary mainly with regard to the time context. They are separated by the decade during which change might have occurred in the power or influence of Japanese foreign policy as well as the overall pattern of international behaviour in North-East Asia.

The outline of this book

In Chapter 1, Tsuneo Akaha analyses Japanese North Korea policy, thereby laying the groundwork for the remainder of the volume. Throughout the cold war period, the improvement of relations with Pyongyang was last on the list of Tokyo's foreign policy priorities. The normalization talks in the early 1990s soon deadlocked and Tokyo was in no hurry to overcome the hurdles. The North Korean missile launch in August 1998, however, heightened the Japanese sense of vulnerability, and subsequent developments surrounding the North Korean nuclear weapons programme added to the urgency with which Tokyo developed a more pragmatic approach to North Korea, including efforts to normalize diplomatic relations. In the Pyongyang declaration of September 2002, the governments of North Korea and Japan made a number of concessions on outstanding bilateral issues. However, Kim's revelation on the abduction issue backfired and gave rise to strong anti-North Korea feelings in Japan. The nuclear issue also soon resurfaced, and Akaha examines the Six-Party Talks from a distinctly Japanese perspective and shows how they are linked with bilateral issues and hinder proposed unilateral Japanese sanctions against North Korea. According to Akaha, Tokyo has not been able to play any significant role in the talks in reducing differences between the United States on the one hand and China, Russia and South Korea on the other on the sequencing and timing of the moves necessary to resolve the nuclear issue. Nor has Japan demonstrated any willingness to forgo an immediate resolution of the abduction issue to enhance the probability of the multilateral talks succeeding in ending the nuclear crisis.

Although this book aims to analyse North Korea policy, North Korea itself is the topic of Chapter 2. The reason for this is obvious: all other countries' policies towards the country are likely to be based, at least partly, on an understanding of Pyongyang's own policy orientations as well as its specific policies and strategies towards them. Contrary to the picture popularly held of North Korea as a closed country which is difficult to understand, Han S. Park claims that the policy of the country is actually very logical and understandable if the state's goals – that is, regime security and system maintenance – are taken into consideration. Park shows how these goals form the basis for Pyongyang's interaction with the governments of neighbouring states, including those of China, Japan, South Korea and the United States. He argues, for instance, that Pyongyang has used its nuclear weapons programme effectively as a source of leverage to induce concessions from the other negotiating parties and to impose its own terms on the negotiations per se. Han also draws attention to the fact that Korea was colonized by Japan and that former North Korean leader Kim Il-Sung won popularity as a freedom fighter – circumstances which have been used to establish a state policy that is based on anti-Japanese sentiment, thus continuously affecting North Korean relations with Japan.

In Chapter 3, Balbina Y. Hwang shows that since the division of Korea – in particular in the post-cold war period – South Korea has been far more independent in its conduct of policies towards the North than conventional theories would predict, especially considering the fact that different great powers have historically played a significant role in determining the fate of Korea. Hwang argues that South Korea's foreign policy independence is due to the fact that norms of identity affect Seoul's response to external forces. She systematically reinterprets the history of Korean contacts with the outside world, and argues that in Korea (before its division, and afterwards in both the northern and the southern halves) there is a deeply embedded strategic culture of 'nationalistic survival'. In the ongoing negotiations for national reunification, for instance, both Korean governments have consistently emphasized that this agenda should be achieved only through the efforts of the Korean people and without outside meddling. In the same vein, Hwang concludes that since the liberation from Japanese occupation at the end of Word War II, Japan's role in South Korean policy towards the North has been negligible, and that Tokyo's inability to exercise independent influence on the Korean Peninsula is likely to continue because of the profound impact of strategic culture in the foreign policy formation of both Koreas.

In Chapter 4, Yoichiro Sato traces the evolution of the USA's North Korea policy. Despite the alleged unilateralist tendency of the present administration of President George W. Bush, Sato argues that the handling of the North Korean nuclear crisis reveals elements of multilateralism, tracing their roots in the USA's global strategic objectives. He then critically examines the US–Japan relationship, and discusses to what extent Japanese interests, for example in regard to the abduction issue, have played into US considerations in the policy coordination with its allies. He finds that changes in Japanese security policy, which have occurred as a result of the ongoing nuclear crises – for instance, the recent upgrading of Japan's military contribution to the bilateral security cooperation – may enhance the US ability to exercise a predominant influence over security matters in North-East Asia. The dispatch of Japan's Maritime Self-Defense Forces to the Indian Ocean and that of its Ground Self-Defense Forces to Iraq for humanitarian reconstruction missions both set important precedents, and were justified with reference to alliance management in the face of the immediate North Korean threat.

US security policy, which is presently undergoing major restructuring at the global level, has acquired greater flexibility through this recent development in Japan's military security policy. Sato concludes by summarizing key developments in US–Japanese military cooperation that may enable US–Japanese co-hegemony in the security arena at both the regional and the global levels.

In Chapter 5, Quansheng Zhao focuses on Beijing's role in the North Korean nuclear crisis. After dealing with problems related to North Korea in a rather passive fashion for a long time, over the past few years Beijing has gone through a major shift in its policy orientation and as a result has even started to act as the host of the highly publicized Six-Party Talks. Although Zhao notes that in the Beijing mindset Japan is second to the United States in importance, in his chapter he analyses Sino-Japanese coordination and the linkage between Beijing's policy towards Pyongyang and the ups and downs of the Beijing–Tokyo relationship. The governments of China and Japan are likely to cooperate when their national interests overlap but they also have different concerns over each of their own respective problems (such as the issue of North Korean refugees for Beijing, and the abduction issue for Tokyo) that may inhibit collaboration. Overall, Zhao argues that the governments of China and Japan have performed different functions in the Six-Party Talks because one is a rising power and the other is a declining one. The talks as such could, however, provide an effective mechanism not only for resolving the nuclear crisis, but also for Beijing and Tokyo to conduct a useful dialogue to resolve their own mutual differences.

In Chapter 6, Alexander Zhebin analyses Russia's interests on its Far Eastern borders. He finds that Moscow wants to preserve the denuclearized status of the Korean Peninsula and has an interest in participating in the development of peaceful cooperation in North-East Asia. From the outbreak of the second North Korean nuclear crisis, there was a tendency in Moscow to approach the situation as mainly a bilateral dispute between the USA and North Korea. Yet Zhebin finds that the Russian government has subsequently taken a rather active and independent position in the process of settling the problem and has stated that the new world order should be based on the broadest kind of multilateral cooperation. This would require serious efforts in harmonizing interests and working out a common strategy for dealing with international problems. According to Zhebin this is the approach used by the Russian government when cooperating with other countries, including Japan, in trying to resolve the North Korean nuclear problem. Japan, however, is the only country in East Asia that Russia was at war with during the last century, and Zhebin argues that the heritage of these old conflicts remains both in the bilateral relations and in the system of international relations in North-East Asia. This is one of the main obstacles to the development of Russo-Japanese political and economic cooperation in the area.

In Chapter 7, Rüdiger Frank argues that the EU's North Korea policy is difficult to conceptualize because the EU is not a single sovereign state. The combination of multilateralism and bilateralism makes the EU a unique case and offers interesting options that are not available to the other parties involved in the policy coordination, but it also limits the potential role that it can play. There are commonalities between the EU and Japan, including the fact that both are economic giants, yet, unlike the United States, their political influence lags behind their economic power. Both are civilian powers and together they account for approximately three-quarters of total funds available for development assistance worldwide (including the bilateral development assistance of the EU member states). Their respective interests in North Korea, however, are characterized by great diversity, both regarding scale and scope. The two actors are also differently perceived in North Korea; while Japanese colonialism is still not forgotten, a positive image of the EU has been created by the economically and psychologically significant support that East European countries – now members of the EU – rendered North Korea in the past. This has created a huge and up to now largely untapped resource of practical, long-term experience with aid and development assistance to North Korea. Frank concludes his chapter by noting that he finds no explicit traces of Japanese influence on the EU's North Korea policy or vice versa. With the dissolution of KEDO, moreover, the only official forum for concrete cooperation on North Korea between Japan and the EU has disappeared.

In the final chapter, Christopher W. Hughes takes issue with the current consensus concerning the significance of the Six-Party Talks and other multilateral approaches in addressing the North Korean security issue. On the basis of a rigorous conceptual framework for multilateralism, however, he takes a more sceptical view of the long-term value of the Six-Party Talks and other current varieties of multilateral frameworks, such as the Trilateral Coordination and Oversight Group (TCOG) and the Proliferation Security Initiative (PSI). Contrary to many other analysts he argues that the Six-Party Talks have hitherto largely served to strengthen the dominant US position in the region and to generate a particular form of hegemonic multilateralism, rather than giving rise to any new and lasting forms of multilateralism or new security architecture. In many cases it is possible to see the virtual death, largely under US direction, of other forms of multilateralism such as KEDO. This chapter also argues that Tokyo has played an implicit role in many of these developments because of its support for the US-inspired format of the Six-Party Talks and the prioritizing of its bilateral alliance with the USA to the detriment of its interests in other non-US inspired multilateral frameworks. Furthermore, the chapter questions whether multilateralism as presented in its current format is in fact the appropriate solution to the Korean Peninsula security issue. The overall conclusion is that a serious rethink of current multilateral approaches may be required, and that Tokyo and other governments need to apply themselves more strenuously to a range of frameworks for resolving the nuclear issue.

Japan and the great powers revisited

Comparing the present-day situation with that immediately after the end of the cold war, it is obvious that the pattern of relationships in North-East Asia has changed considerably. Although the first North Korean nuclear crisis (1993–4) evolved a few years after the end of the cold war, much of the old thinking still prevailed. As Tsuneo Akaha points out, the Japanese government was in no hurry to conduct normalization talks with Pyongyang. Going through secondary sources that analyse Japan's role in the first nuclear crisis, moreover, we find that Japan is largely absent in that literature,[35] or at least described as absent in the policy-making process and dependent on US leadership.[36] Japanese statements also acknowledge the limitations that its foreign policy labours under, stressing that 'Japan's hands were bound', and that the country 'had to follow the US to take any active steps'.[37]

In the early 1990s the Chinese government tended to mind its own business and did not intervene in the affairs of other sovereign states. As Quansheng Zhao points out, this stance has changed in the wake of the 11 September 2001 attacks on Washington and New York, after which China is now fulfilling the role of a partner in the US-led coalition against terror. The Chinese government has become much more proactive especially in Asia where, among other things, it is working on Asian community building. In the case of North Korea, Beijing is currently taking a leadership role, conducting shuttle diplomacy in trying to resolve the North Korean nuclear issue, as well as organizing the Six-Party Talks on behalf of the USA and other great powers in the area. This kind of behaviour would have been virtually unthinkable in the early 1990s.

During the Clinton administration in the USA, there was a clear policy of engagement with and integration of North Korea. With the Bush administration the US position has hardened and there is presently no interest in holding bilateral talks with North Korean representatives or in rewarding the country's 'bad behaviour'. In the Six-Party Talks at the end of 2005 there was eventually an agreement on 'commitment for commitment' and 'action for action', but the US government has taken the position that it is Pyongyang that should take the first step by scrapping its nuclear weapons programme. For Washington, developments in North-East Asia are presently overshadowed by the turmoil in Iraq.

The South Korean position has also changed considerably since the early 1990s with the normalization of diplomatic relations with both Beijing and Moscow, as well as with the establishment of the 'sunshine policy' and a number of concrete measures to engage North Korea. Balbina Hwang points out that in recent years Seoul has taken an increasingly independent position from Washington than Tokyo when it comes to dealing with North Korea. As stated in joint declarations between the two Korean governments, unification is seen as an issue to be resolved by the Korean people themselves without any intervention from the outside.

Moscow is aiming for a Korean Peninsula without nuclear weapons but since the end of the cold war has continuously taken a rather modest position, mostly just watching to see that there is no development unfavourable to Russian interests. Yet, although the Russian government was very little involved in the diplomacy during the first North Korean nuclear crisis, Alexander Zhebin emphasizes that it is now giving more priority to multilateral solutions. As a consequence Russian negotiators are thus participating in the Six-Party Talks.

The EU became engaged in resolving the first nuclear crisis as an executive member of KEDO from 1997 onwards, and although many of its member states have since established diplomatic relations with Pyongyang, and the enlarged EU actually contains many former allies of North Korea, the EU has been less visible during the second crisis. Although it officially takes a firm position on the nuclear issue, Brussels generally favours a policy of engagement over one of containment.

Most chapters of this book concur in the observation that Japan's military role has been expanded in recent years, implying a connection to the increasingly felt security threat from North Korea. The most important developments thus far include Tokyo's decision to proceed with the development of a missile defence system in cooperation with the United States, the passing of national emergency legislation, and the revision of the National Defense Program Guidelines. In the near future, moreover, the North Korean threat could well be used to muster support for revision of the 'peace constitution'.

This expansion of its military role notwithstanding, Japanese North Korea policy actually still seems to be characterized by the inertia of the first nuclear crisis. None of the authors of this book ascribe Japanese foreign policy any real importance in the context of North Korea policy coordination. Japan has 'arguably been the least influential factor in determining the course of the development of the contemporary crisis' (Akaha). The country's influence on North Korea policy has thus been 'surprisingly negligible and far less than traditional theories of power relations might predict' (Hwang). The Japanese 'inputs' into the US North Korea policy, for example, are 'limited mostly to coordinating their respective negotiating approaches and tactics, rather than working on major differences in policy objectives' (Sato), and Japanese participation in multilateral frameworks 'functioned largely to support US influence' (Hughes). Any Russo-Japanese cooperation on the Korean problem, moreover, is likely to be 'more limited than the cooperation between Moscow and the governments of other neighbouring countries' (Zhebin), and 'no explicit traces of Japanese influence' were found on the EU's policy-making process (Frank).

In sum, although North Korea is critically important to Japanese security, none of the chapters find that Tokyo exercises any influence in the North Korea policy coordination process with other actors. Even in the face of a lingering North Korean nuclear threat and despite the enhancement of Japan's military role, the 'Japan factor' still seems negligible.

Why has the policy coordination over the issue of North Korea not witnessed a more independent and proactive Japanese foreign policy? Many of the authors point to historical reasons. The memory of Japanese colonialization and aggression in the twentieth century is not only a driving factor behind the North Korean anti-foreign doctrine and the *Juche* idea of self-determination; it also taints Chinese, South Korean and even Russian impressions of Japan. The 'textbook issue' – the Japanese government's approval of school textbooks that do not include clear information about the Japanese atrocities before and during World War II – and Prime Minister Koizumi's frequent courtesy calls to the Yasukuni shrine, which enshrines the souls of Japanese war dead including

14 convicted Class A war criminals, contribute to deterring any improvement to the situation. So does the occasional eruption of lingering territorial disputes with the governments of China, South Korea and Russia. The Japanese government's lack of sensitivity in regard to these issues clearly creates ill feeling among its neighbours, affecting the bilateral relationships. According to several chapters of this book, Japanese leaders' seeming reluctance to confront their country's history also contributes to reducing Tokyo's role in the coordination of North Korea policy and other issues.

During the cold war and immediately afterwards, Japan was firmly in the Western (US) camp, which made it easy for Tokyo to differentiate between friends and foes, and enabled Japan to profit economically and build up its economic wealth. Since then relationships in North-East Asia have become much more complex and the Japanese government has not been able to build a strong independent position. Instead, Tokyo has drawn even closer to Washington, sharing an increasing number of responsibilities with its ally.

The chapters of this book also return to the topic that Japan has not succeeded in exercising influence independently in the North Korean nuclear crisis. Rather the contrary: the proactive character of US North Korea policy gives 'US allies such as Japan relatively limited manoeuvring room' (Sato). The continuation and strengthening of this asymmetrical relationship, however, 'broadens the USA's options at a time when its military is busy fighting insurgents in Iraq' and thereby plays into the US global strategy (Sato). It also reflects 'the functional role of Japan as the USA's junior partner in a rigid alliance system that was in part designed to limit the breadth and depth of Japanese foreign policy ambitions' (Hwang). The fact that Japan has continued to prioritize its bilateral alliance relationship with the USA, moreover, is allegedly detrimental for 'its interest in other non-US-inspired forms of multilateral frameworks' (Hughes), and several chapters of this book emphasize that other actors in North-East Asia are inclined to be sceptical about the strengthening of the US–Japan alliance, in particular the adoption of the BMD system. The strengthened alliance with the USA, however, has not helped Tokyo's ability to influence US North Korea policy. For instance, Washington has not been willing to take any action on specific Japanese interests, such as the abduction issue.

Many chapters actually allude to the importance of the abduction issue for understanding the Japanese lack of influence in the coordination of North Korea policy. According to one of them, 'Tokyo's North Korea policy has... been hijacked by the Japanese public's preoccupation with the issue of the abductions of Japanese citizens' (Hwang). Although Prime Minister Koizumi's bilateral summitry in 2002 and 2004 might have been intended to tackle this issue, 'in order to free up the domestic constraints on Japan's own diplomacy and rehabilitate it as a more unitary and consistent state actor in Korean Peninsula diplomacy' (Hughes), this design failed. Throughout the Six-Party Talks Japanese negotiators have repeatedly raised the abduction issue to please domestic opinion. This stance, however, has constricted Tokyo's ability to play a flexible and constructive role at the Six-Party Talks, and it is therefore fair to say that 'Japanese Korean policy itself has become a hostage of the abduction issue' (Zhebin). However, the stubborn Japanese stance on the abduction issue has not only limited the potential influence of Japanese foreign policy; it has also 'made an already difficult format even less likely to succeed' (Hughes).

The preceding paragraphs have highlighted different explanations as to why policy coordination over the issue of North Korea has not witnessed the emergence of a more independent and proactive Japanese foreign policy; yet in the end it is not certain that the evidence as summarized does attest unambiguously to the lack of power or influence of Japanese foreign policy. It is probably a fair observation that the abduction issue has prevented Tokyo from playing a constructive role in the coordination of North Korea policy, as well as in the Six-Party Talks; but, to the extent that Tokyo's insistence on the abduction issue has created obstacles for forward momentum in the Six-Party Talks, and this affects other actors in a way that is contrary to their interests,[38] the stubborn Japanese stance could be interpreted as a Japanese exercise of obstructive power. Without progress on the abduction issue, Tokyo has even indicated that it might take sanctions against North Korea. A unilateral move of that kind might further complicate Tokyo's policy coordination not only with Beijing, Moscow and Seoul, but perhaps even with Washington. Although Japanese foreign policy is almost universally known as being in US reins, its North Korea policy accommodates other examples of obstructionism too. For instance, many chapters of this book observe that the Koizumi–Kim summit of August 2002 ran completely counter to US ambitions.

Yet, in the end Japanese policy might not be capable of moving the US one. The North Korean nuclear issue is urgent for Japan but the USA is currently facing more important issues, such as the problems in Iraq. The closer the US–Japan relationship becomes, the more distant is the possibility of an independent Japanese role. This relationship also hinders the Japanese government from creating an independent platform for cooperation with its neighbours. To play a more constructive role in the multilateral North Korea policy coordination process in the future Japanese leaders would probably have to drop the abduction issue and proceed with normalization and economic aid.

Notes

1 For texts emphasizing the limits of Japanese foreign policy, see Kent Calder, 'Japanese foreign economic policy formation: Explaining the reactive state', *World Politics*, 40/4, 1988, pp. 517–41; Kenneth N. Waltz, 'The emerging structure of international politics', *International Security*, 18/2, 1993, pp. 44–79; Akitoshi Miyashita, *Limits to Power: Asymmetric Dependence and Japanese Foreign Aid Policy*, Lanham, Md., Boulder, Colo., New York and Oxford: Lexington Books, 2003. For books that provide an explanation of the limitations under which Japanese foreign policy labours, see Peter J. Katzenstein, *Cultural Norms and National Security: Police and Military in Postwar Japan*, Ithaca, NY and London: Cornell University Press, 1996; and Thomas U. Berger, *Cultures of Antimilitarism*, Baltimore, Md. and London: Johns Hopkins University Press, 1998.

2 For an analysis of this structural change, see Quansheng Zhao, 'The shift in power distribution and the change of major power relations', *Journal of Strategic Studies*, 24/4, December 2001, pp. 49–78.

3 E.g. Clyde V. Prestowitz, *Trading Places: How We Allowed Japan to Take the Lead*, New York: Basic Books, 1988.

4 Quansheng Zhao, 'The shift in power distribution and the change of major power relations', in Quangsheng Zhao (ed.), *Future Trends in East Asian International Relations*, London: Frank Cass, 2002.

5 This development of the Japan image is discussed in J. A. A. Stockwin, 'Why Japan still matters', *Japan Forum*, 15/3, 2003, pp. 345–60; see also Staffan Appelgren, Martin Flyxe, Linus Hagström and Pia Moberg (eds), *Does Japan Matter?*, Special issue of *NIASnytt: Asia Insights*, 1, 2005, available HTTP: <http://nias.ku.dk/nytt/2005_1/20051eALL.pdf> (accessed 6 March 2006).

6 Glenn D. Hook, Julie Gilson, Christopher W. Hughes and Hugo Dobson, *Japan's International Relations Politics, Economics and Security*, London and New York: Routledge, 2001, pp. 8–18.

7 Linus Hagström, 'The Dogma of Japanese insignificance: The academic discourse on North Korea policy coordination', paper submitted to *Pacific Affairs*, Special issue, Linus Hagström and Marie Söderberg (eds), *The Other Binary: Why Japan–North Korea Relations Matter*, under review.

8 On the debates on the rise of China and the possible threat it could pose, see e.g. Denny Roy, 'The "China threat" issue: Major arguments', *Asian Survey*, 36/8, August 1996, pp. 758–71; Herbert Yee and Ian Storey (eds), *The China Threat: Perceptions, Myths and Reality*, London and New York: Routledge, 2002; Byung-Joon Ahn, 'The rise of China and the future of East Asian integration', *Asia Pacific Review*, 11/2, November 2004, pp. 18–35; and David Shambaugh, 'China engages Asia: Reshaping the regional order', *International Security*, 29/3, winter 2004/2005, pp. 64–99.

9 Christopher W. Hughes, *Japan's Re-emergence as a 'Normal' Military Power*, Adelphi Paper 368-9, Oxford: Oxford University Press for the International Institute for Strategic Studies, London, 2004. The idea that Japan is 're-emerging' as a military power clearly refers back to Japan's past. However, it should not be taken to imply that the present authors consider that Japan is now emerging as the same imperialistic kind of military power it used to be.

10 Christopher Layne, 'The unipolar illusion: Why new great powers will rise', *International Security*, 17/4, 1993, pp. 5–51; and Waltz, 'The emerging structure'.

11 Waltz, 'The emerging structure', p. 66.

12 Alan Rix, *Japan's Foreign Aid Challenge, Policy Reform and Aid Leadership*, London and New York: Routledge, 1993; Walter Hatch and Kozo Yamamura, *Asia in Japan's Embrace*, Cambridge and New York: Cambridge University Press, 1996; Ming Wan, 'Spending strategies in world politics: How Japan has used its economic power in the past decade', *International Studies Quarterly*, 39/1, 1995, pp. 85–108; and Reinhard Drifte, *Japan's Foreign Policy for the Twenty-First Century: From Economic Superpower to what Power?*, London: Macmillan, 1998.

13 Richard Rosecrance, *The Rise of the Trading State: Commerce and Conquest in the Modern World*, New York: Basic Books, 1986; cf. Bill Emmott, 'The economic sources of Japan's foreign policy', *Survival*, 34/2, 1992, pp. 50–70.

14 Thomas U. Berger, 'Norms, identity, and national security in Germany and Japan', in Peter J. Katzenstein (ed.), *The Culture of National Security: Norms and Identities in World Politics*, New York: Columbia University Press, 1996, pp. 317–56; Katzenstein, *Cultural Norms and National Security*; and Thomas U. Berger, *Cultures of Antimilitarism*, Baltimore, Md. and London: Johns Hopkins University Press, 1998.

15 Paul Midford, 'The logic of reassurance and Japan's grand strategy', *Security Studies*, 11/3, 2002, pp. 1–43.
16 Jennifer M. Lind, 'Pacifism or passing the buck: Testing theories of Japanese security policy', *International Security*, 29/1, 2004, pp. 92–121.
17 Linus Hagström, *Japan's China Policy: A Relational Power Analysis*, London and New York: Routledge, 2005; and Linus Hagström, 'Relational power for foreign policy analysis: Issues in Japan's China policy', *European Journal of International Relations* 11/3, 2005, pp. 395–430.
18 See Stockholm International Peace Research Institute (SIPRI), 'The 15 major spenders in 2004', <http://www.sipri.org/contents/milap/milex/mex_major_spenders.pdf/download> (accessed 3 March 2006). The link between a country's military expenditure and its denomination, e.g. in terms of 'a power', may seem far-fetched, but defence expenditure is a common 'single-variable indicator of power'. See Richard L. Merritt, and Dina A. Zinnes, 'Alternative indexes of national power', in Richard J. Stoll and Michael D. Ward (eds), *Power in World Politics*, Boulder, Colo.: Lynne Rienner Publishers, 1989, p. 13.
19 Lind, 'Pacifism or passing the buck', pp. 93–101.
20 On 'borrowed power', see Olav F. Knudsen, *Anarki og fellesskap: En innføring i studiet av internasjonal politikk*, Oslo: TANO/Universitetsforlaget, 1994, p. 57.
21 This argument is pursued in Linus Hagström, 'Ubiquity of "power" and the advantage of terminological pluralism: Japan's foreign policy discourse', *Japanese Journal of Political Science*, 6/2, 2005, pp. 145–64.
22 Linus Hagström, 'Japans säkerhetspolitik i stöpsleven', *Internationella Studier*, 4, winter 2005, pp. 20–5; and Marie Söderberg, 'Japan's foreign and security policies', *NIASnytt: Asia Insights*, 1, 2006, pp. 13–14.
23 For discussions of this recent development in Japanese foreign and security policy, see Eugene A. Matthews, 'Japan's new nationalism', *Foreign Affairs*, 82/6, November/December 2003, pp. 74–90; Hughes, *Japan's Re-emergence*; Christopher W. Hughes, 'Japan's security policy, the US–Japan alliance, and the "war on terror": Incrementalism confirmed or radical leap?', *Australian Journal of International Affairs*, 58/4, 2004, pp. 427–45; and Gavan McCormack, 'Remilitarizing Japan', *New Left Review*, 29, Second Series, September/October 2004, pp. 29–45.
24 Fiscal year 2005 starts on 1 April in Japan. Unofficial translations of both the above-mentioned documents are available at <http://www.jda.go.jp/e/index_.htm> (accessed 6 March 2006).
25 E.g. Christopher W. Hughes, 'The North Korean nuclear crisis and Japanese security', *Survival*, 38/2, 1996, pp. 79–103; Jeremy D. Mayer, 'International relations theory and Japanese pacifism: Why didn't Tokyo go ballistic over North Korean nukes?', *Journal of Northeast Asian Studies*, 15/2, 1996, pp. 50–62; and *East Asian Strategic Review 2004*, Tokyo: National Institute for Defense Studies, 2004, pp. 6–27.
26 Mayer, 'International relations theory and Japanese pacifism'.
27 KEDO was founded on 15 March 1995 by the governments of the United States, South Korea and Japan to implement the Agreed Framework. KEDO's principal activity was to construct light-water reactor nuclear power plants in North Korea. Other members later joined the organization. The EU, for instance, became an Executive Board member in 1997.
28 *The Japan Times*, 25 November 2003, available HTTP: <http://search.japantimes.co.jp/cgi-bin/nn20051125b4.html> (accessed 26 March 2006).
29 Although only 15 are officially recognized by the Japanese government, as many as 70 Japanese citizens may have been abducted.
30 On the abduction issue, see Eric Johnston, 'The North Korea abduction issue and its effect on Japanese domestic politics', Japan Policy Research Institute (JPRI)

Working Paper no. 101, available HTTP: <http://www.jpri.org/publications/workingpapers/wp101.html> (accessed 6 March 2006).

31 Tessa Morris-Suzuki, 'The politics of hysteria: America's Iraq, Japan's North Korea', in *Japan in the World*, 13 February 2003, available HTTP: <http://www.iwanami.co.jp/jpworld/text/politicsofhysteria01.html> (accessed 6 March 2006); and Hyung Gu Lynn, 'Vicarious traumas: Television and media in Japan's-North Korea policy', paper submitted to *Pacific Affairs*, Special issue, Linus Hagström and Marie Söderberg (eds), *The Other Binary: Why Japan North Korea Relations Matter*, under review.

32 Sadako Ogata, 'The business community and Japanese foreign policy: Normalization of relations with the People's Republic of China', in Robert A. Scalapino (ed.), *The Foreign Policy of Modern Japan*, Berkeley, Calif., Los Angeles, Calif. and London: University of California Press, 1977, pp. 175–203; and Marie Söderberg (ed.), *The Business of Japanese Foreign Aid: Five Cases from Asia*, London and New York: Routledge, 1996.

33 Marie Söderberg, 'Can Japanese foreign aid to North Korea create peace and stability?', paper submitted to *Pacific Affairs*, Special issue, Hagström and Söderberg (eds), *The Other Binary*.

34 Stanley Lieberson, 'Small *N*'s and big conclusions: An examination of the reasoning in comparative studies based on a small number of cases', in Charles Ragin and Howard Becker (eds), *What Is a Case? Exploring the Foundations of Social Inquiry*, Cambridge: Cambridge University Press, 1992, pp. 105–18.

35 E.g. Leon V. Sigal, *Disarming Strangers: Nuclear Diplomacy with North Korea*, Princeton, NJ: Princeton University Press, 1998; Don Oberdorfer, *Two Koreas: A Contemporary History*, revised and updated edition, New York: Basic Books, 2001; and Leon V. Sigal, 'Nuclear diplomacy with North Korea', in Rudolf Avenhaus, Victor Kremenyuk and Gunnar Sjöstedt (eds), *Containing the Atom*, Lanham, Md., Boulder, Colo., New York and Oxford: Lexington Books, 2002.

36 Michael J. Mazarr, *North Korea and the Bomb: A Case Study in Nonproliferation*, Houndmills, Basingstoke and London: Macmillan, 1995, p. 186; M. Reiss, *Bridled Ambition: Why Countries Constrain their Nuclear Capabilities*, Washington, DC: Woodrow Wilson Center Press, 1995, p. 291; Tsuneo Akaha, 'Japanese security policy in post-cold war Asia', in Tae-Hwan Kwak and Edward A. Olsen (eds), *The Major Powers in Northeast Asia: Seeking Peace and Security*, Boulder, Colo.: Lynne Rienner Publishers, 1996, pp. 24–5; Hughes, 'The North Korean Nuclear Crisis', p. 95; Mayer, 'International relations theory and Japanese pacifism', p. 58; Christopher W. Hughes, *Japan's Economic Power and Security: Japan and North Korea*, London and New York: Routledge, 1999, p. 184; Michael H. Armacost and Kenneth B. Pyle, 'Japan and the unification of Korea: Challenges for US policy coordination', in Nicholas Eberstadt and Richard J. Ellings (eds), *Korea's Future and the Great Powers*, Seattle, Wash. and London: University of Washington Press, 2001, p. 136; C. S. Eliot Kang, 'North Korea and the US grand security strategy', *Comparative Strategy*, 20/1, 2001, p. 38; Tsuneo Akaha, 'Japan's policy toward North Korea: Interests and options', in Tsuneo Akaha (ed.), *The Future of North Korea*, London and New York: Routledge, 2002, pp. 77–80; Isa Ducke, *Status Power: Japanese Foreign Policy Making toward Korea*, London and New York: Routledge, 2002, p. 143; Myonwoo Lee, 'Japanese–North Korean relations: Going in circles', in Samuel S. Kim and Tai Hwan Lee (eds), *North Korea and Northeast Asia*, Lanham, Md., Boulder, Colo., New York and Oxford: Rowman & Littlefield, 2002, pp. 89, 102; Robert A. Manning, 'United States–North Korean relations: From welfare to workfare?', in Samuel S. Kim and Tai Hwan Lee (eds), *North Korea and Northeast Asia*, Lanham, Md., Boulder, Colo., New York and Oxford: Rowman & Littlefield, 2002, p. 67; Victor D. Cha and David C. Kang, *Nuclear North Korea: A Debate on Engagement Strategies*, New York: Columbia University Press, 2003, p. 147; and

Masao Okonogi, 'Dealing with the threat of a Korean crisis', *Japan Review of International Affairs*, 17/2, 2003, p. 75.

37 Isa Ducke, *Status Power*, p. 143; cf. David Fouse, 'Japan's post-cold war North Korea policy: Hedging toward autonomy?', Occasional Paper Series, Asia-Pacific Center for Security Studies, 2004, p. 12.

38 Cf. Steven Lukes, *Power: A Radical View*, rev. edn, London: Macmillan, 2005, pp. 30, 37.

1 Japan and the recurrent nuclear crisis

Tsuneo Akaha

Introduction

From the end of the nineteenth century to the middle of the twentieth century, the Korean Peninsula was the object as well as the battlefield of major-power rivalries, which often turned violent, and Japan was one of the central contenders in those conflicts. Until the mid-twentieth century, Japan held sway in the balance of power game in North-East Asia, militarily defeating China and Russia, seizing territories from them, and colonizing Korea and subjugating its people. Japan then plunged into the bloodiest war it had ever fought in the Pacific, suffering a devastating defeat in the end, and losing the territories it had gained through aggression and greed. After the defeat Japan made its mark by devoting itself to democratization and economic growth, and again shook the landscape of North-East Asia, but this time with its economic and technological prowess. The Korean War in 1950–3 did much to boost Japan's industrial development as the country supplied goods and services to the United States and South Korea, but Japan was both politically and militarily a non-factor in the 'hot' cold war on the Korean Peninsula. Gradually, however, Japan has expanded its military power within the framework of its bilateral alliance with the United States and has become one of the most capable military powers in the region. Nevertheless, in this new era, Japan has been reluctant to assert itself in the politics of the Korean Peninsula.

Another half-century later, the Korean Peninsula has again become a theatre of big-power jockeying for influence, this time over nuclear weapons development in North Korea (the Democratic People's Republic of Korea, DPRK). Unlike in the years before World War II, however, Japan has arguably been the least influential factor in determining the course of the development of the contemporary crisis. But has Japan been totally absent from the scene? Is it doomed to play second or even third fiddle to the other powers? Or are there signs that Japan is ready to play a major role in changing the course of events on the Korean Peninsula? More specifically, is Japan actively promoting change in the behaviour of the North Korean regime, expansion in North–South Korean ties, and improvement in major-power relations surrounding the Korean Peninsula? What contributions is Japan making to the resolution of this, one of the most difficult challenges facing the region's powers? Is Japan presenting any obstacles to solving the problem?

In order to answer these questions, one must analyse what interests the Japanese government is pursuing in its policy towards North Korea and what factors inform the way in which it pursues those interests. This chapter will address these questions. It will also explore Japan's options and what will be the best alternative if it is to contribute to the resolution of the nuclear crisis.

Japan's policy towards North Korea, from the cold war to the post-cold war context

The Japanese government's policy towards North Korea during the cold war was informed by five goals: (a) to maintain a stable and peaceful international environment favourable to its peace and prosperity, (b) to maintain a close alliance with the United States in the interests of its own security and of the peace and stability of the region, (c) to develop friendly relations with its regional neighbours, particularly the Republic of Korea (ROK, South Korea) and China, (d) to enhance its regional security role, and (e) to resolve bilateral issues with North Korea.[1] The first two goals were mutually compatible and reinforcing because of the centrality of the US–Japanese alliance and the US presence in the region to both Japan's peace and prosperity and the region's stability. Since the end of the cold war the bilateral alliance has become even more important, particularly with respect to its role in maintaining regional peace and security. The alliance with the United States remains pivotal in Tokyo's approach to the Korean Peninsula. The Japanese government has also taken steps to ensure that its policy towards North Korea does not harm Japan's bilateral interests with South Korea.[2]

The third goal, to develop friendly relations with its neighbours, was achieved with South Korea in 1965, with China in the 1970s, and with Russia after the end of the cold war. All these states now favour a peaceful, negotiated settlement of the problems with North Korea, as the following chapters will show.

With respect to the fourth goal, enhancing Japan's security role in the region, throughout the cold war period the country relied on the US 'nuclear umbrella' for deterrence against major military threats and concentrated on the development of strictly defensive military capabilities. The end of the cold war has allowed Japan to make substantial progress within the framework of its alliance with the United States. Most important in this context has been the formulation of the 1997 Guidelines for US–Japan Defense Cooperation, which clearly expanded Japan's security role beyond its immediate surroundings.[3] The two countries' concern over the instability of the Korean Peninsula, along with the uncertain relations between the People's Republic of China and Taiwan, provided an important rationale for the strengthening of the bilateral alliance and the expansion of Japan's regional security role.

Throughout the cold war and in the immediate post-cold war years, improvement of relations with Pyongyang was at the bottom of Tokyo's foreign policy priorities in North-East Asia. For many years after establishing diplomatic ties with South Korea in 1965, Japan did virtually nothing to improve its ties with

North Korea. As soon as Japan entered into talks to normalize its relations with North Korea, it ran into obstacles and, as will be discussed below, the government in Tokyo was in no hurry to overcome those hurdles. Japan's first major engagement with North Korea was its participation in the Korean Peninsula Energy Development Organization (KEDO) following the first North Korean nuclear crisis of 1993–4.

By the turn of the twenty-first century, however, North Korea had become an important, if not overwhelming, factor in Japan's security policy. The North Korean missile launch over Japan on 31 August 1998 had heightened Japan's sense of vulnerability. Subsequent developments surrounding North Korea's nuclear weapons programme made it more urgent for the Japanese government to develop a more pragmatic approach to North Korea, including efforts to normalize diplomatic relations with Pyongyang.

It was in this context that the government of Prime Minister Junichiro Koizumi launched a major diplomatic initiative to normalize its relations with the Kim Jong-Il regime in 2002. As will be seen below, however, normalizing relations with Pyongyang has proved a formidable task for Tokyo. The nuclear issue involves factors beyond Japan's control and demands a multilateral approach. The abduction issue is a bilateral issue over which the Japanese government has greater freedom of independent action, but public outcry in the country over this issue has been exploited by right-wing elements in Japan and has frustrated the normalization process.

In the 1990s the Japanese government preferred incremental, evolutionary changes in North Korea to other scenarios, such as a military confrontation between North and South Korea, a collapse of North Korea, or US military intervention. Tokyo supported US President Bill Clinton's selective engagement and South Korean President Kim Dae-Jung's 'sunshine policy' towards North Korea – policies that promised to induce a less bellicose behaviour on the part of North Korea. The Japanese government also believed that improvement in US and South Korean relations with North Korea would have a favourable impact on its own normalization agenda with North Korea. In addition, the government in Tokyo hoped that its rapprochement with Pyongyang would contribute to the opening up of North Korea and an improved regional environment. However, Pyongyang's strategy to drive a wedge between Washington, Seoul and Tokyo frustrated Japan's hopes. Moreover, the inauguration of George W. Bush as US president and his refusal to engage with Kim Jong-Il proved a major challenge in policy coordination between Washington, Seoul and Tokyo.

The 1994 nuclear crisis in North Korea directly threatened the Japanese government's overall goal of maintaining a stable and peaceful international environment. Fortunately for Japan, the Clinton administration responded to the crisis by engaging Pyongyang and producing the Agreed Framework. The United States led the creation of KEDO to implement the bilateral accord. Tokyo agreed to support the Agreed Framework and joined KEDO. South Korea's participation in KEDO was also in line with Tokyo's desire to maintain friendly relations with its neighbour.

The off-again-on-again nature of the talks between the two Koreas had long complicated Tokyo's own approach to Pyongyang. The resumption of high-level talks between Seoul and Pyongyang in December 1990 led to Tokyo's decision to begin normalization talks with Pyongyang, with state-to-state dialogue starting in January the following year. The Japanese government welcomed the simultaneous admission of North and South Korea into the United Nations in September 1991 and was encouraged by the North–South basic agreement and joint declaration on a nuclear-free Korean Peninsula in December. Rapprochement between South Korea and China in 1992 also promised an improving regional environment.

Tokyo's normalization talks with Pyongyang proved formidable. At the most fundamental level, the two sides had a number of legal and jurisdictional disagreements. First, the Japanese government wanted to establish that North Korea's jurisdiction did not extend beyond the 38th Parallel, whereas Pyongyang apparently feared that such an interpretation would justify the division of the Korean Peninsula. Second, Tokyo asserted that the 1910 treaty of annexation of Korea was legally concluded and was therefore a legitimate treaty, while Pyongyang insisted that it was null and void from the very beginning. Third, the Japanese government asserted that the 1951 San Francisco peace treaty was an important consideration in the restoration of diplomatic relations with Pyongyang, but Pyongyang rejected that assertion because it was not a party to the treaty. A more tangible issue related to North Korea's demand for compensation for Japan's colonial rule of the Korean Peninsula until 1945, war reparations and compensation, payment for the losses Japan caused North Korea by recognizing South Korea in 1965, and damages for what North Korea called Japan's complicity in the Korean War. The Japanese government rejected all these demands, and the normalization talks were suspended in 1992. Finally, in March 1995, Tokyo and Pyongyang agreed on the need to resume normalization talks without any preconditions. When talks at political party level resumed in 1997, however, the two sides stuck to their positions on the bilateral issues and government-level talks could not take place.

To make matters worse, on 31 August 1998 the North Korean regime launched a Taepodong missile over Japan, shocking the Japanese and awakening their sense of vulnerability. Tokyo quickly announced unilateral sanctions against Pyongyang. It suspended all chartered flights to Pyongyang, stopped humanitarian assistance to North Korea, froze its financial contributions to KEDO, and froze the normalization talks. Japan also agreed to cooperate with the United States on the research and development of a missile defence system. It was not until December 1999 that a Japanese delegation representing all major political parties visited Pyongyang. The two sides agreed on the need to resume normalization talks.[4] State-level talks resumed in April 2000 in Beijing, followed by another round in Tokyo in August 2000. Tokyo was encouraged by a visible improvement in North–South Korean relations, culminating in the summit meeting between President Kim Dae-Jung and Chairman Kim Jong-Il in June 2000.

At the normalization talks in Tokyo in August 2000, the North Korean side repeated its demand for Japanese apologies and reparations, while the Japanese side raised the issue of ten Japanese citizens believed to have been abducted by North Korean agents in the 1970s and 1980s. At the next round of talks in Beijing in October 2000, the Japanese side proposed a normalization formula similar to its reconciliation with South Korea, including economic assistance, but the North Korean side rejected the proposal.[5] The North Korean side did express appreciation for the Japanese decision to extend food aid to North Korea, but there was no progress on the abduction issue.

The first Koizumi–Kim summit

The inauguration of the administration of President George W. Bush in January 2001, the terrorist attacks in the United States on 11 September 2001, Bush's war on terrorism, and the new doctrine of pre-emptive attack on terrorists and 'rogue states', complicated Japan's policy towards North Korea.

It is not known what caused Kim Jong-Il to seek an opening with Japan in 2002, but the timing of the North Korean overtures would suggest that the decision was a response to the hardening of the US position, as well as the USA's preparation for war against the Taliban and Al Qaeda in Afghanistan in the wake of 11 September.[6]

Besides his fear of the United States, Kim Jong-Il might have had another reason for wanting to mend the relations with Japan, and that is the failure of North Korea's economy. The serious economic problem was the combined result of the loss of advantageous economic relations with other socialist states, the dire shortage of energy and resources, the deterioration of factory operation, the failure of the planned economy, and a series of natural disasters and food crises. The economic reforms that were launched after July 2001 saw the introduction of supply-and-demand principles, but the future of the reforms or their impact remained quite uncertain as the shortage of resources and hyperinflation resulting from the reforms could cause the collapse of the entire North Korean economy. The infusion of capital, technology and resources from Japan through bilateral normalization would be critically important for North Korea's survival.

Developments after 11 September heightened Japan's fear of the dreadful consequences if North Korea refused to give up the development of weapons of mass destruction. The United States and coalition forces destroyed the Taliban regime in Afghanistan in 2001 and then, in 2003, Saddam Hussein's regime in Iraq. In the wake of these developments, many in Japan and elsewhere speculated whether the next target might be North Korea. Since North Korea had already deployed Nodong missiles, the nuclear stalemate in North Korea presented a far more serious security threat to Japan than the earlier nuclear crisis in 1993–4.[7]

In Japan, the abduction issue had become very pressing. Prime Minister Koizumi stated that without progress on this issue Japan would not enter into normalization talks with North Korea, and Pyongyang responded by showing willingness to take action. On 30 August 2002, Koizumi announced that he would meet Kim Jong-Il in Pyongyang in September. Tokyo had officially informed Washington of the planned summit on 28 August. Evidently Washington was not pleased with Tokyo's plan to hold a summit meeting with Pyongyang when evidence was mounting that North Korea might be developing nuclear weapons.[8]

The Japanese and North Korean leaders met on 17 September 2002. The historic summit produced the Pyongyang Declaration, which stated that the two sides agreed to resume normalization talks in October 2002. The Japanese side apologized for the damage and suffering its colonial rule of Korea had inflicted upon the Korean people and agreed that upon restoration of diplomatic ties Japan would extend economic assistance to North Korea. The two sides agreed to 'waive all their property claims and those of their nationals that had arisen from causes which occurred before 15 August 1945'. They also agreed to discuss the status of Korean residents in Japan and the issue of cultural property through normalization talks. They concurred that the two countries would comply with international law and would not engage in conduct 'that would threaten the other side'. Pyongyang confirmed that with regard to the 'outstanding issues of concern related to the lives and security of Japanese citizens' – a reference to the abduction issue – it would take appropriate measures to prevent the recurrence of 'these regrettable incidents' that took place 'under the abnormal relations between the two countries'.[9] To the surprise of the Japanese side, Kim Jong-Il personally admitted and apologized for the North Korean kidnapping of Japanese citizens.

The Pyongyang Declaration stated further that the two sides would cooperate in maintaining and strengthening the peace and stability of North-East Asia, and confirmed the 'importance of establishing cooperative relationships based upon mutual trust among countries concerned in this region' and the importance of building a framework for confidence-building among the regional powers as part of the process of normalizing relations among the countries of the region. The two sides also agreed that 'for an overall resolution of the nuclear issues on the Korean Peninsula, they would comply with all related international agreements', and affirmed 'the necessity of resolving security problems including nuclear and missile issues by promoting dialogues among countries concerned'. Pyongyang stated that it would extend the moratorium on missile launching beyond 2003. Moreover, they agreed to consult each other on security issues.[10] The Japanese also told the North Korean side that it was important for North–South Korean dialogue to move forward and for US–North Korean discussions to reopen.[11]

With respect to the other issues in the Pyongyang Declaration, Japanese analysts welcomed the declaration as an important diplomatic achievement for Japan. A long-term observer of Korean affairs commented approvingly that at the Pyongyang summit Japanese diplomacy had exhibited an unusual degree of independence from the United States.[12] Another academic echoed the same sentiment and stated that the Pyongyang Declaration was an 'epoch-making' document in that it represented Japan's 'first step toward "a new Northeast Asian" regionalism, after 57 years of hiding behind the bilateral relations with the United States since the miserable failure of its "Greater East Asia Co-prosperity

Sphere" scheme'.[13] Another observer of Japan–Korea relations praised the Koizumi government and stated that the declaration opened up a possibility of multilateral talks on the Korean Peninsula. He noted that the document emphasized the importance of solving the nuclear, missile, and other security problems through multilateral dialogues involving North-East Asian countries.[14] A defence analyst concurred and wrote that Japan had succeeded in obtaining North Korea's acknowledgement of the need to develop a multilateral framework for confidence-building and dialogue for peace and stability in the region.[15]

Just when Japan and North Korea were about to enter a new chapter in their relationship, however, the abduction issue quickly moved to the top of Tokyo's agenda towards Pyongyang. Pyongyang revealed that 13 Japanese nationals had been taken from Japan and eight of them had died in North Korea. Following the Pyongyang summit meeting, North Korea announced that the five surviving Japanese abductees would be allowed temporarily to return to Japan. On 15 October the five individuals returned to Japan to a thunderous welcome. At first it was reported that they would stay in Japan for two weeks, but their families and some politicians pressed for their permanent resettlement in Japan. On 24 October the Japanese government announced that the repatriated Japanese could resettle permanently. Pyongyang accused Tokyo of reneging on the agreement to return the former abductees after a brief visit to Japan. The Japanese public was angered by the revelation of the death of eight Japanese abductees and North Korea's less-than-full accounting of the circumstances of their demise.

The second summit

After almost 20 months of suspended negotiations, Prime Minister Koizumi once again visited Pyongyang on 22 May 2004. This visit did not necessarily have new goals, and from the Japanese government's perspective it did not produce nearly as much as the first one.

At the summit, Koizumi and Kim reaffirmed the Pyongyang Declaration. The Japanese prime minister announced his government's plan to extend 250,000 tons of food aid and 10 million US dollars (USD) in pharmaceutical supplies as humanitarian aid through international organizations. The North Korean leader stated that North Korea would maintain a moratorium on missile tests. Kim also stated that North Korea's ultimate goal was the denuclearization of the Korean Peninsula and that his government would work through the Six-Party Talks towards a peaceful resolution of the nuclear issue.[16] The most visible gain from the second summit was the return of the family members of two Japanese abductees who had been repatriated in October 2002. The domestic reaction to the summit was mixed, with the mass media lamenting that the prime minister had paid too high a price for little in return on the nuclear, missile and abduction issues, but a majority of the public praising their leader for bringing home the family members.[17] The American husband and two daughters of a repatriated Japanese abductee, Hitomi Soga, decided to stay behind in Pyongyang for fear that the American, Charles Robert Jenkins, could be extradited and court-martialled by the United States for having deserted the US Army in 1965, ending up in Pyongyang. The three were later reunited with Mrs Soga and now live in Japan.

Conscious of the forthcoming US presidential election in November, North Korea appears to have focused strategically on the timing of the Kim–Koizumi summit, while Japan's diplomacy was affected by domestic political considerations, particularly the House of Councillors elections scheduled for July. In contrast to the first summit, the second meeting in Pyongyang was prepared through informal channels and held without adequate advance negotiations by the Ministry of Foreign Affairs.[18]

The Japanese public's reaction to Koizumi's visit to Pyongyang was mixed. According to a public opinion survey conducted immediately after the second summit, the overall response was rather favourable, with 62 and 67 per cent of those polled evaluating it positively. Only a few people disapproved of Japan's effort to normalize relations with North Korea. However, there was a significant gap between the overall evaluation and the assessment of details. The great majority of the survey respondents were very pessimistic about the prospects of the re-investigation of the fate of the 10 Japanese abductees so far unaccounted for, and about the complete dismantling of nuclear weapons in North Korea. In addition, public opinion remained negative about Japan's humanitarian assistance for North Korea, and most of the mass media also voiced criticism.[19]

Japan at the Six-Party Talks

In October 2002, Tokyo watched US Assistant Secretary of State James Kelly visit Pyongyang and reiterate the US position that Washington would not enter into bilateral talks with Pyongyang until the latter completely, verifiably and irreversibly dismantled its nuclear weapons programme. Tokyo was startled when, following the Pyongyang meeting, Kelly stated that Pyongyang had revealed that it had a uranium enrichment programme. According to Kelly, North Korea proposed the conclusion of a non-aggression pact with the United States and the removal of obstacles to its economic development. Pyongyang's central concern was clearly the survival of the Kim regime – essentially prevention of a US military attack.

In retaliation against the North Korean regime's admission of nuclear weapons development, the US-led KEDO announced on 14 November that it was suspending the delivery of heavy oil to North Korea in December. The North Korean government charged that this was a violation of the Agreed Framework. By the end of the year North Korea had reopened its nuclear facilities at Yongbyong, unsealed the spent fuel rods stored there, and expelled International Atomic Energy (IAEA) inspectors from the country. Pyongyang ratcheted up the pressure by announcing on 10 January 2003 that it was withdrawing from the Treaty on the Non-proliferation of Nuclear Weapons (NPT).[20] Clearly, this was not the development that the Japanese government was hoping to see.

Pyongyang proposed that North Korea and the United States meet bilaterally to discuss the nuclear issue, but the Bush administration insisted on multilateral talks. After weeks of intense behind-the-scenes negotiations, the Chinese government agreed to host a trilateral meeting in Beijing.

The talks took place on 23–24 April, and during them the US representatives learned that Pyongyang had an ongoing nuclear weapons programme. On 15 July, the US government revealed that the North Koreans had notified it that they had completed the reprocessing of 8,000 spent fuel rods. The announcement alarmed Japan and other members of the international community because, if the claims were true, Pyongyang would have enough plutonium to produce six or more nuclear weapons. After the Beijing meeting the North Koreans continued to insist on bilateral talks with the United States, but China and Russia pressed North Korea to accept the participation of other powers in multilateral talks. Pyongyang ultimately agreed.

Representatives of North and South Korea, the United States, China, Russia and Japan met in Beijing on 27–29 August 2003. However, the Six-Party Talks could not bridge what the Chinese host, Wang Yi, called 'comprehensive differences' between the United States and North Korea.[21] The US chief negotiator, James Kelly, insisted that North Korea agree to complete, verifiable and irreversible dismantlement of its nuclear weapons programme before any talks on diplomatic normalization or economic assistance could begin. North Korea's chief negotiator, Kim Yong-Il, startled the other negotiators by declaring that his country had developed nuclear weapons and was prepared to prove its ability to explode and deliver them.[22] However, he denied that North Korea now had a uranium enrichment programme.[23]

Japan's chief delegate, Mitoji Yabunaka, stated that Japan would not accept a nuclear North Korea and urged a peaceful resolution to the problem. He also emphasized the importance of resolving the nuclear, missile and abduction issues in a comprehensive manner, adding that these issues would have to be resolved before Japan would normalize relations with North Korea. Once bilateral relations were normalized, he said, Japan would consider extending economic assistance to North Korea. He also stated that Japan was ready to consider providing energy aid to North Korea if Pyongyang would take concrete steps to end its nuclear programme.[24]

Prior to the Beijing meeting, the Japanese government had hoped to bring the abduction issue to the multilateral talks in Beijing, but China made it clear that it did not want the issue included on the agenda of the Six-Party Talks, apparently out of deference to North Korea.[25] The Japanese government actively sought and won the endorsement of the US and South Korean governments for its position. It also took steps to impress on the international community how much importance Tokyo attached to the abduction issue.[26] In the end, a compromise was reached – to raise the issue during the Six-Party Talks but to discuss it in a separate, bilateral meeting between Japan and North Korea. On the sidelines of the Six-Party Talks, the Japanese delegation pressed the North Korean side to turn over the family members of the five former abductees who were now in Japan and to account for the eight abductees who North Korea had earlier stated had died in North Korea, and for two other Japanese who were suspected to have been kidnapped by North Korea. The North Korean side simply stated that the abduction issue had already been resolved and criticized Japan for reneging on the agreement to return the five Japanese to North Korea.[27]

The second round of Six-Party Talks took place in Beijing on 25–28 February 2004 but the countries were far from finding a solution to the nuclear crisis. The governments of the United States, Japan and South Korea demanded that North Korea halt all its nuclear programmes, but North Korean negotiators offered to freeze the country's nuclear weapons programme – but not its civilian nuclear programmes – in exchange for energy aid, other economic benefits and security assurances. The governments of China and Russia supported the South Korean proposal to provide energy aid after North Korea froze its nuclear programme as a step towards eventual dismantlement, but the US government stated that it would not offer aid at that stage. It also continued to insist on North Korea's commitment to complete, verifiable and irreversible dismantlement of all its nuclear programmes, and Japan supported this position. The governments of Russia and China, however, were agreeable to North Korea's scientific research on civilian nuclear energy development.[28]

Despite the lack of substantive progress, the North Korean government for the first time committed itself publicly to eventual dismantlement of its nuclear programme, although not under the conditions demanded by the United States. Representatives of the six countries also agreed to hold the third round of talks in Beijing no later than the end of June 2004. The six parties agreed to set up a working group or groups to continue discussion.[29]

The third round of the Six-Party Talks was held in Beijing from 23 to 26 June. According to a US proposal, economic aid and investment would only gradually start to flow into North Korea in return for highly intrusive inspections and an agreement for the complete dismantling of all of its nuclear facilities. Pyongyang rejected the proposal and the talks ended without agreement, but the parties did agree to continue to work through the working group and to hold the next round of talks by the end of September. The Japanese government supported the US position on security assurances through the six-party framework. It announced its readiness to join the energy assistance through the six-nation talks on condition that the North Korean regime freeze all its nuclear programmes, including the uranium enrichment programme, declare all nuclear programmes, and submit to adequate verification. The Japanese government also reiterated that it would provide economic cooperation to North Korea only after the nuclear, missile and abduction issues had been comprehensively resolved on the basis of the Pyongyang Declaration and bilateral relations had been normalized. In a bilateral meeting on the sidelines of the multilateral talks the Japanese side urged the North Korean representative to realize the reunion of Mrs Soga with her family in a third country and the swift implementation of a re-investigation into the 10 remaining abductees whose whereabouts remained unknown.[30]

After a long delay, the fourth round of talks took place in Beijing from 26 July to 7 August and from 13 to 19 September 2005. The North Korean regime promised to scrap all its nuclear weapons-related programmes, rejoin the NPT, and allow outside nuclear inspections in exchange for security guarantees and economic aid. The US government pledged not to attack North Korea militarily and to join South Korea, Japan, China and Russia in providing energy supplies to North Korea. These promises led to the announcement on 19 September of a Joint Statement of principles for guiding the parties towards a resolution of the nuclear crisis. According to the statement, the parties agreed on the ultimate goal of verifiable denuclearization of the Korean Peninsula in a peaceful manner. The parties pledged to pursue 'commitment for commitment, action for action' as a guiding principle in implementing eventual agreements concerning North Korea's denuclearization and the normalization of relations among all parties.[31]

The Six-Party Talks were resumed on 9 November 2005, but it soon became apparent that the positions of the North Koreans and the United States remained far apart where the timing of economic assistance to North Korea was concerned, with Pyongyang demanding energy and economic aid in exchange for the suspension of its nuclear programme and Washington insisting on verifiable abandonment of North Korea's nuclear weapons development before it would supply any aid. Moreover, the US government insisted that North Korea scrap both its plutonium and its highly enriched uranium (HEU) programmes, but the North Korean government continued to deny the existence of an HEU programme. By 11 November, the parties had reaffirmed that '[T]hey would fully implement the joint statement in line with the principle of "commitment for commitment, action for action", so as to realize the verifiable denuclearization of the Korean Peninsula at an early date'.[32] However, the parties went into recess on 12 November, with no date set for the resumption of talks. At the time of writing it remained uncertain whether North Korea and the United States could bridge the gap in their positions.

Coordinating policy with the United States and South Korea

By the time the Six-Party Talks resumed in 2005, the positions of Tokyo and Washington had become very close. On the issue of the timing of economic and energy aid to Pyongyang, Tokyo was more flexible than Washington. On the question of denuclearization of North Korea, however, they were in complete agreement. The governments of Japan and the United States also agreed on multilateral security assurances to North Korea. Earlier, however, it had not been easy for Tokyo to adjust to the policy shift from the Clinton administration to the Bush administration. The latter's refusal to engage North Korea until the start of the Six-Party Talks complicated Japanese policy towards North Korea and coordination with South Korea. Although the Japanese, South Korean and US governments shared the same goal of a nuclear-free North Korea, they preferred different approaches. In the first crisis (1993–4), the governments of Japan, South Korea and the United States under President Clinton all believed that engagement with North Korea, whether bilateral or multilateral, was key to resolving the nuclear crisis. During the second nuclear crisis, this view was maintained in Japan and South Korea, but the Bush administration, until 2005, showed no interest in talking directly to the regime in Pyongyang. Japan's concern resonated with former Secretary of Defense William Perry's warning that, in the absence of US engagement with North Korea, Pyongyang was able to proceed with its nuclear weapons development.[33]

The real goal of US policy towards North Korea has been unclear and this has seriously complicated Japan's approach to the North Korean problem. Does the US government want the removal of Kim Jong-Il from power and the collapse of the Stalinist regime regardless of who leads the country, or does it want a change in Pyongyang's policy and behaviour? Japan clearly prefers a peaceful resolution of the nuclear crisis and a peaceful evolution and opening up of North Korea rather than a military conflagration or North Korea's sudden collapse, which would have uncertain but devastating consequences for the neighbouring countries, including Japan. On this, the Japanese government's view is virtually indistinguishable from that of its South Korean counterpart.

Military options are more problematic from Japan's perspective. The Bush administration wants to keep all options open, including that of a possible military strike against North Korea should the regime there launch an attack on its allies in the region. Although the Koizumi government has spoken in favour of the 'carrot and stick' approach, some domestic critics[34] are sceptical about the effectiveness of this approach in changing North Korean behaviour. Moreover, in the present author's view, the crisis atmosphere engendered by the talk of military options encourages Japanese 'hawks' to advocate major rearmament in Japan, including the nuclear option, and this would be very destabilizing for the entire region. In addition, a US pre-emptive attack on North Korea would require the consent of South Korea, but without military provocation by the North, South Korean consent would be difficult to obtain. North Korea could also retaliate by launching some of its 30 Nodong-1 missiles against Japan – a prospect most feared by the Japanese. Nightmarish as the consequences of a US attack on North Korea would be, in this author's view, if it should take place, Japan would have no alternative but to support US action under its security treaty obligations.

Major disagreements between the US and South Korean governments are also troubling to Japan as they will complicate trilateral policy coordination. Trilateral consultations between Japan, the United States and South Korea have become an essential element of Japan's multilateral engagement over the North Korean problem, along with the Six-Party Talks. Between the off-and-on sessions of the Six-Party Talks, the three governments have held both bilateral and trilateral meetings to coordinate their positions on key questions and on how best to keep North Korea at the negotiating table. The trilateral coordination has both a substantive and a symbolic significance. Substantively, it compels Japan, the United States and South Korea to coordinate their positions on the issues of how best to induce North Korea to be less recalcitrant on the nuclear issue. Symbolically, the trilateral coordination helps to highlight the futility of Pyongyang's attempt to drive a wedge between the positions of the three countries.

As of the time of writing, even though North Korea had returned to the negotiating table, it remained doubtful that it would accept the US demand for complete, verifiable and irreversible dismantlement of its nuclear weapons programme.

Nor, as noted earlier, did it appear likely that the US government would agree to enter into a bilateral non-aggression pact with North Korea or offer any economic assistance before North Korea dismantled its nuclear programmes. Meanwhile, Japan and the United States have hinted at the possibility of bringing the North Korean nuclear issue to the United Nations Security Council.[35] Seoul has so far opposed such a move, fearing that it would harden Pyongyang's position even more and further delay resolution of the crisis. Clearly, the move would test the trilateral coordination mechanism.

The abduction issue: debate over economic sanctions

Meanwhile, debate in Japan had turned to the abduction issue and how to force North Korea to account fully for the Japanese abductees. Japan's international appeals, noted above, continued. In March 2003, the family members of the Japanese abductees and their supporters visited the United States and appealed to members of Congress. They also made a presentation to the UN Human Rights Commission's Working Group on Enforced or Involuntary Disappearance. In September, Japanese Foreign Minister Yoriko Kawaguchi raised the abduction issue in her statement to the UN General Assembly and in November Deputy Director-General of the Asian and Oceanian Affairs Bureau of the Ministry of Foreign Affairs Akitaka Saiki addressed the working group and urged prompt identification of the whereabouts of the abductees whose information North Korea had not confirmed.

The Japanese government does not believe what the North Korean government has said on this issue and continues to press it to find out what happened to the other suspected abductees. Those Japanese who were frustrated by the slow progress on the abduction issue were encouraged by the US Congress enacting the North Korea Human Rights Act in October 2004: the act called for more Korean-language radio broadcasts into North Korea and increased funding for non-governmental organizations promoting human rights, democracy, the rule of law and the development of a market economy in North Korea. However, the US government has also officially stated that it supports the Japanese government's position on the abduction issue. The 10 February 2005 joint statement between the Japanese foreign minister and the US secretary of state concerning North Korea noted, '[T]he U.S. Secretary of State reaffirmed the United States' full support of Japan's position' on the abduction issue.[36]

After Pyongyang admitted in 2002 to abducting Japanese citizens in the past, the Japanese authorities tightened baggage screening on North Korean ships visiting Japanese ports. This reduced the amount of cash taken by travellers to North Korea from 4.01 billion yen (JPY) in fiscal 2000 to 2.58 billion yen in fiscal 2003. Remittances to North Korea through financial institutions also dropped, from the peak of 587 million yen in fiscal 2001 to 101 million yen in fiscal 2003.[37] In 2004, the Japanese Parliament approved legislation requiring all foreign ships coming to Japan to carry liability insurance against environmental damage they might cause while in Japanese waters. Scheduled to come into effect on 1 March 2005, the legislation applied to vessels of any nationality, but it was understood that the new law was aimed at North Korean ships, most of which had no such insurance.

Behind these actions is growing public support for economic sanctions against North Korea over the abduction issue. A Kyodo News opinion poll in December 2004 showed that 75.1 per cent of respondents wanted the Japanese government to 'invoke economic sanctions and take a stern posture' against North Korea.[38] Similarly, in a *Yomiuri Shimbun* public opinion poll taken shortly after the North Korean declaration that it had nuclear weapons, 71 per cent of the respondents stated that Japan should set a deadline for resolving the abduction issue and impose economic sanctions.[39] In February 2005, Prime Minister Koizumi received a petition, signed by 5 million people, demanding economic sanctions against North Korea.[40]

The Japanese government has so far been reluctant to impose outright economic sanctions on North Korea, fearing that a unilateral move might complicate Tokyo's policy coordination with Washington and Seoul. For instance, Chief Cabinet Secretary Shinzo Abe, known for his staunch anti-North views, has stated that it would be inevitable for Japan to 'exert pressure' on North Korea if Pyongyang did not come clean on the abduction issue.[41] As noted earlier, the South Korean government opposes economic sanctions, whereas the US government has long maintained economic sanctions against North Korea. Although the Japanese government has not imposed explicit sanctions, it has taken some steps to put pressure on North Korea – for instance, the liability insurance on North Korean (and other foreign) ships visiting Japanese ports. In addition, in 2005 municipal governments in Japan began terminating the preferential tax status of the facilities owned and operated by the pro-North General Association of Korean Residents in Japan (Chongryun).[42] On 6 December 2005, the Japanese government appointed a former ambassador to Norway, Fumiko Saiga, as Japanese human rights ambassador to coordinate Japan's effort to put international pressure on North Korea to improve its human rights record, including the resolution of the Japanese abduction issue. Tokyo supported and welcomed the UN General Assembly's adoption on 16 December 2005 of a resolution criticizing North Korea for its human rights abuses, including the kidnapping of foreign nationals.[43] It should be noted, however, that both China and Russia voted against the resolution and South Korea abstained, clearly a sign of discord among the countries concerned.

After the North Korean declaration that it had nuclear weapons, some Japanese concluded that the utility of Japanese sanctions had weakened further.[44] According to a long-time Japanese observer of Korean affairs, Japan's unilateral economic sanctions against North Korea would not only have limited effect but also give Pyongyang an additional excuse to boycott the Six-Party Talks.[45] Over one-half of North Korea's international trade is with South Korea and China, not including China's delivery of heavy oil to North Korea. In comparison, Japan's trade with North Korea represents a mere 8 per cent of the latter's total trade.[46] Therefore even a complete breakdown of trade between Japan and

North Korea would have only a limited impact on North Korea as long as South Korea and China did not join Japan's trade sanctions, and they are unlikely to do so. Moreover, Pyongyang has stated on several occasions that it would consider economic sanctions against North Korea as an act of war – another justification for boycotting the Six-Party Talks. If Pyongyang's refusal to attend the six-nation talks continued or if the talks were unable to resolve the current impasse, the matter might be submitted to the UN Security Council. However, China and South Korea would oppose such move. In the meantime, as the abduction issue continues with no prospect of solution, domestic calls for sanctions against the North continue.[47]

Meanwhile, the Bush administration is also considering a series of actions designed to choke off North Korea's ability to raise funds for its nuclear programme through illicit drug trafficking, counterfeiting, and the sale of missile and other weapons technology.[48] Even if Japan and the United States agreed to go ahead with their sanctions, serious doubts about their effectiveness would remain. For example, departing US Ambassador to Japan Howard Baker stated, 'Sanctions are a tool, but it is seldom effective unless it's a multilateral undertaking. It probably wouldn't be really effective unless you've got South Korea, China, and maybe Russia on board, and I presently do not see that in the cards'.[49]

Conclusion

The foregoing analysis makes it amply clear that Japan's interest in a non-nuclear Korean Peninsula is shared by the United States, South Korea, China and Russia. It is also evident that the Japanese government and the other powers desire a peaceful, negotiated resolution to the current nuclear crisis. Japan's consistent support of this goal has been its most important contribution to this serious challenge facing North-East Asia. The Japanese government's ability and apparent willingness to extend substantial economic assistance to North Korea if Pyongyang ends and dismantles its nuclear weapons development programme is also very important. Tokyo's coordination of policy with the United States and South Korea has been helpful in demonstrating to North Korea their united stand against a nuclearized North Korea. However, Tokyo has not been able to play any significant role in reducing, much less eliminating, the important difference between the United States, on the one hand, and China, Russia and South Korea, on the other, on the sequencing and timing of the moves necessary on both sides of the crisis to resolve the problem. These crucial questions remain unanswered, and Japan is not in a position to determine the timing or direction of any one of these decisions.

The Japanese government has an additional issue that prevents it from taking concrete steps to help ease North Korea's economic woes. That is the issue of the abduction of Japanese citizens. Tokyo has made the resolution of this issue a precondition for diplomatic normalization with Pyongyang. This position limits Japan's influence over the North Korean nuclear issue inasmuch as it puts a cap on the bottle of economic aid and delays diplomatic normalization with

North Korea. In the author's view, Japan's decision to make the normalization of relations conditional on the resolution of the abduction issue is based more on emotion and domestic public opinion than on strategic calculations regarding the direction of the nuclear crisis. Moreover, in the absence of any progress on the abduction issue, Japan has intimated sanctions against North Korea. However, on this issue, Japan does not see eye to eye with China, Russia or South Korea, thus contributing to the discord among the parties to the Six-Party Talks. It should be added, however, that the United States would probably support Japan's decision to impose sanctions on North Korea as Washington does not seem to be in any hurry to resolve the nuclear crisis.

If Japan is to become a key agent of change in North-East Asia, it needs to reconsider its current policy towards North Korea. In this author's view, Tokyo's best option is to continue trilateral coordination with the United States and South Korea. It must do so, however, while pressing its demand for a non-military solution to the current crisis, urging Washington to engage more actively with Pyongyang, and supporting Seoul's policy of engagement. Tokyo should also encourage Beijing to continue its active role in keeping North Korea engaged in the Six-Party Talks. Additionally, it should demonstrate that it is willing to forgo an immediate resolution of the abduction issue if doing so would enhance the probability of success of the multilateral talks in ending the nuclear crisis. The abduction issue is understandably a very emotional one in Japan and its humanitarian aspects cannot be overstated, but Japan should define the resolution of the abduction issue not as a precondition for the resumption of normalization talks with North Korea but as a part of the talks.

It is also advisable for Japan to consider normalization as an incentive for North Korea to give up the development of nuclear weapons. Considering that its development of nuclear weapons is motivated by a sense of international isolation and vulnerability to US threat, the combination of a US security guarantee and normalization with Japan, accompanied by economic aid from Tokyo on a large scale, would be the best incentive for Pyongyang to give in on the international community's demand for the dismantlement of its nuclear weapons programme.

Although the Pyongyang Declaration between Japan and North Korea is technically a bilateral document, it also calls for steps towards the establishment of multilateral regimes for international peace and stability, including the international nuclear non-proliferation regime and regional security. As part of a comprehensive package of bilateral and multilateral goals and steps, the document points to the possibility that bilateral progress between Japan and North Korea may contribute to and also benefit from the development of a new regional alignment, including improved inter-Korean relations and US–North Korea relations.

From this perspective, improved prospects for bilateral normalization could serve as an incentive for Pyongyang to return to the international nuclear non-proliferation regime and to become a constructive participant in regional realignment. It is conceivable that in this process Japan and South Korea could cooperate in providing North Korea with the financial, technical and human resources it needs to rebuild its economy.

Herein lies the path towards a greater political role for Japan in this region, a path marked by peaceful steps and informed by strategic thinking. If Japan is to move along this path, it must review its current policy, especially with respect to the linkage between the abduction issue and the normalization of diplomatic relations and to the question of multilateral confidence and peace-building in North-East Asia.

Notes

1 Tsuneo Akaha, 'Japan's policy toward North Korea: Interests and options', in Tsuneo Akaha (ed.), *The Future of North Korea*, London and New York: Routledge, 2002, pp. 77–94.
2 Akaha, 'Japan's policy toward North Korea'.
3 Tsuneo Akaha, 'Beyond self-defense: Japan's elusive security role under the New Guidelines for US–Japan Defense Cooperation', *Pacific Review*, 11/4, 1998, pp. 461–83.
4 Tomiichi Murayama, 'Beyond my visit to Pyongyang', *Japan Quarterly*, April/June 2000, pp. 3–10.
5 Nautilus Daily Report, 2 December 2000.
6 Masao Okonogi, 'Niccho Shunokaidan no Seika to Tenbo' [The results of the Japan–North Korea summit and prospects], in Kinhide Mushakoji, Suh Sung, Shuji Matsuno and Xia Gang (eds), *Tohokuajia Jidai eno Teigen: Senso no Kiki kara Heiwa Kochiku e* [Proposal for the era of North-East Asia: From crisis of war to construction of peace], Tokyo: Heibonsha, 2003, p. 47.
7 Masao Okonogi, 'Japan's North Korea policy: Between Koizumi's Pyongyang visits and the Six Party Talks'. Paper presented at the Workshop on Japan, East Asia and the Formation of North Korea Policy, organized by the Swedish Institute for International Affairs and the European Institute of Japanese Studies, Swedish Institute for International Affairs, Stockholm, 17–19 March 2004, p. 4.
8 Katsuyuki Yakushiji, *Gaimusho: Gaikoryoku Kyoka eno Michi* [The Foreign Ministry: The road to strengthening diplomatic power], Tokyo: Iwanamishoten, 2003, pp. 3–6.
9 Japanese Ministry of Foreign Affairs, available HTTP: <http://www.mofa.go.jp/region/ asia-paci/n_korea/pmv0209/pyongyang.html> (accessed 19 March 2004).
10 Japanese Ministry of Foreign Affairs, available HTTP: <http://www.mofa.go.jp/mofaj/ kaidan/s_koi/n_korea_02/sengen.html> (accessed 19 March 2004).
11 Hideji Takesada, 'Kitachosen no Senryaku kara Mita Niccho Shunokaidan no Igi' [The significance of the Japan–North Korea summit meeting from the perspective of North Korea's strategy], in Yoichi Hirama and Yoneyuki Sugita (eds), *Kitachosen wo Meguru Hokutoajia no Kokusaikankei to Nihon* [International relations of North-East Asia surrounding North Korea and Japan], Tokyo: Akashishoten, 2003, p. 35.
12 Okonogi, 'Niccho Shunokaidan no Seika to Tenbo', pp. 47–8.
13 Haruki Wada, *Hokutoajia Kyodo no Ie* [A North-East Asian common house], Tokyo: Heibonsha, 2003, p. 166.
14 Kang Sang-jung, *Niccho Kankei no Kokufuku: Naze Kokko Seijoka Kosho ga Hitsuyo nanoka* [Overcoming Japan–North Korea relations: Why normalization talks are necessary], Tokyo: Shueisha, 2003, pp. 176–81.
15 Takesada, 'Kitachosen no Senryaku kara Mita Niccho Shunokaidan no Igi', p. 35.
16 'Japan–North Korea summit meeting', 22 May 2004, available HTTP: <http:// www.kantei.go.jp/foreign/koizumiphoto/2004/05/22saihouchou_e.html> (accessed 24 May 2005); and 'Press conference by Prime Minister Junichiro Koizumi after the Japan–North Korea meeting', 22 May 2004, available HTTP: <http://www.mofa.go.jp/ region/asia-paci/n_korea/pmv0405/press.html> (accessed 28 May 2005).

17   James Brooke, 'Koizumi's trip gets lukewarm reviews', *New York Times*, 24 May 2004, available HTTP: <http://www.nyhtimes.com/2004/05/24/international/asia/24japa.html> (accessed 24 May 2004). Family members of Japanese still missing after being abducted by North Korean agents expressed dismay and disappointment over the lack of progress on their cases. Akemi Nakamura, 'Pyongyang summit falls short for kin of those still missing', *Japan Times*, 24 May 2004, p. 1.

18   Okonogi, 'Japan's North Korea policy', p. 7.

19   Okonogi, 'Japan's North Korea policy', p. 7.

20   North Korea's withdrawal from the NPT took effect on 10 April 2003.

21   Joseph Kahn, 'Korea arms talks close with plans for a new round', *New York Times*, 29 August 2003, p. A1.

22   Ibid.

23   *Asahi Shimbun*, 29 August 2003, available HTTP: <http://www.asahi.com/international/update/0829/008.html> (accessed 29 August 2003).

24   *Japan Times*, 28 August 2003, available HTTP: <http://www.JapanTimes.com/cgi-bin/getarticle.p15?nn20030828a1.htm> (accessed 28 August 2003).

25   *Yomiuri Shimbun*, 22 August 2003, available HTTP: <http://www.yomiuri.co.jp/politics/news/20030821ia21.htm> (accessed 22 August 2003).

26   *Yomiuri Shimbun*, 25 August 2003, available HTTP: <http://www.yomiuri.co.jp/politics/news/20030825ia23.htm> (accessed 25 August 2003).

27   *Mainichi Shimbun*, 28 August 2003, available HTTP: <http://www.mainichi.co.jp/news/selection/20030829k0000m010069000c.html> (accessed 28 August 2003).

28   Philip P. Pan and Glenn Kessler, 'N. Korea arms talks bring no agreement', *Washington Post*, 28 February 2004, p. A14; Joseph Kahn, 'In Beijing, nuclear talks seem mired in discord', *New York Times*, 27 February 2003, p. A10; and Joseph Kahn, 'U.S. and North Korea agree to more talks', *New York Times*, 29 February 2003, pp. 1–8.

29   *Asahi Shimbun*, 29 February 2004, pp. 1, 2, 4, and 26.

30   'Third round of Six-Party Talks concerning North Korean nuclear issues', 27 June 2004, Japanese Ministry of Foreign Affairs web site, available HTTP: <http://www.mofa.go.jp/region/asia-paci/n_korea/6party/talk0406.html> (accessed 20 February 2005).

31   The full text of the statement is available at the Japanese Ministry of Foreign Affairs home page, available HTTP: <http://www.mofa.go.jp/region/asia-paci/n_korea/6party/joint0509.html> (accessed 22 September 2005).

32   The statement was read by China's chief delegate, Deputy Foreign Minister Wu Dawei, before the other envoys; quoted in an Associated Press report in *International Herald Tribune*, 11 November 2005, available HTTP: <http://www.iht.com/articles/2005/11/11/news/talks.php> (accessed 12 November 2005).

33   William J. Perry, 'Crisis on the Korean Peninsula: Implications for U.S. policy in Northeast Asia', A Brookings Leadership Forum, Brookings Institution, Washington, DC, 24 January 2003 (unpublished).

34   For example, Prof. Izumi of Shizuoka University. Hajime Izumi, 'Kitachosen he no Shin no Atsuryoku wa Nanika: Kokusaiteki Seisai no Michi wo Tozasuna' [What would be genuine pressure on North Korea? Do not close off the path to international sanctions], *Chuokoron*, February 2005.

35   *Yomiuri Shimbun*, 20 February 2005, available HTTP: <http://www.yomiuri.co.jp/politics/news/20050219i115.htm> (accessed 20 February 2005).

36   Japanese Ministry of Foreign Affairs, 'Joint statement on North Korea', 19 February 2005, available HTTP: <http://www.mofa.go.jp/region/n-america/us/fmv0502/n_korea.html> (accessed 21 February 2005).

37   *Japan Times*, 13 February 2005, available HTTP: <http://www.japantimes.com/cgi-bin/getarticle.pl5?nn20050213a2.htm> (accessed 13 February 2005).

38   James Brooke and David E. Sanger, 'Japan urges North Korea to rejoin disarmament talks', *New York Times*, 12 February 2005, available HTTP: <http://www.nytimes.com/2005/02/12/international/asia/12korea.htm> (accessed 12 February 2005).

39 *Yomiuri Shimbun*, 17 February 2005, available HTTP: <http://www.yomiuri.co.jp/politics/news/20050217it13.htm> (accessed 17 February 2005).
40 Brooke and Sanger, 'Japan urges North Korea to rejoin disarmament talks'.
41 *Yomiuri Shimbun*, 21 January 2006, available HTTP: http://www.yomiuri.co.jp/feature/fe4200/news/20060121ia22.htm (accessed 8 February 2005).
42 *Japan Times*, 4 February 2006, available HTTP: <http://search.japantimes.co.jp/cgi-bin/nn20060204a5.html> (accessed 4 February 2006).
43 *Yomiuri Shimbun*, 17 December 2005, available HTTP: <http://www.yomiuri.co.jp/feature/fe4200/news/20051217ia22.htm> (accessed 5 February 2006).
44 Kanako Takahara, 'Pyongyang's nuclear move weakens threat of sanctions over abductions', *Japan Times*, 11 February 2005, available HTTP: <http://www.japantimes.com/cgi-bin/getarticle.pl5?nn20050211a1.htm> (accessed 11 February 2005).
45 Izumi, 'Kitachosen he no Shin no Atsuryoku wa Nanika', p. 149.
46 Ibid., p. 149.
47 For example, on 1 November 2005, the group of members of Japanese abductees and a group formed to support their cause appealed to the Japanese government for sanctions on North Korea if bilateral working-level talks between Tokyo and Pyongyang on the abduction issue failed to resolve the issue. *Yomiuri Shimbun*, 1 November 2005, available HTTP: <http://www.yomiuri.co.jp/feature/fe4200/news/20051101ic22.htm> (accessed 8 February 2006).
48 David E. Sanger, 'US is shaping plan to pressure North Korea', *New York Times*, 14 February 2005, available HTTP: <http://www.nytimes.com/2005/02/14/politics/14korea.html> (accessed 14 February 2005).
49 James Brook, 'US envoy to Japan assails North Korea's arms program', *New York Times*, 17 February 2005, available HTTP: <http://www.nytimes.com/2005/02/17/international/asia/17korea.html> (accessed 17 February 2005).

2 The rationales behind North Korean foreign policy

Han S. Park

The policy of any of the neighbouring states towards North Korea (the Democratic People's Republic of Korea, DPRK) should be based first and foremost on a realistic and in-depth understanding of North Korea's own overall policy orientations and its specific policy strategies and tactics towards the neighbouring states. The purpose of this chapter, therefore, is to shed light on North Korea itself and its government's policy dispositions for dealing with the neighbouring states, including Japan, China, South Korea and the United States.

North Korean nuclear diplomacy: goals and strategies

An understanding of North Korea's policy behaviour must begin with an explanation of how a poverty-stricken country without sound industrial or technological foundations has become a global military power, one that is possibly equipped with nuclear weapons.[1] The roots of this anomaly date back to Japanese colonial rule under which Kim Il-Sung, as a guerrilla fighter in Manchuria, developed an obsessive desire for nuclear weapons when he witnessed the abrupt surrender of the Japanese Empire after atomic bombs were dropped in Hiroshima and Nagasaki in 1945. Once he had established a firm power base in North Korea after the Korean War, Kim focused his efforts on developing nuclear weapons capabilities through an extensive and sustained exchange of scientists with the Soviet Union.

It is not clear exactly when North Korea acquired the indigenous capability to produce the bomb, but the need for such non-conventional weaponry was deeply felt in the late 1960s and early 1970s. During this period, the breach between China and the Soviet Union forced Kim Il-Sung to pursue the means for self-determination and, more importantly, self-defence. It was also during this period that South Korea, the main military threat to the North, took off economically, rapidly passing North Korea. With an economic and industrial base that was inferior to that of the South, Kim Il-Sung was compelled to explore the alternative of a non-conventional military arsenal. The impetus to acquire the bomb was given a further push when post-Mao China abandoned the socialist economy and the whole of the communist bloc was eventually dismantled. North Korea found itself diplomatically isolated, politically alienated and impoverished, while at the same time South Korea was experiencing dramatic economic expansion.

These developments added further urgency to the need for self-reliance in not only the military but also the economic arena.

The evolution of the idea of self-determination, *Juche*, itself reflects the progressive intensification of this doctrine. In the end, the entire North Korean system became a strange hybrid theocracy capable of sustaining a government of anomaly.[2] Without a more complete picture of the factors that have led to and continue to surround the apparent paradox of North Korea's ideological and political posture, the casual observer might easily conclude that the North Korean leadership is irrational, unpredictable, and intent on practising the diplomacy of brinkmanship. It is the contention of this chapter that a more thorough understanding of North Korea's policy orientations and its perceptions of others will yield a credible explanation of Pyongyang's foreign policy behaviour.

Policy goals

The North Korean government has been pursuing a set of goals that are fundamentally aligned with those of other governments – national security and regime survival, political identity as a sovereign state, and economic prosperity to meet the needs of its people.[3] All political regimes pursue these three goals with a variety of strategies depending on the wider context in which they operate.[4] Coping with the context of a volatile security environment has caused tremendous confusion and difficulty for North Korea. Moreover, the United States has fundamentally shifted its North Korea policy – from hostility to rapprochement, then back to hostility – over a span of time ranging from the administration of President Ronald Reagan to that of George W. Bush. The evolution of the South Korean posture towards the North has also shown a great range of diversity, from hostility to competition and to the current co-prosperity. Given the specific context of North Korea in terms of its geopolitical security environment, its economic and material endowment, its cultural heritage and its collective memory of history, the Kim Il-Sung/Kim Jong-Il regime has employed the policy strategies and tactics that it perceived to be most effective in achieving its overall goals.

The North Korean regime has worked consistently to address both the domestic and the foreign sources of the security threat. Domestically, in order to prevent a crisis of legitimacy (which is the most frequent reason for political upheavals and the collapse of political systems), the regime has created a system that is legitimized primarily on the grounds of ideology and not economic prosperity.[5] The legitimacy afforded by the *Juche* ideology became further entrenched once the system became a rudimentary form of theocracy. The extent to which the mass public – as well as the ruling elite – are ideologically socialized defies conventional Western wisdom. As this ideology gives the head of state sanctity as a divine being of sorts, the centre of authority cannot readily be subjected to criticism. This has allowed the regime to remain remarkably stable in spite of the enormous economic and material difficulties suffered by its citizenry. The strategy to cope with external or foreign sources of the security threat has been military self-defence. The regime has been committed to the idea that security deterrence can only be optimized through the possession of nuclear weapon capabilities. The inadequacies of conventional weapons have become increasingly apparent given the threat of the formidable military forces of South Korea and the imposing US military presence. This attitude, stemming from fear of military inferiority, has only been reinforced by the recent display of sophisticated and awesome US military might in Afghanistan and Iraq.

The goal of political sovereignty has been evidenced in North Korea's negotiating strategy in that the government in Pyongyang has insisted on attempting to maintain an equal footing with the United States, defying the practical dynamics of international power politics. This posture has worked to boost national pride and self-esteem, which in turn has helped legitimize the regime: it explains North Korea's insistence on bilateral negotiations with the United States. The government has maintained a consistent policy orientation in which its security is perceived to be threatened only by the United States and not by China, Japan, Russia, or even South Korea. When North Korea participated in several rounds of Six-Party Talks in Beijing in 2003–5, it did so mainly because it expected to convene bilateral negotiations with the United States under the multilateral umbrella.[6]

Finally, the goal of economic prosperity (or, perhaps more appropriately, survival) has produced a measure of pragmatism, especially in the Kim Jong-Il era since 1994. Acute economic difficulties became noticeable in the early 1990s when disastrous natural conditions prevailed for several successive years. At the height of the nuclear controversy at about the same time, North Korea experienced massive starvation and economic dislocation. This prompted the government to wage diplomatic campaigns to attract food aid and economic assistance, causing it serious embarrassment, especially as it had been accustomed to proclaiming, at least to its people, that it had achieved a paradise on earth. Sheer need and the urgency of the situation may have influenced Kim Jong-Il to go as far as to admit to the abduction of Japanese citizens in the hope of receiving economic assistance and achieving diplomatic normalization with other governments, including Japan.

As argued earlier, North Korea's national goals are no different from those of all other political systems. What is unique might be the selection of strategies and tactics to achieve the goals, but each of these can be shown to be rational given the circumstances.

The nuclear strategy

The question is often asked whether North Korea is determined to become a nuclear power at all costs or if the regime is simply using the nuclear card as bargaining leverage. If the former is the case, no negotiated settlement is even conceivable. If the latter carries some degree of validity, then North Korea can give up its nuclear ambitions 'if the price is right'.

It is my contention that North Korea began with the determination to become a nuclear power but eventually changed its position. At the present time it is using the nuclear issue as bargaining leverage. In fact, leveraging its nuclear capabilities became the only viable strategy available to it. This strategic change occurred when Pyongyang's official stance on the existence of a nuclear programme shifted from denial to acceptance. Throughout the 1990s, North Korea had denied any intention of making nuclear weapons, even at the nuclear complex in Yongbyon, in an effort to maintain the confidentiality of sensitive security information; but since North Korea was named as part of the 'axis of evil' by the Bush administration in January 2002 Pyongyang has gradually reversed its position by asserting that nuclear preparedness is its only assured means of deterrence. It has thus made efforts to engage the USA in bilateral dialogue with the intention of using the nuclear issue for the purpose of negotiations.

The change in North Korea's nuclear strategy may have been prompted by four major developments in recent years.

First, the South Korean 'sunshine' policy of co-prosperity made the North Korean leadership reconsider its security preparedness. The Kim Jong-Il government seems to have concluded that South Korea is not realistically a threat to its security, and as a result the arms race with the South may have lost steam. In the decades before Kim Dae-Jung became president in South Korea, the relationship between the two Koreas was one of hostility and competition for legitimacy, fuelling the North's pursuit of a nuclear deterrent, but, as the sunshine policy unfolded in the South during the administration of Kim Dae-Jung, Pyongyang was seemingly persuaded that the demise of the North Korean regime may not even be in the interests of the South. As a result, the regime has also come to realize that a strong South Korean economy is a prerequisite for the provision of the expected economic cooperation and humanitarian assistance to the North.

The second major development that may have influenced Pyongyang's shift in strategic posture was the deterioration in the North Korean economy and its inability to alleviate its chronic food shortages. This desperate situation called for an effective strategy to elicit foreign assistance. In the perceived absence of strategic alternatives, the nuclear issue has again been utilized to gain bargaining leverage. However, it is essential to understand that Pyongyang has no inclination whatsoever to bargain away its nuclear assets for economic gains alone. It cannot be expected to give away its only deterrence mechanism without reliable alternative security assurances. Thus, the North Korean government's insistence on legally binding security assurances from the United States has to be appreciated.

The third important reason for the change in Pyongyang's nuclear strategy involved the US military deployment to invade Afghanistan and Iraq. Here, the Bush administration showed that it was capable of destroying a regime once it had been publicly condemned as 'evil' – a category into which North Korea has also been placed. Perceiving Bush to be insensitive to civilian casualties and physical destruction as 'collateral damage', Pyongyang seems to have realized that a US invasion is a real possibility. The North Korean desire to avoid military confrontation is no less powerful than its desire to survive.

The fourth reason behind the strategic shift may have been Pyongyang's rational calculation that once it 'goes nuclear' and triggers a regional arms race it may not be able to compete with its economically superior neighbours.

North Korea and its neighbours

Given the analysis thus far, a few generalizations can be made regarding Pyongyang's views and perspectives on the role of the neighbouring governments and on the ongoing Six-Party Talks. The North Korean government's perceptions of the foreign governments in addressing the nuclear crisis are quite diverse and yet clear. It insists that different issues surrounding the nuclear stalemate should be treated separately, and delineates the security issue from economic and political issues.

With regard to the security issue, Pyongyang views the matter of its own security as separate from regional security. In Pyongyang's view, its own security is basically a bilateral issue, a good that only the United States can provide. More specifically, North Korea insists that the half-century-old Armistice Treaty, which was meant to be merely a temporary ceasefire, must be replaced by a form of peace arrangement. As the United States and North Korea itself were the only signatories to the Armistice Treaty, changing it remains a bilateral issue. Once this issue is resolved, Pyongyang advocates South Korea's emergence as a legitimate player in securing peace on the Korean Peninsula. Since only three parties – the United States, North Korea and South Korea – maintain uniformed military personnel on the peninsula, it should be these three parties that craft the legal and institutional arrangements for securing peace. North Korea has consistently insisted that the other parties in the six-party format – China, Japan and Russia – pose no security threat to itself or to the Korean Peninsula. The other parties will only become relevant and legitimate for creating and managing a regional cooperative security regime which Pyongyang considers to be a separate issue. Furthermore, Pyongyang seems to expect that China and Japan will become vital partners in economic and political cooperation with North Korea.[7] The following subsections discuss Pyongyang's policy orientations with respect to its bilateral relations in more detail.

Coping with the United States

What does the United States mean to the North Korean leadership, and how are North Korean policies towards the United States articulated? The United States represents an entity that is paradoxical in terms of its implications for North Korea's national interests. On one hand, it is a party that cannot be ignored. Everything that affects North Korea seems to be directly or indirectly linked to the United States. North Korea's security issue is almost entirely a bilateral issue with the United States.

Since Pyongyang rules out South Korea as a source of security threat, it feels that none of the neighbouring states can possibly desire to see North Korea's security threatened or see its regime collapse. At the successive rounds of the Six-Party Talks, North Korean negotiators have insisted consistently that the security issue must be addressed in bilateral negotiations with the United States. Beyond security, Pyongyang is obviously of the view that the United States holds the key to its economic development and prosperity. The regime in Pyongyang realizes that without the support of the USA it cannot obtain development loans from international financial organizations such as the World Bank and the Asia Development Bank. It also realizes that South Korea's economic cooperation with the North cannot be advanced if the United States objects.

Given the dire economic situation and the unpopularity that would result from its becoming a nuclear power in the region, North Korea is seemingly serious about giving up its nuclear programmes and the weapons themselves if 'the conditions are right'. There may be a considerable credibility problem with Pyongyang's pronouncements, but one thing seems to be clear: it is willing to negotiate away its nuclear assets – for two significant reasons. First, it sees the likely regional ramifications: North Korea's becoming a nuclear power will trigger a regional nuclear arms race, as Japan would increase its armament programmes and China would respond. Taiwan and South Korea would also most likely join the nuclear arms race. If this happens, North Korean leaders may feel that the country's economic and industrial base cannot sustain its comparative military advantage vis-à-vis the neighbouring economic powers. Second, even relinquishing the existing programmes and bombs themselves does not mean that North Korea will be stripped of the technical capability, the know-how and the raw material necessary for resuming its nuclear programmes. The continued possession of an inherent nuclear capability seems to give Pyongyang greater flexibility with respect to the negotiations over the existing programmes and products.

The paradox arises when Pyongyang values its ability to resist and stand on an equal footing with the United States. Pyongyang values this ability highly because it is the concrete source of national pride and nationalism not only within its own population but, equally importantly, in the progressive circles of the South. In this sense, North Korea is benefiting from the stalemate and confrontation with the United States, thus being disinclined to soften its negotiating position. In fact, the Kim Jong-Il regime cannot afford to lead the public into thinking that their leadership is giving in to pressure from the United States. It has to be remembered that what sustains the North Korean government and manages to generate support from the people is not its capability to provide them with material comfort but almost exclusively its ideological legitimacy. The ideological legitimacy is founded on *Juche*, which is predicated upon nationalism. In this sense, we might observe that regimes do not collapse simply because of economic difficulties unless those difficulties provoke a crisis of legitimacy.

It is a supreme irony that the United States, intentionally or inadvertently, has provided the North Korean regime with an ideological base upon which to develop nationalism and regime stability with greater ease. By the same token, the United States has recently become a target of criticism and hostility from both North Korea and some youthful progressive circles in the South, which include much of the political leadership. Pyongyang welcomes the emerging and growing anti-American sentiment on college campuses and among young elite groups in South Korea, and to this extent the North Korean leadership may not feel it urgent to improve relations with the United States.

North Korean policy towards the United States since the advent of the Bush administration in 2001 has been affected by two overarching presumptions. First, Pyongyang presumes that the collapse of the Kim Jong-Il regime is a salient policy objective of the United States. Second, Pyongyang believes that the US government in general, and the Bush administration in particular, are not trustworthy. When President Bush labelled the North Korea a 'rogue state' and included it in the 'axis of evil' along with Iraq and Iran in January 2002, Pyongyang expressed deep resentment and disbelief. The president's notion of the 'axis of evil' was designed in conjunction with his 'war against terrorism', with which Pyongyang has nothing to do. In fact, almost immediately after the 11 September 2001 terrorist attacks, North Korea was one of the first countries to send condolences and goodwill messages to the USA. Pyongyang interpreted its inclusion in the 'axis of evil' as the expression of Bush's will to force the North Korean leadership into disintegration and eventually to force a regime change.

Pyongyang contends that the only reason behind Bush's rejection of bilateral direct negotiations with North Korea is that he does not believe that the North Korean government is a sufficiently credible and trustworthy negotiation partner. The US president, according to Pyongyang, thinks that the only just fate for the Kim Jong-Il leadership is the death of the regime. The North Korean leadership feels that as long as the Bush administration does not change its 'hostile attitude' towards Pyongyang, there is no need to proceed with negotiations. It claims that the United States is not to be trusted, as was clearly evidenced by the aborted fate of the Korean Peninsula Energy Development Organization (KEDO). KEDO was set up to administer the Agreed Framework of 1994, which was signed by North Korea and the United States. The latter, however, chose not to live up to the terms of the framework once the presidency shifted from one political party to another. Pyongyang voices further frustration over the recent Six-Party Talks in Beijing. According to the Agreement of Principles in September 2005, North Korea agreed to dismantle and suspend all nuclear programmes, facilities and weapons in several reciprocal phases in accordance with the principle of 'commitment for commitment and action for action'. This reciprocity and simultaneity were embedded in the agreed document, but the Bush administration insists that Pyongyang must comply with its commitments first before the United States can consider reciprocal actions. Pyongyang notes that no sovereign government is expected to strip itself of its means of national security when its security is threatened, and insists that the Bush administration is undermining the terms of the agreement. It appears that the governments of both China and South Korea agree with Pyongyang's interpretation of the outcome of the Six-Party Talks.

North Korea is often criticized for resorting to what many refer to as 'brinkmanship diplomacy' in declaring that there is no room for further negotiation and in refusing to compromise its stance with respect to the negotiations surrounding the nuclear crisis. Pyongyang, in turn, blames the USA for not being flexible and for attempting to 'strangle' North Korea. The leadership in North Korea has clearly demonstrated its frustration with the current US policy, predicated as it is upon the belief that Kim Jong-Il is an evil man and that his regime should not be allowed to remain in power. It is evident that Pyongyang feels that being a nuclear power is its only means of deterrence, and thus for survival. Under these circumstances, North Korea is not expected to compromise its nuclear stance without the assurance of regime survival through some type of security guarantee.

Although much has been written and said about Pyongyang's demand that the United States can and should be the guarantor of North Korean security, Kim Jong-Il is not easily persuaded to give up the doctrine of military self-reliance. To the extent that this is the case, the North Korean government is not likely to abandon its nuclear deterrence capabilities. This does not mean that it will not negotiate away the existing weapons and programmes, because the capability to develop and manufacture weapons would remain within North Korea itself. That capability cannot be neutralized by external powers through negotiation.

What Pyongyang seeks from the United States in the short run with regard to the security issue is US consent to replacing the current armistice agreement with a more durable peace arrangement. With the Korean Peninsula still technically at war, and US ground troops equipped with sophisticated weapons (which the North Korean government believes include tactical nuclear weapons), Pyongyang senses a very real and dangerous security threat. As a result, it is diverting an enormous amount of resources and manpower to its military – resources that could be better used to build its economy. Realizing that the improvement of bilateral relations beyond the security arena carries profound implications for its economic development, the North Korean leadership seeks to normalize relations with the United States as the first and foremost goal of its diplomacy.

Japan: managing a perplexing political culture

Policy is formed and implemented in the wider context of history and political culture. Nowhere is the relevance of the context as crucial as in the case of North Korean policy towards Japan.

The denunciation of Japan was the underlying basis for legitimizing the regime created under the charismatic leadership of Kim Il-Sung. Since North Korea came into existence, the atrocities committed by Japan during colonial times have been the subject of condemnation, the energizer of nationalism, and the content of civic and political education. Anti-Japan sentiment was effectively mobilized even before Kim Il-Sung came to power: it was used to justify the creation of the regime itself with Kim Il-Sung as the centre of authority. The historical fact that Kim Il-Sung was involved in a leadership capacity with guerrilla warfare in sporadic events in Manchuria has been grossly amplified, to the extent that he is said to have crushed the Japanese imperialists single-handedly. Numerous anecdotal and historical accounts portray Kim as an unmatched hero who emancipated his motherland from the 'yoke' of Japanese imperialism. In this way, Japan has been used as a vital source of regime and leadership legitimacy. To the extent that this anti-Japan sentiment has been invoked and used for political ends, the government of North Korea will find it difficult to change its attitudes towards the former colonial power.

Another factor that makes Japan central to North Korea is that Pyongyang has always been wary about the possibility of a resurgent Japan as a dominant regional power that might one day threaten the security of North Korea itself. This concern has been reinforced by the presence of the US military in Japan and the US–Japanese security alliance. An intriguing factor in this regard is the fact that North Korea's desire to build a nuclear weapons capability was initially prompted by Kim Il-Sung's witnessing of its awesome destructive power in Hiroshima and Nagasaki. For Kim, it was the surrender of imperial Japan to the might of the atomic bomb that established the immense value of nuclear-based deterrence. In short, the saliency of Japan in the mindset of North Koreans, and especially the leadership, can never be overstated: the very origin of the *Juche* idea is the anti-foreign doctrine in which Japan occupies a central position.

The relevance and significance of Japan to North Korea cannot be completely understood without examining the status and political orientations of Koreans living in the former colonizer while still sympathizing and identifying themselves with the northern part of the peninsula. The *Chosen Soren* community has had strong ties with North Korea since the very beginning of the Kim Il-Sung regime. When the regime of Syngman Rhee in South Korea (1948–60) virtually ignored some 600,000 Koreans living in Japan following Japan's surrender in World War II, many of whom had been taken from Korea forcibly by the Japanese government, North Korea made concerted efforts to care for their well-being. It was Kim Il-Sung's regime that provided them with schools at all levels, including a university in Tokyo (*Chosen Daikaku*). It was North Korea that helped them establish ethnic organizations in Japan and provided them with subsidies. The functional interaction between *Chosen Soren* and the North Korean government has thus been remarkably congenial. Over the years, the pro-North Korea community of Koreans has succeeded in establishing a solid economic base throughout Japan by monopolizing the pin-ball (*pachinko*) parlours industry, which is extremely lucrative. Their social and cultural status in Japan has never been commensurate with their economic achievement, as they lack self-esteem and social respect, but the North Korean government has not overlooked them – in fact it has given recognition and a hero's welcome to these visiting overseas compatriots from Japan. Kim Il-Sung's government created a cabinet-level quasi-official organization, the Committee on Overseas Compatriots, to accommodate and ensure their well-being. These Korean–Japanese, in return, have brought in such considerable sums of cash that they have at times been North Korea's largest source of foreign currency income.

Since the advent of Kim Jong-Il as the undisputed leader, and especially since 1998, North Korea has shown a heightened interest in opening an economic relationship with Japan. The period between 1994, when Kim Il-Sung died, and 1998, when the new constitution was adopted, coincides with the consolidation of power and leadership, involving purges of the political and military leaders of the 'old guard'. Once the leadership was consolidated, government policies showed greater pragmatism. It was the newly emerging pragmatism that led to Kim Jong-Il's inviting Japan's Prime Minister Junichiro Koizumi to Pyongyang in September 2002 and to the shocking surprise admission of the kidnapping of Japanese citizens. The admission of kidnapping itself was also intended to solidify the basis of legitimacy for the new leadership by demonstrating that it was dissociating itself from the old guard. Kim Jong-Il took upon himself the embarrassment and humiliation of not only admitting to the kidnapping to Koizumi but also promising, with an apology, that such misguided actions would not happen again. He also said that he had already punished those 'zealous military old guards' who were responsible for the inhuman abductions.

It seems important to consider the 'zealous military old guards' in terms of who they were and why they might have committed such a deplorable act as kidnapping innocent civilians, including children.[8] Setting aside the moral and political concerns surrounding the kidnapping, one might attempt a 'clinical' assessment of their mindset and motives. The present author had the opportunity of having a casual conversation with one of the key people who would have represented the old guard military leadership before 1994. This man recalled his two sisters being forcefully dragged away by imperial Japanese soldiers in front of his own eyes, never to be heard from again, during the period of colonial rule. He said that numerous similar atrocities that he had witnessed had led him to regard the Japanese as 'subhuman animals' and to believe that they 'deserved to be treated accordingly'.[9] I have little doubt that some of the old guard had such a mindset and that it may have been instrumental in the abducting of innocent Japanese citizens. One official in a recent conversation offered the observation that the abducted Japanese were used for 'instruction of Japanese language, not for forced prostitution or enslavement'.[10] The fever of hatred for Japan still runs high among North Koreans, especially the older generation, as the colonial time is still part of living memory.

Considering the anti-Japan sentiment in North Korea, Kim Jong-Il's unexpected departure from his previous denial of North Korean involvement in the kidnapping suggests that his desire to enhance bilateral relations with Japan may have been intense. This may have been necessitated primarily by economic need; however, Kim's desire to stimulate economic and political relations with Japan was frustrated, as Japanese public opinion and the media gave the government no room to expand any relationship with North Korea without a conclusive resolution of the abduction issue. Japanese public sentiment is clearly against improving relations with the Pyongyang regime unless this and other pending issues are resolved.[11] The government of Japan is virtually paralyzed by the abduction issue and unable to proceed with any policy towards North Korea. At the same time, Pyongyang is unwilling and unable to 'satisfy' Japan's demands. So the stalemate continues.

China and the resurgent fraternal relationship

China is a country of continuous importance to North Korea's economy and diplomacy. Since the end of the Soviet Union, Pyongyang has not felt the need to maintain equidistance with Beijing and Moscow. While China has prospered since the end of the cold war, Russia has been plagued by economic problems and political unrest, to such a point that North Korea has became only a peripheral concern. Pyongyang has adopted economic policies from China in the area of establishing special economic zones to attract foreign capital and investment. When the Rajin–Sonbong Special Zone did not bear fruit – due, among other things, to the general lack of legal and institutional infrastructure conducive to foreign economic activity – a range of economic and legal reforms were undertaken. However, the regime's inability to expose the social and economic system to foreign investors, coupled with the fact that North Korea is regarded by many as an unstable system, has continued to plague the economy.

Pyongyang sees China as a desirable model for its own economic development and modernization, a model that would allow the coexistence of a central political system and an open economic one. It is no secret that Kim Jong-Il is impressed with what China has accomplished in the fields of technological and economic development. His visit to Shanghai in 2001 resulted in North Korea crafting policies and reform measures in which information technology, managerial skills and limited market mechanisms were given greater attention. When the prospect of economic assistance that was expected to result from the previous Six-Party Talks diminished, Kim Jong-Il initiated a visit to China in January 2006 for the purpose of surveying the Chinese experience with economic development strategies. This trip suggests that North Korea is prepared to launch economic expansion plans with which China is willing to cooperate. North Korea has been sending scores of students and scientists to China for training as technocrats and experts. Due to the severe restrictions on the export of dual-use technology from the Western world, North Korea has opted to exploit China as a source of such technology. Pyongyang is also favouring China as a source of food supply and a partner for trade and economic collaboration. The volume of trade with China has shown a steady increase, reaching nearly one-third of the North's total trade turnover. A relatively stable fraternal relationship with China is expected to continue, as is evidenced by Beijing's sympathetic orientation towards North Korea in the Six-Party Talks. It is clear that the Chinese government desires to play a leadership role in the multilateral efforts to alleviate the North Korean nuclear crisis; yet Beijing also makes it clear that it has its own national agenda which may not be consistent with that of the Bush administration. The North Korean leadership seems to be convinced that it has an ally in this regard.

The epoch-making visit to Pyongyang by Chinese President Hu Jintao in October 2005 has been interpreted by the US government and its allies in Tokyo and Seoul as an effort to pressure Kim Jong-Il to fully dismantle all nuclear programmes and existing bombs. Pyongyang, however, has credited the Hu–Kim summit talks as having laid the basis for a stable bond between the two countries in the areas of security and the economy. There seems to have been serious discussion on the feasibility of patterning North Korea's economic development strategies after the Chinese model, and on the principle of economic cooperation between the two countries. Given this, it is highly likely that China will play a pivotal role in developing the North Korean economy. However, China could be discouraged from helping the North if doing so would adversely affect its relations with South Korea. Its economic ties with South Korea are significant to the Chinese government, and it would not choose economic cooperation with Pyongyang at the expense of its relations with the South, but since the sunshine policy of the late 1990s, South Korea has been successfully pursuing economic rapprochement with the North at a remarkable pace. The development of this inter-Korea relationship makes it easier for Beijing to be proactive in engaging itself with the economic opportunities and challenges in North Korea.

One fundamental consideration with respect to China's role in the development of North Korea and other Third World countries is the undeniable truth that all large nations possess the ambition to expand the sphere of their power and influence. This fundamental tenet of international relations has persisted throughout history, and China is hardly an exception. However, the North Korean government is seemingly more comfortable with the influence of China in forging its economic policies. This is mainly because China's economic expansion since the adoption of its outreach policy in the last quarter of a century represents a curious mixture of political communism and economic capitalism, accommodating an open economic system without compromising the communist one-party political system. North Korean leaders have seen China accumulate abundant material assets and display a great political mobilization capacity, both of which will enable the Chinese leadership to plan and implement massive initiatives in future. Given the relatively small size of the North Korean economy, it will hardly be an insurmountable burden for China to 'carry' North Korea, and the leadership in Pyongyang is well aware of this. At the same time, unlike the United States, China is not likely to interfere with North Korea's internal politics or ideological orientations – a fact which North Korean leaders will find comforting.

South Korea and inter-Koreas relations

To North Korea, South Korea is not just another neighbouring state. It has always been regarded as the other half of the nation. Pyongyang has never doubted that national unification will be realized when the South is liberated from the peril of US imperialism. The North Koreans believe that national division has been maintained because of the forcible occupation of the southern half of the peninsula by US forces and that reunification of the nation is impeded by the grand imperialist design of the United States. In this regard, South Korea's distancing itself from the United States, as seen in the sunshine policy of the government of President Roh Moo-Hyun, is considered encouraging.

The goal of reunification by means of socialist premises or on North Korea's terms has virtually been replaced by a more pragmatic premise of nationalist prosperity. Since the advent of the sunshine policy in South Korea, and especially since the inter-Korea summit meeting in 2000, Pyongyang has gradually changed its orientation towards the South in that it no longer considers the government in Seoul as a source of military or security threat. Rather, Pyongyang regards the South as a source of economic assistance and cooperation. This political and security 'comfort zone' has expanded into the social, academic and cultural arenas during the administration of Roh Moo-Hyun.

Sensing that the Roh government with its conciliatory policies towards the North may not last indefinitely, Pyongyang seems to be more motivated to move ahead with collaborative projects in Kaesong and elsewhere. Regarding the Roh government's promotion of more and more collaborative and cooperative measures in promoting inter-Korean relations, especially in the economic sector, the North Korean government has responded with reciprocally positive policies and attitudes. Beneath these seemingly conciliatory developments, however, there are some sources of continuing tension. One of these is the Roh government's domestic political problems; its sliding popularity coupled with rising conservatism and anti-sunshine policy sentiment, especially among the economic elite, does not bode well.[12] Another factor is Pyongyang's keen awareness of the danger that might accompany the flourishing economic and political interaction in the form of consumerism and 'spiritual pollution', which could eventually lead to the collapse of the regime itself.

While Pyongyang is obviously benefiting from the progressive policy of the Roh government, it is guarding itself against the possible overexposure of its people to new ideas – especially its government officials who are working directly with South Koreans. In this regard, North Korea is not being driven into the Kaesong industrial complex project, which could hold multiple dangers for the regime, without a plan. The plan is to preserve the ideological upper hand in its interactions with the South. The ideology that legitimizes politics in North Korea is primarily nationalism. Pyongyang seems to believe that an overwhelming majority of South Koreans, especially the younger generation, tends to be more nationalistic. It seems to be comforted by the opinion polls in the South that consistently show that a majority of the people find themselves in sympathy with the North, rather than with the United States.[13]

As long as the Pyongyang leadership feels that South Korea's sunshine policy brings economic benefit, and also possibly helps in winning the nationalist ideological war with the South, it will continue to seek an enduring economic relationship with the Roh government. Pyongyang believes that if Roh and his political party lose elections in future all the 'sunshine' measures will inevitably be rolled back; consequently, it is an opportune time for Pyongyang to maximize the collaborative economic programmes with the South, and it is imperative for it to do so as quickly as possible. The North therefore has an interest in preventing a breakdown of the Six-Party Talks so as to avoid a chilling effect on inter-Korea relations. Nevertheless, as observed above, the Kim Jong-Il government, owing to its being deeply entrenched with the country's military leadership, is mindful of the scenario of the sunshine policy possibly eventually inducing reforms that open up the North Korean system, which in turn could threaten the survival of the regime itself. They are also mindful of the fact that the South Korean government, no matter how nationalistic and sympathetic to the North, cannot turn its back against the United States. As a result, North Korea will pursue a

Southern policy that is based on the premise that Seoul's relationship with the United States should remain friendly, for the sunshine policy cannot withstand objections from Washington. These complex dynamics involving the United States, South Korea and North Korea represent new phenomena unprecedented in the cold war era.[14]

Conclusion

From this discussion it should be clear that North Korea's foreign policy orientations and policy statements are hardly inexplicable. In fact, with respect to the state's goals and how it seeks to achieve them, North Korea is not an atypical system. It has been consistent in pursuing the maintenance of the system and regime security. It has shown focused efforts to seek solutions to its economic difficulties without undermining the very survival of the system itself. The North Korean government has, indeed, shown an array of 'rational' choices of policy strategies and tactics that have yielded the greatest benefit to its national interests in that it has used the leverage of the nuclear programme most effectively to induce concessions from, and impose its own terms on, the negotiating parties in the region. As observed above, its foreign policy strategies and tactics have shown sensitivity to the changing environment of the region and the neighbouring states themselves, and these strategies are hardly beyond comprehension.

Yet the very dynamic nature of the power structure in post-cold war politics has given a new meaning to each of the political systems in East Asia, which makes the issue of the nuclearization of North Korea a complex conundrum that defies a simple, one-dimensional analysis. In this conundrum, Pyongyang is surprised by its ability to attract the attention of the world and to stand up to the power of the United States.

Notes

1 This apparent anomaly is discussed more fully in Han S. Park, 'Human needs, human rights, and regime legitimacy: The North Korean anomaly', in Moon Jung-in (ed.), *Understanding Regime Dynamics in North Korea: Contending Perspectives and Comparative Implications*, Seoul: Yonsei University Press, 1998.

2 The present author has advanced the theme that the ideology of *Juche* has evolved into a theological perspective. See Han S. Park, *North Korea: The Politics of Unconventional Wisdom*, Boulder, Colo.: Lynne Rienner, 2002, Chapter 4.

3 The satisfaction of human needs as the base of legitimacy is espoused extensively in Han S. Park, *Human Needs and Political Development*, Cambridge, Mass.: Shenkman Books, 1984.

4 For a comprehensive application of this concept of foreign policy goals, see William O. Chittick, *American Foreign Policy: A Framework for Analysis*, Washington, DC: CQ Press, 2006.

5 Ideology and performance are recognized as two different ways in which governments have sought legitimacy for power. John Schaar makes an excellent discussion on the concept of legitimacy in his book, *Legitimacy in the Modern State*, Brunswick, NJ: Transaction Books, 1981.

6 When the Six-Party Talks were deadlocked after the initial meeting in Beijing in 2003, a high-ranking government delegation from North Korea participated in an informal seminar with American participants in Athens, Georgia, USA, in November 2003. In the meeting, the North Koreans expressed the intention to come to the subsequent round of the Beijing talks only after assurances by American participants that there would be time for bilateral talks with the US delegates. There have been numerous other venues where Pyongyang has expressed the desire and necessity for direct negotiations with the United States.

7 The primary reason for Kim Jong-Il's inviting the Japanese prime minister was the fact that the North Korean leadership anticipated economic assistance and collaborative economic programmes from Japan. The series of recent visits by Kim Jong-Il to China have also been prompted by the prospects for economic assistance and cooperation from China.

8 A credible account of North Korea's motives for abducting Japanese citizens is that it wanted to train its spies to South Korea so that they could be disguised as Japanese. See *Nihon Keizai Shimbun*, 19 January 2003.

9 Although the identity of this general is not revealed here, anyone who is familiar with the nature of the atrocities committed by the Japanese imperial army will be aware of the widespread anti-Japan sentiment among the old generation in both North and South Korea.

10 Senior Researcher Pak Chol at the Korean Asia–Pacific Peace Committee made this observation in February 2004 when I visited Pyongyang.

11 Following the Koizumi visit, Takashi Shiraishi observed that 'the vast majority of Japanese still feel deep distrust toward North Korea for its role in the abductions and other problems ... It is hard to see the Japanese government moving ahead with the normalization and bilateral relations in the face of this kind of public sentiment'. *Japan Echo*, 29/6, December 2002.

12 Roh's dipping popularity has taxed his ruling Uri Party to the extent that the party leadership wants him to dissociate himself from the party if he is to help the party retain the presidency at the next election.

13 An opinion poll in South Korea showed that most people believe that the United States is primarily responsible for the division of Korea and is the greatest hindrance to unification. KSOI (The Korea Social Opinion Institute), 12 September 2005.

14 Of the six parties to the Beijing talks, Russia is not given separate analysis here because it seems to have only limited significance in relation to the North Korean nuclear conundrum. North Korea's policy towards Russia is of only marginal importance. The volume of their bilateral trade has dropped to under 4 per cent of North Korea's total trade in recent years. The fact that Russia is a neighbouring state and a significant nuclear power helped it to be included in the six-party 'club', but it will probably be a peripheral party to the negotiations.

3 Seoul's policy towards Pyongyang: strategic culture and the negligibility of Japan

Balbina Y. Hwang

In the study of international relations, the prevailing view about the characteristic of small states is their relative inability to conduct independent foreign policies due to constraints imposed by the structure of the international environment. This axiom is particularly accepted in the analysis of the foreign policies of Korea (both South and North). The common supposition about Korea is that, as a small power surrounded by major powers, the fate of this 'shrimp among whales' has for centuries been determined at various times by China, Japan, Russia and the United States. Moreover, geographically centred at the nexus of Great Powers' interests, the Korean Peninsula has been valued more for its strategic than for its intrinsic value. This being so, the conclusion often drawn about both the formation and the implementation of Korean foreign policies is that they are wholly dependent on the machinations or vagaries of its more powerful neighbours. These immutable traits cause Korean foreign economic policy to be determined in a reactive fashion, responding to the exigencies of the situations thrust upon the country. According to this capabilities-based argument, the only way Korean (again, both South and North) foreign policy formation can become more proactive is with a corresponding elevation of Korea's status and power in the regional hierarchy.

However, the argument presented in this chapter is that such a viewpoint is an incorrect characterization of the foreign policies of South Korea (the Republic of Korea, or ROK), particularly towards North Korea (the Democratic People's Republic of Korea, DPRK). While the structure of the international system – for example, the cold war structure – has been an important influence on policy formation in South Korea, it has not always had a direct causal effect on the resulting policy. For example, in 1998, President Kim Dae-Jung implemented and continued to promote his 'sunshine policy' despite criticism and scepticism in the region, particularly from Japan and the United States. Moreover, Kim's successor, Roh Moo-Hyun (inaugurated in February 2003) has continued to promote a policy of active engagement despite the eruption of a nuclear crisis and growing tensions between North Korea and the United States, and between North Korea and Japan.

This is because norms of identity within South Korea affect the responses to external forces in sometimes surprising and even unpredictable ways. Both global factors outside the state's control and internal elements within the domestic society have worked in South Korea to modify the foreign policy process. While this is not an unusual dynamic in the formulation of a state's foreign policies, it is surprising in the case of Korea because of the extraordinary influence that its neighbouring states have exerted in determining Korea's fate throughout its history. Korea's important geographic position in the region – as the 'dagger pointed at the heart of Japan', or Japan's stepping-stone to mainland Asia, depending on the point of view – and its relative weakness compared to neighbouring great powers have always made the peninsula a tempting battleground for control and influence by external powers, in particular Japan. The relative ease with which Japan annexed Korea in 1910 and its bitter legacy of brutal colonial rule for the next 35 years left a profound scar on the national Korean psyche that has remained long after 1945, and remains largely unhealed today.

While lingering historical bitterness is not unique to Korea, the unusual feature of Korea–Japan relations is the unexpected lack of influence that the former colonial power has over Korean policies (both South and North) despite the fact that Japan continues to dwarf Korea in relative strength and power. For example, considerations of Japan have indeed influenced inter-Korean dynamics, but it is not their effects alone that are interesting. Rather, it is how the domestic political society in Korea internalizes and modifies these pressures instead of merely responding to them passively. Such analysis reveals that the real significance of the 'Japan factor' is not that it has influenced South Korea's policy towards the North, but how little the real impact has been, given conventional predictions to the contrary.

This chapter therefore seeks to explain how and why Japan has played an ancillary role in the inter-Korean dynamic by first analysing the role of strategic culture in the creation and formation of South Korea's policy towards the North, and second examining the tumultuous history of Japanese–Korean relations and its significance for North–South relations. It concludes by discussing the implications for the future role of Japan on the Korean Peninsula and the regional security environment.

Strategic culture

Conceptual framework

In order to understand the foreign policies of a nation, one must first assess the state's inherent disposition and strategic goals in order to explain the desired outcomes and the policies that are chosen to pursue them. Only then is it possible to address the fundamental questions such as: What role does the external environment play in foreign policy formation? Why and when do external powers have an intervening effect in independent foreign policy decision making? For the purposes of this chapter, these questions are applied to analyse what role, if any, considerations of Japan have had on South Korea's policy towards North Korea.

In order to answer these questions, one must first understand how a state – in this case, South Korea – determines its security, particularly when it feels threatened.

How do such assessments or beliefs concerning threats inform decision makers' views about the strategic priorities regarding the state's security? And how do such understandings of priorities become manifested in fixed strategy, or policy? An understanding of how intentions are formed by strategic culture allows an explanation of policy actions not as isolated events but as part of a broader pattern of strategic calculations. It can also explain why one course of action was chosen over a range of other available alternative strategies. Perhaps more significantly, strategic culture can explain puzzling outcomes that do not seem to respond to conditions in the international system, such as why the Japan factor has not mattered more in inter-Korean dynamics, as one would have expected of a former colonial power and a critical democratic and capitalist ally of the United States.

Strategic culture is conceptualized here as 'an integrated system of symbols that establish pervasive and long-lasting strategic preference'[1] in a state's key decision makers, by formulating notions of the role and efficacy of the state in interstate political and economic affairs.[2] The symbols derive from the state's self-perceived identity or 'memory' thereof, which is made up of the most important geographical, societal, cultural and ideational influences in a state's history.

Factors such as geography, history and culture are important because, as Chung-In Moon observes, they 'inform threat perception by identifying sources and types of outstanding and potential threats' to the state's security. Ideas provide a set of 'norms, beliefs and value orientations that shape a society's understanding of the security concerns'. And, finally, identity itself is important because it 'offers a critical referent for defining the contents and scope' of the security threat in question.[3] All these factors combine to create what Alexis de Tocqueville terms mores, or 'habits of the heart', that is, the sum of ideas that shape mental habits among men and includes 'the whole moral and intellectual state of a people'. It is precisely mores, de Tocqueville argues, that form the basis of the support of political institutions within a state.[4]

The system of symbols becomes embedded in the domestic state, as Charles Kupchan argues, because their 'images and symbols at once mould public attitudes and become institutionalized and routinized in the structure and process of decision making'.[5] The symbols in turn affect political leaders, government bureaucracies and business leaders by defining their central roles and missions. These decision makers then rank grand strategic preferences[6] according to a shared central paradigm of assumptions about the nature of the competition and the competitors.[7]

The case of Korea

Korea's (before its division, and afterwards in both the North and the South) national strategy has always been to maintain independence in its domestic and foreign policies, a posture which stems from a deeply embedded strategic culture of nationalistic survival. This term describes the acute sense of Korean insecurity born of a continuous historical pattern of territorial invasions and assaults that have challenged the existence of an independent, sovereign kingdom and relatively homogeneous society.

In its 2000 years of recorded history, Korea has suffered over 900 foreign invasions, great and small. It has experienced five major periods of foreign occupation – by China; the Mongols; Japan; and, after World War II, the United States (in the South) and the Soviet Union (in the North). Of these experiences, those with Japan have remained the most bitter. When unified Japan began its major expansion in the sixteenth century, its leader, Hideyoshi Toyotomi, attacked Korea as the first phase of an invasion of the Chinese mainland. Eventually the Japanese were driven out with an early class of ironclad (turtle) warships but only after laying waste to the land, thus setting a lasting pattern of enmity. In the wake of the Japanese invasion and a subsequent invasion by the Manchus, who were soon to take power in China, Korea established a rigid policy of excluding foreigners.[8]

Korea was the last of the major cultures in East Asia to be 'opened' by Western imperialism, not necessarily because it was stronger, but 'perhaps because it was more recalcitrant', observes Bruce Cumings.[9] Korea did not enter into its first international treaty until 1876, not because it wanted to, but because it was forced to under foreign pressure. On 22 February the Treaty of Kanghwa was signed under Japanese pressure, or 'diplomacy with a gun to the temple, an offer Korea couldn't refuse', as Cumings observes, and featured provisions typical of an unequal treaty.[10] The most important of its 12 articles proclaimed that, as an autonomous nation, Korea possessed 'equal sovereign rights' with Japan. The objective behind this declaration of Korean independence was to open the way for Japanese aggression without inviting interference from China, which had historically claimed suzerainty over Korea. Korea would be officially annexed by Japan on 22 August 1910 under the Treaty of Annexation.[11]

The year 1876 marked the beginning of 'modern' Korea – a country whose leaders could no longer shape events as they wished: 'For the first time in its history, the country was shaped from without more strongly than from within'.[12] Other treaties followed in short order, more as defensive measures than anything: in 1882, Korea signed a Treaty of Amity and Commerce with the United States, and a treaty with Tsarist Russia to build the Trans-Siberian railway.[13]

In the ensuing years, with China's relative decline, Russia and Japan exercised direct power in Korean affairs, with Japan warring against China (the Sino-Japanese War, 1894–5) and then sponsoring epoch-making reforms on the Korean Peninsula, and Russia offering King Kojong the shelter of its legation from the Japanese, and for a time involving itself in Korean politics. In the Treaty of Shimonoseki, which concluded the Sino-Japanese war on 17 April 1895, the Chinese government formally ceded its influence over Korea, repudiating age-old Sino-Korean tributary ties, and solidifying Japan's foothold on the Korean Peninsula.[14]

In 1902, Japanese decision makers carved out a stronger position for their country by entering into an alliance with Britain, the most important European power in the region. The Japanese government recognized British interests in China in return for British recognition of Japan's 'special interest' in Korea. Sensing weakness along the rim of the Chinese mainland, Tsarist Russia began moving forces into Korea and immediately came into conflict with Japan. In an attempt to head off a clash, the Japanese government proposed that the two countries carve up Korea into spheres of influence, with the dividing line at the 38th Parallel.[15] The negotiations eventually failed, however, and the rivalry evolved into the Russo-Japanese War in 1904, when the Japanese navy launched a successful surprise attack on the Russian fleet at Port Arthur, stunning Asia by becoming the first non-Western nation to subdue one of the 'great Western powers', and putting the Japanese in a powerful position to dominate the Korean Peninsula.

The Russian government recognized Japan's paramount rights in Korea under the Portsmouth Peace Treaty, signed in 1905 and brokered by Theodore Roosevelt, who won the Nobel Peace Prize for it. Diplomatic notes exchanged between Roosevelt and the Japanese – known to every Korean schoolchild as the Taft–Katsura Agreement – acknowledged a trade-off between the Philippines and Korea: Japanese leaders would not question American rights in its colony, the Philippines, and the US leaders in turn would not challenge Japan's new protectorate, Korea. The Japanese government thus had a 'free hand' in Korea after 1905, as the diplomatic historians say, because of its victories over China and Russia, and because of the support of Britain and the USA (the Anglo-Japanese Alliance had been concluded in 1902). As long as the direction of Japanese imperialism was towards Korea and Manchuria, which kept it at a distance from the Philippines or the many British colonies, it had the blessing of London and Washington.[16]

In some ways, the 'real story' behind Korea's century-long development was, as Cumings observes, 'indigenous Korea and the unstinting Koreanization of foreign influence, not vice versa'.[17] This is precisely the basis for Korea's deeply embedded strategic culture of 'nationalistic survival', which shapes national identity and acts as a mediational filter. At times, this filter produces 'logical' outcomes, meaning those that are commensurate with the state's international position. But at other times the state's foreign policies may be unexpected in nature or seemingly not derived from international pressures. These latter cases are the clearest indication of the critical role of domestic–ideational factors as a mediating force in strategic choice. A broader implication of the role of strategic culture is that, regardless of immediate changes in the external environment – such as the end of the cold war – because of Korea's immutable relative position in the region, South Korea's strategic culture will continue to prevail, producing predictable, although not necessarily logical, foreign policy outcomes, particularly in its policy towards North Korea.

The following section traces the evolution of the South's policy towards the North, revealing that South Korean strategies have been far more consistent and independent than conditions in the external environment might imply.

The formation of South Korean policy towards the North

Since 1945, when the Korean Peninsula was essentially divided by foreign powers at the end of World War II, the Korean people have harboured a deep yearning for the reunification of their country and a return to their historical status as a homogeneous nation of nearly five millennia. This desire has been equally intense on both sides of the 38th Parallel; indeed, the only differences have been over the means and method, resulting in a costly three-year fratricidal war that tragically only maintained the status quo division. Since the end of the Korean War in 1953, successive governments in both North and South Korea have pursued policies on unification, the achievement of which has been their respective national priorities.

Such a prevailing nationalist goal has dominated the South Korean pursuit of four foreign policy goals since the inception of the Republic in 1947: national security, economic prosperity, national prestige and peaceful reunification. Throughout the decades, South Korea's political systems have evolved from authoritarianism to democracy, but these four foreign policy goals have essentially not changed.[18] In pursuit of these goals each successive regime has resorted to a strategy of supremacy, emanating from the premise that the only way to make the North Korean regime abandon its policy to communize South Korea by all means and seek peaceful coexistence is to make South Korea's economic and military capabilities and its diplomatic position irrevocably superior to North Korea's.

Even more remarkable than the fact that these four foreign policy goals remained unchanged throughout the changes in regime is that they have remained constant despite dramatic changes in the external environment with the end of the cold war, which conventional wisdom argues should have inexorably altered the parameters, if not the actual calculations, of Korean foreign policies. Shifting power relations in the region, after all, are considered by most Koreans to be the cause of their country's division. The political characters of the two Koreas were determined in many ways from the outset by the ideological rivalry between East and West, and both the North and the South Korean states found an external guarantor for their own security. Consequently, the foreign policies of both Koreas were largely dominated by the ebb and flow of East–West competition.

The division of two Koreas

As World War II drew to a close in August 1945, the Korean Peninsula was divided into two 'temporary' spheres of influence by the *de facto* Soviet occupation of the northern half of the peninsula, and a hastily made decision by the United States to occupy the southern half below the 38th Parallel.[19] In November 1947, upon the failure of the US–Soviet Joint Commission to reach agreement on the establishment of a unified government in Korea, the United Nations General Assembly adopted a resolution calling for free general elections in both halves of Korea under UN supervision, as an initial step towards inaugurating a unified Korean government.

The North, however, by now firmly under the political control of Kim Il-Sung, rejected this resolution, and a general election was held only in the South on 10 May 1948 under the auspices of the United Nations Temporary Commission on Korea (UNTCOK). The result was the establishment of the ROK government, which proclaimed its sovereignty on 15 August, and the election of Syngman Rhee as the country's first president.[20]

From the beginning of his tenure in 1949 until he was ousted from power by a student-led revolt in April 1960, Rhee maintained a posture of implacable hostility towards North Korea and pursued a policy of reunification through a victory over communism. The intervention by the US government and 15 other UN members to aid South Korea in the aftermath of the North Korean attack on 25 June 1950 helped to bring Rhee's objective of defeating the communists and presiding over a unified Korea tantalizingly close to realization, but ultimately failed.

Stalemate and continued division

After seizing control of the South Korean government on 16 May 1961 in a relatively low-key coup, Park Chung-Hee implemented a policy that prioritized economic reconstruction of the South while maintaining an uncompromising attitude of 'unification through victory over communism (*sunggong t'ong il*)' towards the North.[21] Park's emphasis on strengthening the South Korean economy as part of the strategy towards the North was not surprising given South Korea's precarious position in the region. In 1961, South Korea was politically and socially unstable, with an economy that was almost entirely dependent on the United States. More than 40 per cent of all households were living below the poverty line, and the average per capita income was less than 100 US dollars (USD) per annum.[22] Just as worrisome to Park was his country's complete dependence for military support on the United States, a foreign backer whom he fundamentally mistrusted.[23] Thus, Park's intensive efforts to focus on economic growth were in large part an effort to increase his independence from Washington, particularly in an era when the US willingness to protect the country against the North seemed to be waning.[24] The focus on rapid economic development was a clear manifestation of the strategic culture of nationalistic survival, which recognized that the building of national power, with emphasis on economic power, was a necessary prelude not only to enhancing national security but also to establishing independent security options, including the issue of reunification.

By the late 1960s, after consolidating his domestic political power base, Park was able to implement his blueprint for economic modernization and development. One of the key efforts as part of this strategy was the massive influx of foreign capital and technology, as a result of the conclusion of the South Korea–Japan normalization treaty in 1965. Despite fierce domestic opposition based on hostility to the former colonial master, the Seoul–Tokyo normalization initiated by Park (and strongly encouraged by Washington) brought an immediate Japanese assistance package of 800 million USD and millions more in Japanese investments and valuable economic cooperation projects with Japanese firms.[25] This is an important example of how pragmatism derived from the strategic culture of national survival trumps ideological or emotional currents that are often argued to be the sources of 'irrational' Korean foreign policy outcomes.

The 'Nixon shock'

In fact, rather than Japan, it was actions taken between the governments of the United States and China that had the most far-reaching and profound impact on

South Korean policies towards the North. On 9 July 1971, Us National Security Advisor Henry Kissinger landed secretly in Beijing to begin the historic Sino-US rapprochement. As Don Oberdorfer notes, Korea probably did not figure in US President Richard Nixon's desire to end the USA's two decades of hostility with China, which had begun with China's intervention in the Korean War.[26] Rather, among the factors uppermost in Nixon's triangular diplomacy with Beijing and Moscow was its potentially alarming effect on North Vietnam, another Asian client of the two giants of international communism. By simultaneously improving ties with both Hanoi's sponsors, Nixon hoped to demonstrate that North Vietnam was expendable and vulnerable in a larger game being played by major players.

Although probably unintended, the same sets of pressures were felt in North Korea and, to Washington's eventual dismay, in South Korea as well. As a result, both Korean regimes felt more insecure than ever before, with fears of abandonment by the great powers increasing acutely.[27] Both Korean governments would thus attempt to parlay their vulnerability by venturing into seemingly more flexible strategies towards reunification, but with little result.

In Seoul, Park was shocked by the news of Nixon's opening to China, and, with no advance notice from Washington, it raised profound doubts about the constancy and reliability of US sponsorship. For Park, the rapprochement implied US acceptance of a hostile, powerful and revolutionary country in South Korea's immediate neighbourhood, doubly more dangerous because it was tied with a military alliance to North Korea. With the 'Nixon Doctrine' in mid-1969 – that Asians should provide the manpower for their own wars – the United States had appeared to be moving steadily towards disengagement from Asia. Early in 1971, over Park's vehement objections, Washington had withdrawn two divisions – approximately 20,000 of the 62,000 US troops – stationed in South Korea since the Korean War, at the same time as it was pulling back US forces from South Vietnam. Finally, the breakdown of the Bretton Woods dollar-gold international financial system, also in 1971, seemed to portend the beginning of the end of the global system of US economic and military hegemony on which the South Korean state had been founded, and on which it continued to depend.[28]

Despite the reassuring words of US political leaders and diplomats, Park took these developments as 'a message to the Korean people that we won't rescue you if North Korea invades again'. Park later described the manoeuvring surrounding the US rapprochement with China: 'this series of developments contained an unprecedented peril to our people's survival... [The situation] almost reminded one of the last days of the Korean Empire a century earlier, when European Powers were similarly agitating in rivalry over Korea'.[29]

Korean détente

When Pyongyang began to soften its posture, Seoul's swift response took the form of first proposing Red Cross-sponsored humanitarian talks, followed by secret high-level exchanges in Pyongyang in May 1972, which proved to be remarkable not for having any lasting impact but for the expression of shared antipathy to the major powers and the heavy emphasis by both Koreas on reaching accords and eventual reunification.[30] Shortly thereafter, following the secret visit to Seoul by the North Korean deputy premier, who conferred with President Park, the governments of North and South Korea surprised the outside world by publicly issuing a North–South Joint Statement on 4 July 1972, a date that seemed to have been chosen to punctuate the symbolism of declaring independence from a great power.[31] The statement, 'pursuant to the intention of their respective superiors', declared that the two sides had reached an agreement on three principles for achieving unification: independence from foreign interference, peaceful means, and national unity transcending differences in ideology and system.[32]

The astonishing joint statement did little to reduce the confrontational stance or fundamental disagreements between the two states, thus indicating that that statement was much more likely a product of desperate pragmatism derived from the compelling strategic culture of nationalistic survival. Both governments felt immense pressure and insecurities from the momentous actions taken by their respective great power patrons, and the statement was more a declaration of Korean independence from external machinations than any concrete attempt at reunification.

The puzzle most commonly expressed about the aftermath of the 1972 agreement is 'why did the initial attempt at North–South dialogue suddenly flower and then wither?', but this is in fact the wrong question. The more fundamental and relevant puzzle is why the seemingly revolutionary agreement did not produce the expected changes in attitude and stance between the two parties. The answer lies in the reality that for both governments the tentative agreement on reunification was the result not of true readiness or willingness to reunify, but of the attempt to do so on their own terms, and for the first time without external influence which was mutually considered the ultimate threat to their own security.

The paradox is that, in order for each side to maintain its strength and ability to thwart domination by the other, each had to rely on the support of the great powers – China and the Soviet Union for North Korea, and the United States and Japan for South Korea – the very support that both sides fundamentally chafed at and resented. Thus, at the height of the cold war, when a unique confluence of great-power withdrawal seemed to be occurring, both Koreas made the surprising push for rapprochement which was driven by intense insecurity.

Some argue that 'without a strong push from the outside powers, who had conflicting interests and who were paying little attention to the Korean peninsula, the two rival states were incapable of sustaining their dialogue'.[33] Yet it was precisely this fear of great-power inattention that had led the two Koreas to reach a tentative agreement, at least temporarily. Instead, the ensuing decade saw the pursuit of military strategies by both Koreas that prioritized military build-ups, which at first glance may seem counter-intuitive and illogical given the simultaneous move towards a thawing of relations. But, within the context of the strategic cultures of nationalistic survival, both Korean leaders formulated and pursued long-term strategies for reunification based on conspicuous strength; this would be achieved by increasing national power through directed efforts towards economic modernization.

Nordpolitik

The basic tenor of the static nature of inter-Korean relations would remain largely unchanged through the 1980s, and it was only with the stunning democratic election of Roh Tae-Woo as president of South Korea, in December 1987, that a new era of activity with the North began to emerge. On 7 July 1988, Roh formally elaborated this new national policy towards the North in what would become known as the *Nordpolitik* (*Bukbang Jeongchek*) speech.

Of the Roh administration's outreach efforts, one of the most significant was the establishment of full diplomatic ties with Moscow in 1990.[34] Much of the *Nordpolitik*'s success for South Korea was based on major openings in Eastern Europe following the fall of the Berlin Wall in 1989, the unification of Germany in 1990, and the dissolution of the Soviet Union in 1991.[35] Following on the heels of Mikhail Gorbachev's perestroika and glasnost of the late 1980s, the Roh government stressed the importance of exploiting new opportunities with the Soviet Union as part of a calculated strategy of attrition diplomacy towards the North.

Perhaps most notably, the Roh government's engagement of the communist camp resulted in a major environmental shift around the Korean Peninsula, and in principle established the possibility for the United States and Japan to establish diplomatic ties with North Korea and finally realize Kissinger's cross-recognition proposal first proffered in 1973.[36] This is yet another example of how South Korean policy towards the North affected Japanese policy, rather than the more predictable inverse causal relationship.

In advance of the historic Gorbachev–Roh San Francisco summit meeting in June 1990, uncertainty about how North Korea would react caused worry in Washington and Seoul, with speculation that Pyongyang might strike out 'irrationally'. In fact, rather than turn inward or 'lash out', as feared after the setback caused by Moscow's rapprochement with Seoul, Pyongyang sharply intensified a flurry of diplomatic activism with the governments of China, Japan and South Korea in an effort to match the diplomatic accomplishments of its rival south of the 38th Parallel.

Kim Il-Sung initiated his new diplomatic initiative in dramatic fashion with an overture to Japan. On 24 September 1991, as a result of contacts that had begun earlier in the spring and accelerated after the Gorbachev–Roh meeting in June, 44 members of the Japanese Diet – the most important official mission to date – visited Pyongyang. Over the next four days, the Great Leader deployed all his personal charm and diplomatic skill to negotiate an unexpected breakthrough with the country he had fought in World War II and had long treated as an 'unregenerate antagonist'.[37]

The 'Japan factor' in inter-Korean wrangling

The Japanese government had normalized its relations with South Korea in 1965, expressing regret for the 'unfortunate period' of Japanese occupation from 1910 to 1945, and providing 800 million USD in grants and credit assistance. In the ensuing years, Japanese trade, investment and technology were important factors in the rapid economic development of the South. Allied with both countries, the US government strongly supported South Korean rapprochement with Japan and over the years worked quietly to reduce tensions that might threaten the relationship.

Japan–North Korea relations had been much more contentious. Kim Il-Sung had made modest overtures to Tokyo in the early 1970s, at the time of the US–Sino détente and the initiation of the North–South talks, but a rapprochement between Pyongyang and Tokyo had been vehemently opposed by Seoul and was given no encouragement from Washington. Thus, while stunning in its boldness, Kim Il-Sung's fresh overture to Japan in 1991 should not have come as a surprise given the renewed sense of superpower betrayal, this time from the Soviets. During the Japanese visit in 1991, Shin Kanemaru, considered the most powerful figure in Japanese politics at the time and the head of the delegation, met with Kim Il-Sung and recounted that Kim was furious at the Soviet Union and spoke of the necessity for 'yellow skins' to stick together against 'white skins'.[38]

Kim Il-Sung then proceeded to propose an immediate normalization of relations with Japan. Reversing Pyongyang's previous position, this proposal implied forthright Japanese acceptance of two Koreas, which North Korea had always vehemently opposed. The pay-off for North Korea would be a large sum of Japanese reparations, in keeping with the precedent of the 1965 Japan–South Korea accord. The Japanese delegation, comprising members of the Diet from the ruling Liberal Democratic Party (LDP) and the Socialist Party, issued a three-party declaration with the North Korean Workers' Party. Among other points, the joint statement declared that Japan should fully and formally apologize and compensate North Korea for the 36 years of Japanese occupation of Korea and also for the 45 years of 'abnormal relations' after World War II.[39] Additionally, Kanemaru personally made astonishing and profuse apologies for past Japanese sins, of the kind that South Korea had long demanded from Japan but had never received. Further, Kanemaru indicated a readiness to provide reparations not only for the colonial period, as had been done at the time of normalization with South Korea, but also – inexplicably – for the abnormal relations with Pyongyang in the post-war period.

This created an unprecedented uproar in Tokyo and Seoul because the statement was issued without coordination, either with the Japanese Foreign Ministry or with the South Korean government, and because it went well beyond what the South had received as part of the 1965 Tokyo–Seoul Normalization Agreement. Moreover, Washington joined the concern that some of the Japanese funds would be used to support North Korean military and nuclear weapons programmes. As a result of the furore, Kanemaru later flew to Seoul to express his regrets for having sidelined South Korea, but the damage had been done. The incident fed South Korean suspicions of Japanese duplicity and was interpreted as evidence of a two-Koreas policy designed to perpetuate the division of the peninsula.[40]

Ultimately, Japanese negotiations with North Korea were turned over to Japan's Foreign Ministry. During the next eight rounds of normalization talks, over a period of two years from January 1991 until November 1992, Pyongyang demanded, above all, that Tokyo recognize it rather than Seoul as the only lawful government in Korea, which effectively ended prospects for normalization given that Japan would never be able to honour it – a fact that North Korean leaders most likely knew, which implies that it was deliberately raising a barrier to negotiations for normalization.[41] The negotiations thus failed to make any progress in ties between Tokyo and Pyongyang, and succeeded only in raising scepticism of Japanese motives in Seoul, and to a lesser extent in Washington.

In some respects, this fiasco only served to increase Seoul's leverage over Tokyo in its policy towards Pyongyang. In an effort to make amends for the damage done to relations with South Korea over the Kanemaru fiasco, the then Japanese Prime Minister, Toshiki Kaifu, acted quickly to close off another issue of discord by formally agreeing the following year to a request from President Roh to approach Pyongyang only after prior consultation with Seoul. Kaifu also agreed that any efforts to improve Japanese relations with North Korea must be preceded by meaningful progress in the inter-Korean dialogue, and agreed to provide economic assistance and aid to North Korea only after normalization was achieved. The agreement, as Armacost and Pyle observe, was a simple recognition of the fact that Japan had a lot more at stake with South Korea than with the North.[42] This commitment to coordinate Japan's policy towards North Korea closely with Seoul and make it dependent upon the progress of North–South relations has been repeated by subsequent Japanese prime ministers, and illustrates further the constraints on independent Japanese policy on the peninsula, as well as the limits to Japanese influence on North Korean policy.

Return to the status quo

Roh's North Korea policy seemed to mark a significant shift from containment to engagement, and from confrontation to reconciliation and cooperation. This new stance ostensibly allowed for the launch of new rounds of public and secret negotiations with North Korea, eventually leading to by far the most important document adopted by the North and South since their joint statement of 4 July 1972 – the December 1991 Agreement on Reconciliation, Nonaggression and Exchanges and Cooperation between the South and North.

Yet, as with the earlier, 1972, declaration, although the 1991 agreement did mark an important milestone in inter-Korean relations, it was not for the reasons most commonly assumed; while it did indeed formalize a policy of engagement, more importantly, it did not alter the zero-sum competition with the North. Primarily driven by concerns of relative gains *vis-à-vis* North Korea, President Roh's seemingly sudden shift in policy towards the North did not occur in a vacuum, nor in isolation from external influences and opportunities. Much like the impetus for rapprochement in the early 1970s that drove the two Koreas together, compelling factors in the global and regional environment in the late 1980s and early 1990s provided the unique opportunity for Roh's calculated policy of engagement to gain traction. As Oberdorfer observes, it was one of those rare periods when the policies of the two Koreas were in alignment for conciliation and agreement, with all the major outside powers supportive or at least neutral.[43]

Post-cold war uncertainty on the Korean Peninsula and the 'Japan factor'

Throughout the post-World War II period, Japanese interests on the Korean Peninsula have been dominated by two overarching principles: preventing a war on the Korean Peninsula and supporting South Korea as the only lawful government on the peninsula. Firm adherence to these principles effectively prevented Japan from having much influence on the Korean Peninsula, in the first case because it has no ability to project military capabilities beyond its borders, and in the latter because of the rigidity of the cold war structure.

Following the collapse of the Soviet Union, however, and the initiation of *Nordpolitik* by Seoul in the early 1990s, Japanese decision makers were finally able to initiate tentative efforts to keep official and unofficial channels open for talks with North Korea. However, diplomatic efforts, including the botched 1991 trip to North Korea by Shin Kanemaru, did not reach fruition, despite increasing alarm in Japan about North Korea's development of nuclear weapons and missile programmes. The asymmetry between Japanese concerns and the country's decreasing ability to influence developments on the Korean Peninsula is a powerful example of the diminutive effect of the 'Japan factor' in inter-Korean relations.

Since the end of World War II, Japanese leaders had generally deferred to the South Korean insistence that matters having to do with the reduction of tensions or a peace mechanism on the Korean Peninsula must be resolved through inter-Korean dialogue, because of the Korean sensitivity to what may be perceived as Japanese interference in peninsular affairs. This feature of Japanese policy was also based on Tokyo's gradual realization that it has little choice but to coordinate its policy closely with Seoul and not attempt initiatives towards the North without consulting the South. This position was confirmed in the aftermath of Tokyo's failed initiative in 1990 to normalize relations with Pyongyang.[44]

Such deference on the Japanese part also effectively shut the country out from the pursuit of independent policies towards Pyongyang. Two developments in the aftermath of the 1994 nuclear crisis offered tantalizing opportunities to alter this pattern. The first was the establishment in April 1999 of the Trilateral Coordination and Oversight Group (TCOG) through the 'Perry Process'. Based on a report issued by former US Defense Secretary William Perry, who had been tasked by the US Congress to conduct a complete review of US policy towards North Korea, one of its strongest achievements was institutionalizing trilateral policy coordination through the creation of the TCOG, whose aim was to narrow the policy gaps among its three members, the governments of the United States, South Korea and Japan. During President Kim Dae-Jung's historic visit to Tokyo in October 1998, the two governments had agreed to increase defence consultations and to establish regular bilateral cabinet meetings, and in 1999 Japanese and South Korean warships conducted their first joint exercises, which were focused on humanitarian search and rescue operations. This process gradually moved a step further with discussion of a trilateral joint defence framework.

The fruit of this solidarity was clearly evident in their coordinated response to North Korea's plan to launch a Taepodong-2 long-range missile, which had been expected on or around 9 September 1999, the 51st anniversary of the North Korean communist government. Since the preparations for the launch were detected in mid-June, and North Korean sources confirmed the plan in early July, the three countries deepened their coordination and issued strong warnings against another missile launch, which ultimately never occurred.[45] The trilateral coordination culminated in the summit meeting of Japanese Prime Minister Keizo Obuchi, US President Bill Clinton and South Korean President Kim Dae-Jung on the occasion of the Asia–Pacific Economic Forum (APEC) meeting on 12 September 1999, where they reiterated their determination to penalize North Korea if it proceeded with the planned missile launch.[46]

This unity also greatly facilitated the Berlin agreement of 13 September 1999 in which Pyongyang agreed to halt testing of long-range ballistic missiles in exchange for a commitment from Washington and Tokyo to move forward with economic assistance to North Korea.[47] After the agreement, Japan lifted the sanctions it had imposed on North Korea after the August 1998 missile launch. Indeed, through the TCOG, Tokyo joined Washington and Seoul in sending North Korea the message that it had more to gain through cooperation than confrontation and that the three countries were united in their resolve to counter any North Korean provocation.[48]

The second development after the 1994 nuclear crisis that offered an opportunity for an independent Japanese policy towards Pyongyang was the launching of Kim Dae-Jung's 'sunshine policy' of engagement in 1998. Although the national interests of South Korea, the United States and Japan have coincided throughout the decades in terms of primary objectives – such as maintaining peace and stability on the Korean Peninsula and in the region – differences between the three began to emerge and became starker after Seoul launched its engagement of Pyongyang in earnest. Given the alarming nature of North Korean missiles, the Japanese government was reluctant to embrace the South Korean government's engagement by mirroring it with its own conciliatory gestures towards Pyongyang. During his visit to Japan in September 2001, some three months after the historic inter-Korean summit, Kim Dae-Jung expressed the hope that relations between North Korea and Japan would be improved as expeditiously as possible, as this would contribute substantially to the advancement of South Korea's national interests, security and future development.

The then Japanese Prime Minister, Yoshiro Mori, stated that he was willing to assist the North Korean government build up its infrastructure. However, he noted that it would be difficult to convince the Japanese public to support the provision of such fundamental economic assistance to North Korea, given the concern that such economic aid could benefit the North's military build-up. His statement was interpreted to mean that large-scale assistance from Japan would not be provided until Japanese concerns about the threat presented by North Korea were resolved, thus putting a serious damper on South Korean euphoria over improved relations with the North.[49]

North Korea's nuclear challenge

Since then, and with the recurrence of another nuclear crisis with North Korea in 2002, the national priorities of the three governments have increasingly been divided. While all three still prioritize avoiding war on the Korean Peninsula, there is less agreement on the priorities of preventing a collapse of the regime in Pyongyang and other issues such as human rights. Moreover, divisions exist among the three countries over how to address the ever-present North Korean threat – such as its nuclear weapons missile programmes, and illicit activities – as well as their expectations of each others' roles in addressing these issues. Some examples have been the Japanese government's increasing assertiveness – supported widely by the Japanese public – in pursuit of defensive measures, such as the launching of its own national intelligence satellites[50] to better monitor North Korean missile activities, and legislation to make remittances to North Korea more difficult. Perhaps the starkest example of a key difference in policy with South Korea has been Tokyo's decision to proceed with development of a missile defence system in cooperation with United States – a programme that the South Korean government has publicly criticized as being unnecessarily provocative of North Korea.

The so-called Six-Party process was launched in 2003 to address precisely these coordination concerns, and to bring together the even more disparate interests of China, Russia and North Korea, all with the aim of permanently denuclearizing the Korean Peninsula. The TCOG process was superseded by the Six-Party format, and Japan's voice has diminished even further, as the Six-Party Talks have evolved to allow little consideration for specific issues that are considered bilateral in nature, such as that of the kidnapped Japanese citizens. Thus, while arguably Japan is the single other government that shares with the United States the greatest sense of urgency about ridding North Korea of its nuclear weapons programmes, Tokyo's North Korea policy has in fact been hijacked by the Japanese public's preoccupation with the issue of the abductions of Japanese citizens.

New regional dynamics

When Prime Minister Junichiro Koizumi came into office in Japan in 2001, hopes were high that he would launch a new era in relations with the Korean Peninsula.

Had he been successful, it would have effectively helped Tokyo overcome a sense of diplomatic passivity during this period of rapid change in the political environment surrounding the Korean Peninsula. However, with the re-emergence of the issue of North Korea's nuclear weapons, and a public that was demanding a strong attitude towards North Korea, the Japanese government naturally conformed to the tougher US stance, which was in stark contrast to the South Korean approach aimed at resolving the nuclear crisis through continued engagement and dialogue. Thus, Japanese policy makers were again unable to forge an independent policy towards the North.

Instead, Koizumi has addressed the new insecurities posed by North Korea by strengthening Japan's long-standing bilateral military ties with Washington in an effort to shore up its defence capabilities. In the past, Japanese leaders had been reluctant to increase the country's security cooperation with the United States for the fear of 'entrapment', but given the severe nature of the threats in the new security environment, the Japanese government now believes that the benefits of a closer military alignment with the United States in case of a contingency on the Korean Peninsula outweigh the potential costs.[51]

Ironically, closer Japanese cooperation with the United States and the country's movement away from ambiguity in defining the threats posed by North Korea may have contributed to a regional atmosphere in which Tokyo's ability to act on its concerns is diminishing, rather than increasing.

For the governments of Japan and the United States, closer bilateral coordination is a positive move that enhances deterrence to curb North Korea's adventurous provocation while promoting stability on the Korean Peninsula, but other actors of the North-East Asian region have regarded this development with greater scepticism. This closer bilateral coordination comes at a time when Koizumi's insistence on continued visits to the Yasukuni shrine – a memorial to Japan's war veterans but an affront to many Asians because it also enshrines several Class A war criminals – and the publication of several primary school textbooks that feature distorted interpretations of the Japanese role in World War II, have heightened tensions and sensitivity and evoked suspicions among Japan's regional neighbours about the true ambitions of its government and people. Combined with flare-ups with China and South Korea over lingering territorial disputes, Japanese leaders' seeming reluctance to confront the country's history once and for all has again become the focal point, drawing energy away from the cooperation required to pursue the Six-Party process effectively. Clearly, any tensions and South Korean and Chinese disagreements with Japan have the effect of boosting Pyongyang's ability to maintain a hard-line stance towards Tokyo.

Two other areas of Japanese cooperation with the United States have elicited negative reactions among the regional neighbours – missile defence and the Proliferation Security Initiative (PSI). Japan has become the first country officially to begin joint development with the United States on a missile defence system, despite predictably negative reactions from regional neighbours China, North Korea and Russia. More surprising has been South Korean criticism of the missile defence system, which views the system as an unnecessary provocation of

North Korea. Many in South Korea argue that pursuit of a defence system that will effectively make North Korean missiles an obsolete threat only spurs Pyongyang to pursue aggressively other deterrent capabilities, including nuclear weapons programmes.

Another area of US–Japanese cooperation that has produced consternation in the region has been the Japanese government's early support of the PSI, a rapidly growing multilateral regime that emerged as a new response to the proliferation of weapons and illicit materials in the aftermath of the 11 September 2001 terrorist attacks. Its aim is interdict the illicit trafficking of weapons of mass destruction to 'states and non-state actors of proliferation concern' by incorporating cooperative actions and coordinated training exercises. Since the PSI's inception on 31 May 2003, in stark contrast to Japanese support, Seoul has resisted US pressure to join, citing concerns about the adverse reaction from North Korea.[52] The current South Korean government has publicly expressed scepticism about the true motives behind the PSI, arguing that its intent is to force a regime change in Pyongyang, a prospect that many South Koreans find dangerous and destabilizing. Such deep divisions between Japan and South Korea pose profound challenges to the future cooperation that is necessary to thwart North Korean threats.

Conclusion

Despite the end of the cold war more than a decade ago, North-East Asia remains one of the most volatile regions in the world, with the Korean Peninsula the pivotal point for potential disaster. While inter-Korean relations and the future of the peninsula can be considered an internal issue for the Koreas to resolve, the resolution of the division of the peninsula is key to the future of political order and stability in East Asia. Accordingly, all the major powers of the region, including the United States, have a key stake in its peaceful resolution.

Yet, as this chapter has attempted to argue, despite the historically significant role the great powers have played in determining the past fate of Korea, since its division, and in particular in the post-cold war period, consecutive South Korean governments have been far more independent in their conduct of policies towards the North than conventional arguments would predict. Moreover, since Korea's liberation from Japanese occupation at the end of World War II, Japan's role and influence on policy towards the North have been surprisingly negligible and far less than traditional theories of power relations might predict.

Indeed, despite the critically important economic role that Japan plays in the region, it has had little direct influence in Seoul's policies towards North Korea. While both Koreas have consistently prioritized strategic calculations of the external environment in their policies towards each other, ultimately Japan has had little independent effect beyond its position as one of the great neighbouring powers of the Korean Peninsula. In part, this is a natural reflection of Japan's peculiar position in the international order as an economic powerhouse but not a 'normal' political actor. It has also reflected the functional role of Japan as the

USA's junior partner in a rigid alliance system that was in part designed to limit the breadth and depth of Japanese foreign policy ambitions.

Although North-East Asia is undergoing dynamic change, the Japanese inability to have independent influence on the Korean Peninsula will probably remain unchanged, in large part because of the profound impact of Korean strategic culture in both Koreas' foreign policy formation. In spite of, or perhaps because of, the overwhelmingly dominant role that Japan has historically played on the peninsula, Korea (either separately, or as a unified country) will endeavour to limit the impact of a 'Japan factor' on Korean policies. In this regard, Japan will continue to be an important, but ultimately secondary, player in the future of Korea.

Notes

1 An 'integrated system of symbols' means a kind of meta-structure, or unified set of images and symbols that shape how the state – both state elites and the public – understands the nature and scope of the relationship between national security and governmental policies, and the position of their state *vis-à-vis* the international system. In addition, the meta-structure provides a cognitive map that guides decision makers as they assess threats and formulate and implement policy. Note that Chung-In Moon uses the term 'meta-structure' as one particular angle with which to analyse security practices. Chung-In Moon, 'South Korea: Recasting security paradigms', in Muthiah, Alagappa (ed.) *Asian Security Practice: Material and Ideational Influences*, Stanford, Calif: Stanford University Press, 1998.

2 This definition is adapted from Alastair Iain Johnston, 'Cultural realism and strategy in Maoist China', in Peter Katzenstein (ed.), *The Culture of National Security*, New York: Columbia University Press, 1996, pp. 222–3.

3 Moon, 'South Korea: Recasting security paradigms'. For a detailed discussion of the role of identity in security, particularly within the constructivist perspective, see Alagappa, *Asian Security Practice*, Chapter 1; and Alexander Wendt, 'Constructing international politics', *International Security*, 20/1, 1995, pp. 71–81.

4 Alexis de Tocqueville, *Democracy in America*, transl. George Lawrence, New York: HarperCollins, 1966, Vol. I, Part II, Chapter 9, p. 287.

5 Charles Kupchan, *The Vulnerability of Empire*, Ithaca, NY: Cornell University Press, 1994, pp. 5–6.

6 I use the official US government definition of 'grand strategy' as 'the coordination of all elements of national power, including economic, political and military to accomplish national goals, primarily security against external threats'. US Department of Defense, *Dictionary of Military and Associated Terms*, 1987, pp. 350–1. For a more qualified and subtle debate on the differences between the components of 'military strategy' versus 'national strategy', see Barry Posen, *The Sources of Military Doctrine: France, Britain, and Germany Between the World Wars*, Ithaca, NY: Cornell University Press, 1984; and Alastair Johnston, *Cultural Realism: Strategic Culture and Grand Strategy in Chinese History*, Princeton, NJ: Princeton University Press, 1995, pp. 36–7.

7 Johnston, *Cultural realism*, p. ix. Note that Johnston defines strategic culture using the terms 'conflict' and 'enemy' where I substitute 'competition' and 'competitors', respectively. I do so because I believe these terms are more appropriate in the discussion of economic strategies.

8 The only foreign enclaves that were allowed to remain were a Chinese enclave and a small Japanese one that had been established at the southern port of Pusan. Don Oberdorfer, *The Two Koreas: A Contemporary History*, Reading, Mass.: Addison-Wesley, 1997, p. 4.

9 China was the first to succumb to the West during the Opium Wars of 1839–42, and Japan came next when Commodore Matthew Perry's 'black ships' appeared in Tokyo Bay in 1853. Bruce Cumings, *Korea's Place in the Sun: A Modern History*, New York: W. W. Norton, 1997, p. 86.

10 Cumings, *Korea's Place in the Sun*, p. 102.

11 Carter J. Eckert *et al.*, *Korea Old and New: A History*, Seoul: Ilchokak Publishers, 1990, pp. 200–1. See also Martina Deuchler, *Confucian Gentlemen and Barbarian Envoys: The Opening of Korea, 1875–1885*, Seattle, Wash.: University of Washington Press, 1977, pp. 47–9.

12 Cumings, *Korea's Place in the Sun*, p. 86.

13 In this treaty, Korea's first with a Western power, the United States promised to provide 'good offices' in the event of external threat, presumably from Korea's neighbours. Cumings, *Korea's Place in the Sun*, p. 86.

14 Eckert *et al.*, *Korea Old and New*, p. 223.

15 Note that Cumings disputes the historical accuracy of the 38th Parallel being the line of division during these negotiations. Nevertheless, the significance of this latitude would reverberate profoundly a half-century later, in 1945, when Russia (the Soviet Union) once again played a part in partitioning Korea at the 38th Parallel, along with the United States. Another agreement, in 1896, to create a demilitarized zone between the Russian and Japanese armies, was also to resonate during the Korean War. Cumings, *Korea's Place in the Sun*, p. 123.

16 Akira Iriye, *Pacific Estrangement: Japanese and American Expansion, 1897–1911*, Cambridge, Mass.: Harvard University Press, 1972, pp. 47–8; and Cumings, *Korea's Place in the Sun*, pp. 141–2.

17 Cumings, *Korea's Place in the Sun*, p. 20.

18 Sang-Seek Park, 'Determinants of Korean foreign policy', *Korea and World Affairs*, 10/3, fall 1986, pp. 457–83.

19 For further details, see Cumings, *Korea's Place in the Sun*, pp. 185–2; and Oberdorfer, *The Two Koreas*, pp. 5–10.

20 Yu-Hwan Koh, 'Unification policies of two Koreas and the outlook for unity', *Korea Focus* [Seoul: Korea Foundation] 8/6, November/December 2000, p. 91.

21 Park introduced this phrase in a speech on 25 June 1966. B. C. Koh, 'Policy toward reunification,' in Youngnok Koo and Sung-joo Han (eds), *The Foreign Policy of the Republic of Korea*, New York: Columbia University Press, 1985, p. 82.

22 Mark Clifford, *Troubled Tiger*, New York: M. E. Sharpe, 1994, pp. 50–5.

23 Oberdorfer, *The Two Koreas*, p. 33.

24 Note that in the North, in a similar way, Kim Il-Sung also struggled during this period to gain independence from his Soviet and Chinese supporters.

25 For further details on the normalization see Youngnok Koo, 'Conduct of foreign affairs', in Edward Wright (ed.), *Korean Politics in Transition*, Seattle, Wash.: Royal Asiatic Society/University of Washington Press, 1975, pp. 217–18; 222–5.

26 Oberdorfer, *The Two Koreas*, pp. 11–12.

27 Ibid., pp. 12–13.

28 Eckert *et al.*, *Korea Old and New*, p. 364.

29 Park Chung-Hee, *Korea Reborn*, New York: Prentice Hall, 1979, p. 48.

30 From 2 to 5 May 1972, Lee Hu-Rak, director of the South Korean Central Intelligence Agency (KCIA), visited Pyongyang in utmost secrecy and met North Korean leader Kim Il-Sung. A transcript of their discussion can be found at *Monthly Joongang*, March 1989 (in Korean); the North Korean version can be found in *KIS Works* 26, 1989, p. 134ff; and Oberdorfer, *The Two Koreas*, pp. 23–4.

31 For Seoul's version of these contacts, see *Confrontation with Dialogue*, Korea Policy Series no. 5 (Seoul: Korean Overseas Information Service, 1972); B. C. Koh, 'Policy toward reunification', p. 88; and Oberdorfer, *The Two Koreas*, p. 24.

32 *Nodong Shinmun,* 4 July 1972 and *Dong-A Ilbo,* 4 July 1972. For further details, see Yu-Hwan Koh, p. 94; and B. C. Koh, 'Policy toward reunification', p. 88.
33 Oberdorfer, *The Two Koreas,* p. 46.
34 See Ho Joong Cho, 'The road toward South Korea–Soviet recognition', *Shin Dong-Ah,* August 1994, pp. 453–67 (in English).
35 Lee, Chung Min, 'Neighbors, friends and allies: From the outside looking in', in Chung-In Moon and David Steinberg (eds), *Kim Dae-Jung Government and Sunshine Policy,* Seoul: Yonsei University Press, 1999, pp. 88–9.
36 Perry Wood, 'The strategic equilibrium on the Korean Peninsula in the 1990s', in James Cotton (ed.), *Korea Under Roh Tae Woo,* St Leonards: Allen & Unwin, 1993, p. 194.
37 Oberdorfer, *The Two Koreas,* pp. 220–1.
38 Ushio Shioda [What was discussed by the 'Kanemaru North Korean Mission'?], *Bungei Shunju,* August 1994, as translated in Oberdorfer, *The Two Koreas,* pp. 221–2.
39 Masao Okonogi, 'Japan–North Korean negotiations for normalization', in Manwoo Lee and Richard W. Mansbach (eds), *The Changing Order in Northeast Asia and the Korean Peninsula,* Boulder, Colo.: Institute for Far Eastern Studies, Kyungnam University/Westview Press [1993], pp. 195–216.
40 Michael Armacost and Kenneth Pyle, 'Japan and the unification of Korea', in Nicholas Eberstadt and Richard Ellings (eds), *Korea's Future and the Great Powers,* Seattle, Wash.: National Bureau of Asian Research, 2001, pp. 136–7.
41 Okonogi, 'Japan–North Korean negotiations for normalization', p. 216.
42 Armacost and Pyle, 'Japan and the unification of Korea', p. 138.
43 Oberdorfer, *The Two Koreas,* p. 260.
44 Armacost and Pyle, 'Japan and the unification of Korea', pp. 136–7.
45 Japan warned North Korea on 5 August 1999 that it would suspend all cash remittances and goods shipments by Koreans living in Japan to North Korea if North Korea proceeded with its plan to test-fire a new long-range ballistic missile. *New York Times,* 9 August 1999.
46 C. S. Eliot Kang and Yoshinori Kaseda, 'Japanese security and peace regime on the Korean Peninsula', *International Journal of Korean Unification Studies,* 9/1, 2000, pp. 127–8.
47 *New York Times,* 13 September 1999.
48 Kang and Kaseda, 'Japanese security', p. 129.
49 Hosup Kim, 'Korea–Japan relations and tasks for the Roh administration', *Korea Focus,* 11/3, May/June 2003, pp. 80–1.
50 This move required reinterpretation of a 1969 Diet resolution against the military use of space.
51 For a discussion on the concept of 'entrapment', see Victor Cha, *Alignment Despite Antagonism: The United States–Korea–Japan Security Triangle,* Stanford, Calif.: Stanford University Press, 1999, pp. 38–43.
52 Kyudok Hong, 'South Korea's dilemma on the Proliferation Security Initiative', *Korean Journal of Defense Analysis,* XVII/1, spring 2005, p. 105.

4 US North Korea policy: the 'Japan factor'*

Yoichiro Sato

Introduction

North Korea is the most visible and immediate factor driving recent changes in Japanese security policy. The renewed threat of North Korea developing nuclear weapons has been a major catalyst in bringing Japan's basic defence policies up to speed and motivating Japan to make larger commitments to providing logistical support to US forces in the event of a military contingency in the region.[1]

While steps to fortify the US–Japan alliance have been well appreciated, Japan's apparent desire to move towards normalization of relations with North Korea, despite its intransigence on the nuclear issue, has raised criticism in some parts of Washington. As these critics perceive it, Prime Minister Junichiro Koizumi's announcement that he would visit Pyongyang in the autumn of 2002 ran counter to a series of US efforts to plug the loopholes in the 1994 Agreed Framework.

In addressing such criticism in the United States, a senior Japanese diplomat argued that Japan's policy towards North Korea had been erroneously characterized as ambiguous in the United States, noting that, whereas the US government tended to focus exclusively on the nuclear issue, the Japanese one was concerned with a wide range of issues, including medium-range missiles, espionage efforts, and the abduction of its citizens by North Korean agents. Tokyo, it was argued, hoped to resolve these issues in the long term by establishing better relations with North Korea while at the same time maintaining a deterrent capability.[2]

While this comment justified Koizumi's visit to Pyongyang in the light of the highly complex interests of Japan, it did a disservice by oversimplifying the US interests and policy on the Korean Peninsula. After all, the differences between Tokyo and Washington over the issues on the peninsula were differences of degree, priorities and approaches, rather than of fundamental strategic interests. The transition from the Clinton administration to that of President George W. Bush in 2000 was not the only factor behind the changes in US policy. Rather, such changes were driven by a multitude of factors. They included North Korean behaviour during the last few years of the Clinton administration; US domestic (particularly Republican) criticism of President Clinton's North Korea policy; events that were largely external to the security of North-East Asia but important to US global strategy (such as the 11 September 2001 terror attacks and Iran's suspected nuclear weapons development); US global responses; and inputs from key allies of the USA. Inevitably, the policy process is evolutionary.

This chapter seeks to do three things. First, it traces the evolution of the Bush administration's North Korea policy with its main focuses on nuclear weapons and ballistic missile proliferation, as well as its priorities among the related issues and negotiation strategies. Despite the alleged unilateralist tendency of the Bush administration, its handling of the North Korean nuclear crisis reveals elements of multilateral diplomacy. In addition to describing such multilateral elements, this chapter explores their roots in the US global strategic objectives and their relevance to the North Korean crisis.

Second, the chapter examines whether the concern that is unique to Japan (the abduction of its citizens) and Japan's different priorities (with greater emphasis on missile development) played or did not play into US considerations in the process of policy coordination among the allies. Critical examination of the 'special relationship' between the United States and Japan which developed during the tenures of President George W. Bush and Prime Minister Koizumi requires that we look not only at the issues of convergence, but also at the divergences.[3] This will allow a deeper and more nuanced understanding of the extent of policy coordination.

Finally, the chapter describes the 'outcome' of the ongoing nuclear crisis – changes in Japan's security policy – which may in turn directly affect the future course of this crisis and US policy for dealing with it. The long-held paradigm about the relations between the USA and Japan – that Japan is a 'reactive state'[4] – has led scholars to look at US policy preferences as exogenous inputs into Japanese foreign policy. To examine this view critically, others have focused on endogenous sources of Japanese foreign policy, from the perspectives of both material interests[5] and intangible values and ideologies.[6] However, little consideration has been given to Japan's role as an exogenous causal factor in US foreign policy. There is a continuous reciprocal causal relation between Japanese foreign policy as an input into US foreign policy and US foreign policy as an input into Japanese foreign policy. The recent upgrading of Japan's military contributions to the bilateral security cooperation, in which the North Korean crisis was one of the key exogenous factors, may in turn enhance the United States' ability to exercise a predominant influence over security matters in North-East Asia, including the ongoing nuclear crisis on the Korean Peninsula. I therefore summarize the key development in the US–Japanese military cooperation that may enable US–Japanese co-hegemony[7] in the security arena.

The evolution of the Bush administration's North Korea policy

Despite criticizing the 1994 Agreed Framework before assuming office, the George W. Bush administration's North Korea policy did not make a drastic departure from the framework until early in 2002.[8] The Trilateral Coordination and Oversight Group (TCOG) meeting on 26 May 2001, for example, issued a joint statement in which the three parties 'expressed their strong continued support for the Republic of Korea's policy of reconciliation and cooperation with North Korea and President Kim's leading role in resolving inter-Korean issues', and 'reaffirmed' their commitment to continue the Agreed Framework.[9] The US and Japanese delegates expressed hope that the second inter-Korean summit would reduce tensions on the peninsula, and the US delegates 'presented *preliminary elements* of the Administration's review of policy toward North Korea' and 'invited the ROK and Japan to provide comments and suggestions'.[10] The 'axis of evil' speech by President Bush in January 2002 was followed by the administration's announcement that it could not certify North Korean compliance with the Agreed Framework. In the same month George Tenet, director of the US Central Intelligence Agency (CIA), told the Senate Armed Services Committee that 'North Korea continues to comply with the terms of the Agreed Framework *that are directly related to the freeze on its reactor program*'.[11]

In contrast to the common view that North Korea's highly enriched uranium (HEU) programme was suddenly discovered in the summer of 2002, it was the cumulative intelligence that can be traced back as early as to 1999 which led to the administration's decision to confront North Korea with this new charge.[12] US Deputy Secretary of State Richard Armitage commented in February 2003 that the 'bold new approach' the US government was about to propose towards a comprehensive normalization of the relationship with North Korea was 'derailed... by our discovery of a covert uranium enrichment program for nuclear weapons'.[13] This statement, however, needs to be clarified by the more detailed testimony of US Assistant Secretary of State for East Asian and Pacific Affairs James Kelly in the same month – that 'last summer we concluded that Pyongyang had moved from R&D to construction of a plant that could produce enough weapons-grade uranium for two or more nuclear weapons per year when fully operational – which could be as soon as mid-decade'.[14] The need for closer cooperation with key North-East Asian allies (Japan and South Korea) was heightened by the US military engagement in Afghanistan and Iraq.[15] It was in this context that the United States proposed multilateral talks to North Korea.

In March 2003 Kelly stated:

> [T]o achieve a lasting resolution, this time, the international community, particularly North Korea's neighbors, must be involved. While the Agreed Framework succeeded in freezing the North's declared nuclear weapons program for eight years, it was only a partial solution of limited duration. That is no longer an option. That is why we are insisting on a multilateral approach, to ensure that the consequences to North Korea of violating its commitments will deny them any benefits to their non-compliance. It was easier for North Korea to abrogate its commitments to the United States under the Agreed Framework, thinking it would risk the condemnation of a single country.[16]

The consolidation of what would later be known as the key element of US policy – CVID (complete, verifiable and irreversible dismantlement) *before* discussion of rewards for North Korea – can be seen during this period. Likewise, the US negotiating approach – to focus on the nuclear weapons first, and then incrementally link the rewards to North Korea's progress in other issue areas such as human rights, missiles, chemical and biological weapons, support of terrorism, and conventional force posture – emerged during the same period in close consultation with the governments of South Korea and Japan.[17] Thus, the administration's decision to pursue North Korea's acceptance of a more comprehensive set of regulations started to take shape in the spring of 2002, and although the new decision was soon communicated to the Japanese counterpart, the new policy was still in an evolutionary state until about the spring of 2003.

The United States and Japan in the evolution of the Six-Party multilateralism

The end of the cold war did not stabilize the Korean Peninsula. Quite the contrary: 'the loss of economic assistance and a restraining hand from Moscow' led North Korea to seek to 'compensate for its failure of governance and loss of economic viability by seeking to develop nuclear weapons, and by developing and exporting missiles and other weapons of mass destruction'.[18]

As Robert Manning correctly points out, 'North Korea's nuclear problem was but a symptom of the larger Korean problem, not the source of it'.[19] The 1994 Agreed Framework was successful in 'freezing North Korea's *known* nuclear weapons program', but did not 'seriously reduce tensions, the conventional military threat, or advance North–South reconciliation'.[20] Assuming that North Korea is willing to trade its ultimate security guarantee (its nuclear weapons programme) 'for security assurances and a new economic and political engagement with the United States, South Korea, and Japan',[21] 'the absence of a larger strategy beyond the nuclear accord has [nonetheless] allowed the DPRK to set the diplomatic agenda since 1993'.[22]

Despite policy consultations between the United States, Japan, South Korea, other Western states and (to a limited extent) China, the Agreed Framework was in essence a bilateral agreement. To be sure, it had some limited multilateral characteristics: (a) it made reference to the North–South agreement of December 1991 to keep the Korean Peninsula free of nuclear weapons; (b) it included multilateral financing of the Korean Peninsula Energy Development Organization (KEDO); and (c) the framework was to bring back North Korea under the multilateral International Atomic Energy Agency (IAEA) inspection regime. On the other hand, enforcement of the Agreed Framework was largely left to North Korea's counterpart in the agreement, the United States. Despite its military supremacy, US military action against North Korea would incur substantial costs to its forces and allies. Other proactive but non-military options, such as economic sanctions or rewards, required coordination with Japan and South Korea.[23] The US influence over North Korea by diplomatic and economic means was therefore limited. The absence of significant economic relations between the United States and North Korea, due to the economic sanctions that were already in place (in contrast to North Korea's sizeable and growing economic relations with China and South Korea), left the United States little room for additional economic sanctions.

The same was true for Japan, despite its more extensive economic relations with North Korea; hence Japan refrained from unilaterally imposing official and full-scale sanctions. Japan's involvement with North Korea has oscillated during and after the cold war. Its non-confrontational and conciliatory approach (although limited), starting with Prime Minister Kakuei Tanaka's policy shift from an exclusive focus on South Korea's security to the peace and stability of the whole Korean Peninsula, fluctuated with the rise and easing of cold war tensions.[24] The start of diplomatic normalization talks in the early 1990s was seen as an extension of this historical pattern. However, the revelation within a few years of North Korea's nuclear and missile development led the Japanese to identify North Korea as a threat.[25] The availability of US protection and Japan's self-imposed constitutional restrictions against the use of military forces went hand in hand in leading Japan to entrust its security policy to the US lead. By avoiding otherwise necessary high military expenditure of its own, which would inevitably chill relations between Japan and South Korea, Japan also benefited economically from its relations with South Korea.

Coordination between the USA and Japan in matters of the Korean Peninsula is not entirely independent of South Korean preferences. South Korean leaders used to see Japan as a possible security back-up (although they preferred US protection),[26] but with a growing confidence in their ability to manage the relationship with the North, they began to try to limit the involvement of external actors during the 1990s, beginning with Russia and Japan. US policy makers had to be careful in their handling of the repeated South Korean proposals for four-party talks (between the USA, China, South Korea and North Korea) on issues of the Korean Peninsula and efforts to enlist the United States as a co-sponsor of such a proposal.[27]

These basic frameworks still hold, and the Japanese government is therefore hedging against both shortcomings in US protection (due to divergent interests) in the immediate term and a loss of political influence and economic stake in post-reform North Korea (if that happens) in the medium term.[28]

Prior to the Koizumi visit to Pyongyang, Tokyo was reluctant to emulate the bilateral summit approach of South Korean President Kim Dae-Jung to engage the North, which the Clinton administration welcomed:[29] US Secretary of State Madeleine Albright visited Pyongyang in late 2000. The Japanese government was unwilling to start normalization talks with North Korea during the second half of the 1990s while North Korea denied abduction of Japanese citizens. If nothing else, Koizumi's announcement in the autumn of 2002 that he was to visit Pyongyang, which completely reversed Japan's previous approach, caused a degree of confusion at the least.

Japan's preparation for the 2002 summit meeting of Koizumi and North Korean leader Kim Jong-Il was an effort not to be left out by its TCOG partners. President Kim Dae-Jung's 'sunshine' policy towards North Korea was replacing

South Korea's earlier resentment at a perceived overzealous US-led engagement policy towards North Korea. Japan was thus caught in a dilemma, between on the one hand opposing the US/South Korean engagement policy on the basis of its own unresolved agenda and priorities, and on the other hand the risk of losing a voice (if not a seat) in the emerging multilateral framework for dealing with problems with North Korea (including those unique to Japan). It moved, rather belatedly, towards engaging North Korea – at the same time as the United States started critically reviewing its own engagement policy.

Japan in US North Korea policy

The US policy towards North Korea is guided by several identifiable global strategic considerations, in addition to the regional considerations of North-East Asia. The proactive stance taken by the United States on the North Korean problems, moulded in these global considerations, gives US allies such as Japan relatively limited manoeuvring room. At the same time, a high degree of convergence between Japan's global interests and those of the United States – the foundation of the expanding scope of the bilateral alliance – means that the US regional policy is still highly consistent with Japanese interests. Japanese 'inputs' into the US policy towards North Korea are thus limited mostly to coordinating their respective negotiating approaches and tactics, rather than working on major differences in policy objectives.

The 'Japan factors', therefore, should be viewed from the 'outputs' perspective as well. The North Korean crisis has without doubt accelerated Japan's enhanced military cooperation with the United States.[30] While many point to the underlying and more long-term projections of China's ascent to the status of regional giant as the main driver of Japan's growing security consciousness, North Korea has demonstrated more visible and unanimously recognized threats to the Japanese people, helping the decision makers forge a domestic consensus on Japan's expanded military roles.[31] This, in return, broadens US options at a time when its military is busy fighting insurgents in Iraq.

The Bush administration has identified Japan as the cornerstone of US alliances in the Asia–Pacific. The close personal ties that developed between Prime Minister Koizumi and President Bush were further supported by a well-known Japan hand, Richard Armitage. Close policy coordination between the governments of Japan, the United States and South Korea was institutionalized in the form of the TCOG during the second Clinton administration, but tripartite coordination based on engagement of North Korea (centred around the sunshine policy of South Korean President Kim Dae-Jung) was drastically revised by the incoming Bush administration, due to North Korea's defiance of IAEA inspections and its provocative ballistic missile testing (among other actions) during the second Clinton administration. Within the trilateral TCOG, close coordination between the governments of Japan and the United States has continued, but signs of South Korean divergence from the other two have become more visible.

Despite the departure of Armitage, the second Bush administration continues to view Japan as a key partner in Asia. In the words of Assistant Secretary of State for East Asian and Pacific Affairs Christopher Hill, the US–Japan alliance 'represents more than a defensive balance of power. It is also a positive force of progress. We now have a historic opportunity to transform our alliance to meet the challenges of the 21st century – including both traditional and new security, economic, and transnational challenges'.[32] The close bilateral coordination between the governments of Japan and the United States was possible because the divergence of interests between them was minimal.[33] Issues around North Korea other than its nuclear weapons development clearly carry differing weights for Tokyo and Washington.[34] On the other hand, the predominance of the nuclear weapons issue as the number one priority for both countries has worked to smooth out most of their differences on the other issues – such as North Korea's ballistic missiles and the abduction of Japanese citizens.

The Japanese government consulted its counterparts in the USA about the plan for Prime Minister Koizumi's 'surprise' visit to Pyongyang in the summer of 2002. The groundwork for the visit was carefully prepared by the Ministry of Foreign Affairs for almost a year.[35] The conventional public wisdom that the US government was told of the forthcoming Koizumi visit to Pyongyang only three days in advance, and that the US government only then informed the Japanese government about North Korea's HEU programme,[36] is inaccurate, as this information was exchanged at least a few months earlier than is commonly acknowledged.

The US government had by that time decided to add North Korea's HEU programme to the expanded list of charges against it and warned Koizumi about the existence of the HEU programme in the summer of 2002. However, it did not explicitly oppose Koizumi's decision. During the summit meeting in Pyongyang in September 2002, Koizumi won from Kim Jong-Il the return of five abductees. Unfortunately, Koizumi's gambit – to resolve the abduction issue completely and normalize the relationship with North Korea before (or in parallel to) addressing the nuclear issue – failed, as conflicts over the remaining abductees and those unaccounted for halted the bilateral normalization talks. As alternative models for multilateral negotiations started emerging with strong Chinese brokerage, the Japanese government had to be rescued by its US ally from diplomatic isolation by the Chinese and South Korean preference for 'four-party' (United States, China, North Korea and South Korea) talks, which would have excluded Japan and Russia.

The US global agenda, North Korea policy, and Japan

Among the numerous issues that involve North Korea, the most important for the United States is the development of nuclear weapons by North Korea. From the standpoint of non-proliferation, the United States has opposed known and suspected nuclear weapons development by North Korea, India, Pakistan, Libya, Iraq and Iran since the early 1990s. While the first North Korean crisis in the mid-1990s was averted by the Agreed Framework, actual testing by India and Pakistan in 1998 led them to declare themselves nuclear weapon states. Internationally coordinated economic and military sanctions in which the United States took part did not alter the two states' behaviour. The sanctions were considerably eased after Pakistan expressed its cooperation with the United States in the war on terrorism.[37]

In his famous 'axis of evil' speech of January 2002, President Bush identified three states (North Korea, Iran and Iraq) as developing nuclear weapons, while at the same time working on the 'Libyan model' of dissuasion combined with positive inducements of improved political and economic ties, and initiating proactive policies to induce these countries to roll back their nuclear development efforts. While the US government seeks ways in which to enhance multilateral management of fissile material, it also focuses on the underground market for the transfer of nuclear technology, the danger of which was amply demonstrated by the revelation of the network of a Pakistani nuclear scientist, A. Q. Khan. Under the Proliferation Security Initiative (PSI), the United States also leads efforts by the 'coalition of the willing' to interdict shipments of fissile material, weapons of mass destruction (WMD) components, and components for the enrichment of fissile material.

The US government identified North Korea as a state sponsor of terrorism because of its involvement in several incidents which have concerned the US allies in the region – providing a sanctuary for Japanese Red Army members, an attempt at the assassination of South Korean President Chung Doo-Hwan in Rangoon in 1983, and the bombing of a Korean airliner in 1987. Kim Jong-Il's admission during the September 2002 summit with Koizumi that Japanese citizens had been abducted and active lobbying by the abductees' families contributed to the US State Department listing North Korea as a sponsor of terrorism in April 2004.[38]

Enhancing the control of fissile material

While North Korea's nuclear weapons development has exposed major weaknesses in the nuclear non-proliferation regime, US efforts to enhance the control regime require careful consideration of its allies' interests. Japan's dual identity as one of the foremost anti-nuclear-weapon states and one of the foremost users of nuclear energy complicates its non-proliferation stance and hence policy coordination with the United States.

In the aftermath of the 1991 Gulf War, IAEA inspectors discovered evidence of 'an ambitious clandestine nuclear weapons program in Iraq, involving a number of undeclared installations'.[39] The IAEA Safeguards Protocol only mandates ensuring the non-diversion of nuclear material from declared installations. To rectify its inability to detect clandestine programmes, the IAEA, with strong backing from the US government, successfully negotiated a Model Additional Protocol in 1997, which included broadened requirements on the member states to submit information and give additional access rights to IAEA inspectors.

While the 1968 Treaty on the Non-Proliferation of Nuclear Weapons (NPT) assured the peaceful use of nuclear energy for states that gave up nuclear weapons, 'the NPT was threatened by the actions of a number of states that sought – without ostensibly violating the treaty – to come very close to complete acquisition of the nuclear fuel cycle, that would put them in what we call a "breakout" position... and that's why the President said that the only really sure way to prevent this kind of problem is not to have countries develop uranium enrichment or plutonium reprocessing capabilities if they don't already have it'.[40] In return for their refraining, participating countries would be assured of a stable supply of nuclear fuel according to the concept of multilaterally managed nuclear fuel pooling.

This extended call for the proliferation of nuclear material enrichment technology to be stopped initially placed Japan in an awkward position. Only when the United States agreed voluntarily to abide by the inspection requirement for its non-sensitive nuclear facilities were countries like Germany and Japan convinced that they did not need to fear commercial disadvantages and persuaded to accede to the original NPT[41] (nuclear-weapon states are not bound by the same mandatory IAEA inspections). Japan was the only non-nuclear-weapon state in possession of commercial uranium enrichment and reprocessing technology. One newspaper reported that the Japanese government feared that joining the extended anti-proliferation initiative might force it to shut down the existing enrichment plant at Rokkasho and cancel the planned reprocessing plant expected to be operational by 2007, but the Ministry of Economy, Trade and Industry (METI) decided to participate in the new initiative in the expectation that placing Japan's programmes under international management would avoid the country's isolation.[42] As matters stand at the time of writing, the proposal by IAEA Director General Mohamed El Baradei that the nuclear fuel bank be placed under the IAEA's jurisdiction conflicts with the US proposal for an international consortium led by the energy industries of the Nuclear Suppliers Group (NSG) countries, and the conflict will have to be resolved before the initiative proceeds further.[43]

Some observers take an even more critical view of Japan's nuclear capability. They argue that Japan has an interest in maintaining its nuclear material stockpile and enrichment technology, which can be converted into a weapons programme if deterioration in its security environment makes the possession of nuclear weapons necessary.[44]

Measures to counter the proliferation of ballistic missiles

Ballistic missile technology has proliferated more extensively than nuclear material enrichment technology. Although ballistic missiles per se pose threats to the states within their ranges, it is the combination of ballistic missiles with the so-called ABC (atomic, biological, and chemical) weapons that make them truly weapons of mass destruction.

The governments of Japan and the United States have differing degrees of priority over the North Korean missile issues. Tokyo is more concerned about the

North Korean missiles (together with the abduction issue) and therefore less enthusiastic about South Korean and US summit diplomacy with North Korea from 1998 to 2000.[45] However, a growing recognition that any positive inducement to North Korea requires financial cooperation with Japan, and, more importantly, the Bush administration's review of US policy, led to gradual narrowing of the gap between Japan and the United States after 2000.

In August 1998, North Korea tested its newer Taepodong missile, with an extended range, over the Japanese archipelago. In response to the test, Japan suspended payment of its KEDO contribution for about two months. The US Senate attached additional conditions to the US contribution to KEDO for heavy oil supply, including a ban on North Korean export of missiles to states that sponsored terrorism, and delayed its fiscal year 1999 disbursement.[46] Despite congressional opposition, the Clinton administration was still willing to defend KEDO. Its agreement with North Korea in September 1998 to speed up the delayed construction of the light-water reactor at a time when Japan was still recovering from the fury over the Taepodong incident was particularly upsetting for the Japanese.[47] In an attempt to persuade the Japanese government to resume its contribution, the Clinton administration agreed to take a firmer stance against the further testing, production and export of ballistic missiles by North Korea and to consult closely with Japan and South Korea on these issues.[48]

North Korea claimed that the Taepodong test was a successful satellite launch, and later made a proposal to Russian President Vladimir Putin that it would forgo its long-range missiles if the Western countries agreed to launch North Korean civilian satellites. During US Secretary of State Albright's visit to Pyongyang in 2000, North Korea reiterated its proposal that it would forgo missiles with a range of over 300 kilometres – that is, missiles that could threaten Japan and US bases in Japan – in return for the USA launching two to three North Korean satellites per year, and, more importantly, US assurances of North Korea's sover-eignty and security. Kim Jong-Il also expressed willingness to stop all missile exports – including exports of components, technical advice and brokering services – in return for economic aid.[49]

The Japanese fear was that the US government might accept a deal with North Korea which did not address the existing Nodong missiles.[50] Newly in office, the Bush administration decided in the spring of 2001 to include in its security agenda 'verifiable constraints on North Korea's missile programs and a ban on its missile exports'.[51] However, US policy on North Korea's missiles (like the case of US policy on North Korean nuclear weapons) had to wait for the result of the policy review during 2001.[52] The Japanese government's frustration at the absence of a new US policy to deal with North Korea's ballistic missiles became increasingly visible. It was reportedly examining the possibility of buying the existing North Korean missiles (through economic aid) in order to scrap them.[53]

Prime Minister Koizumi's summit meeting with Kim Jong-Il in September 2002 resulted in the Pyongyang Declaration, which included a North Korean moratorium on missile launching 'in and after 2003'.[54] This was not very new, as Kim Jong-Il had previously committed himself to a moratorium on the launching of long-range missiles until 2003,[55] except that the new statement could be interpreted as an indefinite moratorium. Furthermore, the evolving US decision taken later to address the nuclear weapons development issue first in the Six-Party Talks, and the suspension of the bilateral normalization talks between Japan and North Korea due to the complication of the abduction issue, have put progress on the missile issue on hold. Since then, Pyongyang has threatened at times to resume long-range missile testing. Meanwhile the Bush administration's decision to deploy a missile defence system was met with the Japanese decision to buy and deploy currently available US systems, while continuing on the joint research and development.

Despite Japan's hope for a more explicit US commitment to remove the existing North Korean ballistic missiles, US policy on this point remains ambiguous. In the wake of the inconclusive third round of the Six-Party Talks, Kelly stated: '[T]o achieve full integration into the region and a wholly transformed relationship with the United States, North Korea... needs to... eliminate its illegal weapons of mass destruction programs, put an end to the proliferation of missiles and missile-related technology...'.[56] After the fourth round, Assistant Secretary of State Hill commented, 'as a necessary part of the process leading to [US–DPRK] normalization, we must discuss important issues including... biological and chemical weapons, ballistic missile program...'.[57]

The Proliferation Security Initiative and Japan

On 31 May 2003, President Bush announced the Proliferation Security Initiative to seek new agreements on searching ships and aircraft suspected of carrying illegal weapons or missile technologies. The PSI seeks the partnership of states to 'develop legal, diplomatic, economic, military, and other tools to interdict threatening shipments of WMD and missile-related equipment and technologies'.[58] The PSI was an urgent reaction to a missile proliferation incident involving North Korea,[59] but it aims to stop any would-be proliferator. It consists of sharing of information to facilitate interdiction within the sovereign land, water and air space of the member countries, or any state cooperating on a case-by-case basis, and interdiction on the high seas of vessels registered in a member state or operating under another state that is willing to authorize interdiction by PSI members on a case-by-case basis.[60]

Japan was involved in the development of the PSI, but its initial participation was limited by both domestic–legal factors and external relations. Domestically, Japan's Self-Defense Forces Law did not allow its Maritime Self-Defense Forces (MSDF) to engage in maritime inspection activities in peacetime. (The Coast Guard is authorized to conduct such activities under Japanese law.) As a result, Tokyo sent a civilian Coast Guard vessel and SDF observers to the first PSI exercise in the Coral Sea in September 2003. The Japanese government planned to host a multilateral maritime exercise, to be held in May 2004, but postponed the plan because it anticipated negative effects on the ongoing discussions with North Korea over the nuclear weapons and abduction issues, and reluctance on the part of Asian countries to join the PSI. However, when an MSDF vessel and aircraft participated for the first time in the PSI exercise off Tokyo Bay in October 2004, the absence of enabling domestic law meant that the role of the Self-Defense Forces (SDF) was limited to patrolling and intelligence-sharing.[61]

North Korea denounced the Japanese hosting of the PSI exercise as a violation of the Pyongyang Declaration.[62] In James Kelly's words, '[w]hile not directed at North Korea, North Korea is affected by PSI because it is the world's leading proliferator of missiles and missile technology'.[63] In August 2005, for the first time one Japanese MSDF ship, one Coast Guard ship and two MSDF aircraft were sent to a PSI exercise in Singapore, fully participating in the boarding inspection drill.[64]

From the standpoint of counter-proliferation, efforts to stop proliferation do not have to, and should not, await a complete resolution of the North Korean nuclear weapons development programme. While an overly aggressive counter-proliferation policy runs a risk of retarding the progress in negotiations to abolish the nuclear weapons development programme, to disregard the proliferation risk completely was not acceptable to the US government.

The PSI aims to use both the existing national regulations of the cooperating states and developing international law to plug the loophole on interdictions on the high seas and provide basis for additional national legislation. Stephen G. Rademaker, Assistant Secretary of State for Arms Control, characterizes the PSI as 'an activity, not an organisation'.[65]

The expansion of the PSI activities into the domains of civilian law enforcement has enabled Japan to increase its participation. In addition to the Coast Guard and SDF participation already mentioned, the Japanese government pursues control of illicit activities through its own export control and anti-money laundering measures, as well as bilateral cooperation with Association of Southeast Asian Nations (ASEAN) countries in these areas.[66]

Although PSI exercises are conducted in a multilateral format, the Japanese participation directly contributes to improving the country's capability in a regional contingency over the Korean Peninsula and to its bilateral military cooperation with the United States in maritime interdiction.

The humanitarian issues in US policy and the abduction of Japanese citizens

By the mid-1990s, North Korea's food shortage was clearly apparent to outsiders. Both Japan and the United States separated humanitarian aid to North Korea from the nuclear issue. It was only after North Korea shot a Taepodong missile over Japan in 1998 and returned the alleged ashes of a Japanese abductee, Megumi Yokota (which, the Japanese government claimed, belonged to someone else) that Japan suspended food aid.

North Korea's stubborn refusal during the first Bush administration to agree (even in principle) to the abolition of its nuclear weapons programmes meant that the human rights issues (if brought to the table at the Six-Party Talks) would only further complicate the already difficult negotiations. Although this continues to hold true, the exclusion of the humanitarian issues from the agenda of the Six-Party Talks was not meant to be permanent. Quite the contrary: US officials have repeatedly emphasized that the humanitarian issues are among the list of issues on which North Korea must alter its current behaviour.[67] North Korea's agreement during the fourth round of the Six-Party Talks in July–September 2005 to (in principle) dismantle all nuclear weapons and nuclear weapons programmes has given the humanitarian issues a more concrete place among the US list of foreign policy priorities. The human rights issues are more explicitly linked with the diplomatic normalization process which (according to the sequence of events which the USA prefers) would follow North Korea's dismantling of its nuclear weapons programmes and facilities.

The consistent emphasis of James Kelly and Christopher Hill on the human rights issue did not guarantee rock-solid convergence of the United States and Japan on the abduction issues. Both the US support for and distancing from the issue of the Japanese abductees are based on its own calculations of the overall negotiation objectives, and divergence of opinions within the US administration has affected the nuances of official pronouncements. In March 2004, John R. Bolton (then Under Secretary for Arms Control and International Security in the State Department) in his testimony before the House International Relations Committee explicitly referred to the 'abduction of Japanese citizens' as being among 'other critical issues of concern', but noted:

> We do not raise these issues because we want to set the bar higher for any negotiated settlement with North Korea. While our long-term goal remains the peaceful reunification of the peninsula, we know that any interim solution will require a comprehensive change in North Korean behavior. Given its past violations of agreements, its extensive, well documented program of deception and denial, its dangerous proliferation activities, as well as its terrorist activities and its egregious human rights record, North Korea must know that relations with the United States can only become fully normalized when it deals with all of our concerns.[68]

Although generally supportive of the Japanese effort to address the abduction issue, Kelly's testimony before the same committee on 2 June 2004 kept some distance from the Japanese cause:

> We have been fully supportive of Prime Minister Koizumi's visit to Pyongyang. We are pleased that five abductee family members were allowed to go to Japan and that the Prime Minister reinforced the CVID message in his face-to-face discussions with D.P.R.K. leader Kim Jong-Il. Japan has kept the abductee issue on the agenda with the D.P.R.K. even as they continue to press for denuclearization. Similarly, we maintain our human rights concerns with North Korea as part of our broad agenda for discussions. Our bilateral cooperation with Japan and trilateral cooperation with Japan and South Korea continue to anchor our approach to the Six-Party Talks.[69]

The Kelly testimony illustrated the dilemma the United States faced –
between on the one hand lending support to the cause of its key ally (at a time
when bilateral negotiations between Japan and North Korea on the abduction
issue were deadlocked and suspended), and on the other hand risking giving
the North Korean government an excuse not to attend the third round of
the Six-Party Talks. In contrast, Bolton's press conference comment at the
US embassy in Tokyo on 10 February 2005, amid uncertainty about the sched-
uling of the fourth round of the Six-Party Talks, more explicitly supported
the Japanese government's raising of the abduction issue in the next round.[70]
However, mainstream US thinking on the abduction issue seems to have been
represented by Hill's comment in June 2005, a month prior to the fifth round
of the Six-Party Talks, which, although only indirectly, referred to the abduction issue as a step towards full normalization, after resolution of the nuclear
problems:

> The United States, working with allies and others, remains committed to
> resolving the nuclear issue through peaceful, diplomatic means. While we
> are not prepared to reward the D.P.R.K. for coming back into compliance
> with its international obligations, we have laid out the path to a peaceful
> resolution of the nuclear issue. Of course, to achieve a wholly transformed
> relationship with the United States, North Korea must address other issues
> of concern to us and the international community as well. It must change its
> behavior on human rights, *address the issues underlying its appearance on
> the U.S. list of state-sponsored terrorism*, eliminate all its weapons of mass
> destruction programs and missile technology proliferation, and adopt a less
> provocative conventional force disposition.[71]

At the fourth round of the Six-Party Talks (26 July–7 August and 13–19
September 2005), Japanese negotiators raised the abduction issue, despite the
opposition and reserved 'understanding' of other members. Pyongyang attempted
to avoid the abduction issue by refusing to hold bilateral talks with Japan during
the Six-Party Talks, but with US urging it met the Japanese delegate, if only to
promise to convey the Japanese message to the home government in Pyongyang.
The fourth round produced a joint statement of principles in which the six
parties agreed to prompt and verifiable denuclearization of North Korea, aid
measures, and the normalization of diplomatic relations with North Korea.
Japan's effort to include the abduction issue in a comprehensive solution was
partially supported by other members, including the United States, by including
in the agreed statement from the talks language which pertained to the commitment of North Korea and Japan to pursue normalization in accordance with
the 2002 Pyongyang Declaration 'on the basis of settlement of the unfortunate
past and outstanding issues of concern'.[72] In his closing remarks the Japanese
delegate made direct reference to the abduction issue separately from the agreed
text. Likewise, Hill in his remarks explicitly listed 'human rights, biological and
chemical weapons, ballistic missile programs, proliferation of conventional

weapons, terrorism and other illicit activities' as 'longstanding concerns' of the United States that must be resolved before full normalization of relations with North Korea.[73] That these concerns (shared by Japan) were not in the agreed joint statement was a result of the difficult negotiations, not of the United States giving these concerns lower priority than Japan.

The Japanese position that there should be no aid to North Korea until the abduction issue has been resolved constricts the country's own ability to play a flexible and constructive role at the Six-Party Talks. While the Japanese proposal during the fifth round of the Six-Party Talks to create separate issue-based working groups to simultaneously draw road maps towards a comprehensive resolution of the problems of the Korean Peninsula and full normalization of relations with North Korea[74] might have been signalling a willingness to decouple economic/energy aid from the abduction issue, the round failed to agree on such a process and to set the date for the next round.

The upgrading of US–Japanese military cooperation: the utility of Japan for US policy towards North Korea (and beyond)

North Korea is the most visible and immediate factor driving recent Japanese policy changes. As mentioned above, the renewed threat of North Korean nuclear weapons development has been a major catalyst in bringing Japan's basic defence policies up to speed and motivating the Japanese government to make larger commitments to providing logistical support to US forces during a military contingency in the region. The threat of North Korea developing nuclear weapons, in conjunction with its ongoing missile programme, played a major role in spurring the Japanese government to agree in late 2003 to purchase from the United States SM-3 intercept missiles for its Aegis warships along with Patriot 3 (PAC-3) anti-missile batteries.[75]

Tokyo took a series of measures to enhance its military cooperation with the United States during the period of crisis over the Korean Peninsula. The timing was not a coincidence. There is a clear causal relationship between the perceived threats from North Korea and the upgrading of the bilateral US–Japanese cooperation, although there are also other relevant causes. At the very least the enhanced bilateral cooperation allows the United States better preparation in the event of North Korean aggression and allows it to negotiate with North Korea backed by solid deterrence. It is therefore essential to look at the 'Japan factors' from the viewpoint of their utility for the United States.

The Anti-Terror Special Measures Law

In November 2001, the Diet passed the Anti-Terror Special Measures Law, which enabled the Japanese SDF to engage in 'cooperative and supportive activities'. Article 1 of the law cites UN Security Council resolutions 1267, 1269 and 1333 (which denounced terrorism in general and called for all UN members to take appropriate measures for prevention) and 1368 (which specifically identified the 11 September 2001 terror attacks as threats to international peace and stability) as justification for Japanese participation.[76]

A centrepiece of Japan's support to the Coalition maritime patrol in the Indian Ocean has been the refuelling of US and other Coalition ships belonging to France, Germany, New Zealand, Italy, The Netherlands, Spain, Greece and Canada. The aim of the Coalition effort was to intercept smuggled weapons and components, which could end up in the hands of terrorists, at sea.[77]

The Acquisition and Cross-Servicing Agreement

The SDF's expanded activities beyond territorial defence necessitated smoother cooperation in procurement and cross-servicing with the United States. The 1999 Law to Assure Peace and Safety of Japan in Contingencies in Adjacent Areas allowed SDF supplies to and servicing of the US forces based on the Acquisition and Cross-Servicing Agreement (ACSA). Although it is deliberately left ambiguous, the scope of the law is broadly understood to be North-East Asian security situations, and it was not invoked in Japan's support for the maritime patrol in the Indian Ocean and the post-war reconstruction of Iraq. Refuelling and servicing of aircraft to be ready for combat missions and supplies of weapons and ammunitions were explicitly excluded. These bans were explicitly included in the Anti-Terror Law and continued in practice under the 2003 Iraq Humanitarian Reconstruction Law.

The revised ACSA was signed on 27 February 2004. The original ACSA defined procurement and cross-servicing in joint training, UN peace operations, international humanitarian relief activities, and 'contingencies in the adjacent areas'. The revision added direct or imminent armed attack on Japan as an enabling condition. The revised ACSA continues explicitly to exclude Japanese supply of weapons to the US forces, but a subtle change expanded its scope to include the supply of ammunition in the event of direct or imminent armed attack on Japan.

On 14 June 2004 the Japanese Diet passed the Law on Measures Japan Implements along with US Military Actions in Situations of Armed Attacks against Japan, which extended the applicability of the ACSA to situations of direct and imminent armed attacks against Japan. The supply of arms is explicitly excluded, but the supply of ammunition is not, in order to match the revised ACSA. As regards the servicing of aircraft during such emergency scenarios, there is no longer a distinction between combat and non-combat missions. On the same day the Diet passed another law to amend the Self Defense Forces Law in order to further extend the coverage of the ACSA to US forces participating in disaster relief activities requested by the Japanese government, emergency evacuations of Japanese nationals – which has been a major concern in the event of armed conflict on the Korean Peninsula – and routine activities, including training and communications. Supply of weapons and ammunition in these non-combat situations is explicitly excluded.

Maritime interdiction

The 1999 Law to Assure Peace and Safety of Japan in Contingencies in Adjacent Areas, which enabled the SDF's rear support roles in regional contingencies, deliberately excluded SDF participation in maritime interdiction in order to smooth the passage of the bill through Diet.[78] However, after the Liberal Democratic Party (LDP) victory in the House of Representatives elections in 2000, the law was amended to add maritime interdiction to the list of authorized SDF activities. Anticipating a possible maritime blockade of North Korea, this change has equipped Japan with an expanded list of available military options.

The whole process of reviewing the 1976 Guidelines on US–Japan Security Cooperation was a direct response to the anticipation of military conflicts on the Korean Peninsula at a time when tensions over the North Korean missile and nuclear development were escalating in the mid-1990s. The fear of a rupture in the alliance in the event of Japan remaining a bystander again (as during the first Gulf War) drove the leaders of the two countries to revise the guidelines, on which the Contingency in Adjacent Areas Law was to be based.[79]

While this legislation laid a foundation for SDF cooperation with the US forces in the event of military confrontation on the Korean Peninsula, it is still viewed as a bare minimum by security practitioners in both countries. As Japan has built up a record of dispatching troops overseas under the 1992 law on peacekeeping operations and other emergency legislation, and as tensions both on the Korean Peninsula and in the Taiwan Strait heighten, the two countries are about to revise the guidelines for their security cooperation once again. Nevertheless, Hughes and Fukushima are cautious in their prediction about growth in the bilateral cooperation, citing the Japanese government's additional preference for hedging against 'entrapment' into unwanted conflicts via the alliance and for maintaining some ambiguity in its commitment to respond to regional contingencies.[80]

Conclusion

The US policy towards North Korea is influenced by both regional considerations and its global commitments. Where the removal of nuclear weapons capabilities from North Korea is concerned, Japanese interests largely converge with those of the United States. The concerns of the Japanese government revolve around how the US negotiating strategy towards this common goal affects Japan's other issues with North Korea. Thus, one way to look at the 'Japan factors' in US policy towards North Korea is to look at Japanese inputs into US policy (and conversely US consideration of Japanese interests). Minor differences between the two countries (if one goes down to the sub-national actors' level) still exist over the abduction issue, but this is more a matter of negotiating tactics than an overall strategic disagreement. The failure of Koizumi's two visits to Pyongyang to solve the abduction issue allowed China to take over the overall brokerage on the nuclear issues. Domestically, Koizumi's failure stopped the politicians from support-ing the 'engagement school' vocally. Although hard-line politicians have gained a stronger voice in Japan's North Korea policy, so far the prime minister and the Ministry of Foreign Affairs have contained their influence in order not to divert the focus of the Six-Party Talks from North Korea's nuclear weapons programmes.

The governments of Japan and the United States have demonstrated slight differences of view on the missile and fissile material control issues. In the mid-1990s, a considerable gap existed between their degrees of concern about the existing Nodong missiles. This gap has since narrowed as North Korea has tested missiles with longer ranges. On the issue of fissile material control, Japan's attempt to join the nuclear material enrichment business is competing against US efforts to stop proliferation of such technologies.

The other way to look at the 'Japan factors' in US policy towards North Korea is to look at what Japan has to offer US policy. The Japanese government resented the engagement diplomacy of the Clinton administration and its requests to Japan for financial aid to North Korea. This gap widened after the Taepodong launch in the summer of 1998 and the deterioration of the normalization talks between Japan and North Korea. By contrast, the Bush administration's revised approach to North Korea defers the issue of financial aid to North Korea to the future: it is contingent on North Korean compliance with CVID. Japan's immediate utility instead is its military cooperation with the United States in the event of a military contingency over the Korean Peninsula. The process of upgrading US–Japanese security cooperation has been boosted by a long-term geopolitical shift in East Asia and other events inside and outside the region. A series of perceived provocations by North Korea has been a major factor in boosting the upgrading of the bilateral military cooperation.

Japan's increased military cooperation with the United States has enhanced the bilateral alliance at both regional and global levels. Japan's dispatch of the MSDF to the Indian Ocean set an important precedent of de facto multilateral patrol activity.[81] The cautious yet bold initiative to dispatch the Ground Self-Defense Forces (GSDF) humanitarian–reconstruction troops to Iraq was also explained in terms of alliance management in the face of immediate North Korean threats.[82] Provisions on the transport of arms and ammunition to US troops were gradually upgraded through the two special measure laws (the Anti-Terror Law and the Iraqi Humanitarian Reconstruction Law) to the Law on Armed Attacks against Japan. Moreover, the Japanese government is also planning to further revise the guidelines for US–Japan security cooperation. These developments in Japan's military security policy in turn give more flexibility to the US security policy making, as its military goes through a major restructuring at the global level.

Notes

*The views expressed in this chapter are personal opinions of the author and do not reflect the official policy or position of the Asia–Pacific Center for Security Studies.

1 Yoichiro Sato, 'Will the US–Japan alliance continue?', *New Zealand International Review*, 24/4, July/August 1999, pp. 11–12.

2 'Four views of the Pyongyang summit', *Japan Echo*, December 2002, pp. 43–7.
3 Akitoshi Miyashita, 'Introduction: A framework for analysis', in Akitoshi Miyashita and Yoichiro Sato (eds), *Japanese Foreign Policy in Asia and the Pacific: Domestic Interests, American Pressure, and Regional Integration*, New York and Houndmills: Palgrave Macmillan, 2001, p. 4.
4 Kent E. Calder, 'Japanese foreign economic policy formation: Explaining the reactive state', *World Politics*, 40, 1988, pp. 517–41.
5 Miyashita and Sato (eds), *Japanese Foreign Policy in Asia and the Pacific*.
6 Peter Katzenstein and Nobuo Okawara, *Japan's National Security: Structures, Norms and Policy Responses in a Changing World*, Ithaca, NY: Cornell University, East Asia Series, 1993.
7 Robert Gilpin, *The Political Economy of International Relations*, Princeton, NJ: Princeton University Press, 1987, pp. 6–7.
8 David Kerr, 'The Sino-Russian partnership and US policy toward North Korea: From hegemony to concert in Northeast Asia', *International Studies Quarterly*, 49/3, September 2005, pp. 422–3.
9 US Department of State, 'Joint statement on North Korea by the US, the Republic of Korea, and Japan', 26 May 2001, available HTTP: <http://www.state.gov/p/eap/rls/rm/2001/3115.htm> (accessed 8 February 2005).
10 US Department of State, 26 May 2001 (italics added).
11 Tenet, cited in Kerr, 'The Sino–Russian partnership and US policy toward North Korea', p. 422 (italics added).
12 Jonathan Pollack, 'The United States, North Korea, and the end of Agreed Framework', *Naval War College Review*, 56/3, summer 2003, p. 24.
13 US Department of State, 'Weapons of mass destruction developments on the Korean Peninsula', Testimony by Richard L. Armitage, Deputy Secretary of State, before the Senate Foreign Relations Committee, 4 February 2003, available HTTP: <http://www.state.gov/s/d/rm/17170.htm> (accessed 8 February 2005).
14 US Department of State, 'A peaceful resolution of the North Korean nuclear issue'. Remarks by James A. Kelly, Assistant Secretary of State for East Asian and Pacific Affairs, to the House International Relations Committee, 13 February 2003, available HTTP: <http://www.state.gov/p/eap/rls/rm/2003/17754.htm> (accessed 8 February 2005).
15 Kerr, 'The Sino–Russian partnership and US policy towards North Korea', p. 423.
16 US Department of State, 'Regional implications of the changing nuclear equation on the Korean Peninsula'. Testimony by James A. Kelly, Assistant Secretary of State for East Asian and Pacific Affairs, before the Senate Foreign Relations Committee, 12 March 2003, available HTTP: <http://www.state.gov/p/eap/rls/rm/2003/18661.htm> (accessed 8 February 2005).
17 US Department of State, 12 March 2003.
18 Richard P. Cronin, 'Challenges of governance in Asia: Significance for regional security and stability', in Yoichiro Sato (ed.), *Growth and Governance in Asia*, Honolulu: Asia–Pacific Center for Security Studies, 2004, pp. 10, 12.
19 Robert A. Manning, 'Waiting for Godot? Northeast Asian future shock and the U.S.–Japan alliance', in Michael Green and Patrick M. Cronin (eds), *The US–Japan Alliance: Past, Present and Future*, New York: Council on Foreign Relations Press, 1999, p. 48.
20 Manning, 'Waiting for Godot?', p. 48 (italics added).
21 Ibid., p. 49.
22 Ibid., p. 50.
23 Yutaka Kawashima, *Japanese Foreign Policy at the Crossroads: Challenges and Options for the Twenty-first Century*, Washington, DC: Brookings Institution Press, 2003, pp. 87–9.

24 Matake Kamiya, 'Japanese foreign policy toward Northeast Asia', in Takashi Inoguchi and Purnendra Jain (eds), *Japanese Foreign Policy Today*, New York and Houndmills: Palgrave, 2000, pp. 242–3.

25 Kamiya, 'Japanese foreign policy toward Northeast Asia', p. 244.

26 Jung-Hoon Lee and Chung-In Moon, 'Responding to Japan's Asia policy: The Korean calculus', in Takashi Inoguchi (ed.), *Japan's Asian Policy: Revival and Response*, New York and Houndmills: Palgrave Macmillan, 2002, pp. 138–9, 151.

27 Yoichi Funabashi, *Alliance Adrift*, New York: Council on Foreign Relations Press, 1999, pp. 83–6. North Koreans were conversely trying to improve relations with first (bilaterally) the United States, then Japan, and face South Korea (Funabashi, p. 87), playing upon both the South Korean fear of abandonment by the United States and the Japanese fear of being excluded from peninsula matters.

28 David Fouse, *Japan's Post-Cold War North Korea Policy: Hedging Toward Autonomy?*, Asia–Pacific Center for Security Studies Occasional Paper Series, February 2004, Honolulu: Asia–Pacific Center for Security Studies, available HTTP: <http://www.apcss.org>; and David Fouse, 'Japan's post-cold war North Korea policy: Hedging toward autonomy?', in Yoichiro Sato and Satu Limaye (eds), *Japan in a Dynamic Asia*, Lanham, Md., Boulder, Colo., New York and Oxford: Rowman & Littlefield, 2006 (forthcoming).

29 Ted Osius, *The US–Japan Security Alliance: Why It Matters and How to Strengthen It*, West Port and London: Praeger and Washington, DC: Center for Strategic and International Studies, 2002, p. 12.

30 Sato, 'Will the US–Japan alliance continue?', pp. 10–12.

31 Fouse, 'Japan's post-cold war North Korean policy', February 2004, pp. 10–11; and Michael Green, *Japan's Reluctant Realism*, New York and Houndmills: Palgrave Macmillan, 2003, p. 126.

32 US Department of State, 'U.S. relations with Japan', Remarks by Christopher R. Hill, Assistant Secretary for East Asian and Pacific Affairs, to the Senate Foreign Relations Committee, 29 September 2005, available HTTP: <http://www.state.gov/p/eap/rls/rm/2005/54110.htm> (accessed 26 October 2005).

33 Osius, *The US–Japan Security Alliance*, p. 13.

34 Michael Green, 'The challenges of managing US–Japan security relations after the cold war', in Gerald L. Curtis (ed.), *New Perspectives on US–Japan Relations*, Tokyo and New York: Japan Centre for International Exchange, 2000, pp. 257–8.

35 Kerr, 'The Sino-Russian partnership and US policy toward North Korea', p. 424.

36 Ibid.

37 Satu Limaye, 'Japan and India after the cold war', in Sato and Limaye (eds), *Japan in a Dynamic Asia*.

38 *Asahi Shimbun*, 30 April 2004.

39 US Department of State, 'U.S.–IAEA Additional Protocol', Testimony by Susan F. Burk, Acting Assistant Secretary for Nonproliferation, before the Senate Foreign Relations Committee, 29 January 2004, available HTTP: <http://www.state.gov/t/np/rls/rm/29249.htm> (accessed 26 October 2005).

40 US Department of State, 'Press roundtable with Japanese media', John R. Bolton, Under Secretary for Arms Control and International Security, US Embassy, Tokyo, 10 February 2005, available HTTP: <http://www.state.gov/t/us/rm/42197.htm> (accessed 14 February 2005).

41 US Department of State, 'U.S.–IAEA Additional Protocol', 29 January 2004.

42 *Asahi Shimbun* 25 October 2005.

43 *Asahi Shimbun* 27 September 2005.

44 Morton H. Halperin, 'The nuclear dimension of the U.S.–Japan alliance', section 4, 'Japanese nuclear option', available HTTP: <http://www.nautilus.org/archives/library/security/papers/US-Japan-4.html> (accessed 2 December 2005).

45 Green, 'The challenges of managing US–Japan security relations after the cold war', pp. 257–8.
46 Hidekazu Sakai, 'Continuity and discontinuity of Japanese foreign policy toward North Korea: Freezing the Korean Energy Development Organisation (KEDO) in 1998', in Miyashita and Sato (eds), *Japanese Foreign Policy in Asia and the Pacific*, p. 68.
47 Green, 'The challenges of managing US–Japan security relations after the cold war', p. 257.
48 Sakai, 'Continuity and discontinuity of Japanese foreign policy towards North Korea', pp. 68–9.
49 Osius, *The US–Japan Security Alliance*, pp. 16–17.
50 Ibid., p. 12.
51 'Statement by the president', 6 June 2001, available HTTP: <http://www.usinfo. state.gov>, cited in Osius, *The US–Japan Security Alliance*, p. 17.
52 US Department of State, 'Briefing on policy toward North Korea'. Press briefing by James A. Kelly, Assistant Secretary of State for East Asian and Pacific Affairs, following the Trilateral Coordination and Oversight Group (TCOG) Meeting, 26 May 2001, available HTTP: <http://www.state.gov/p/eap/rls/rm/2001/3114.htm> (accessed 8 February 2005).
53 *Tokyo Shimbun* 4 June 2001.
54 'Japan–DPRK Pyongyang Declaration', 17 September 2002, available HTTP: <http:// www.nautilus.org/DPRKBriefingBook/agreements/CanKor_VTK_2002_09_17_pyon gyang_declaration_japan_dprk.pdf> (accessed 14 November 2005).
55 US Department of State, 'U.S. policy toward the Democratic People's Republic of Korea', Testimony by Charles L. Pritchard, Special Envoy for Negotiations with the DPRK. and US Representative of KEDO, before the Subcommittee on East Asia and the Pacific, House Committee on International Relations, 26 July 2001, available HTTP: <http://www.state.gov/p/eap/rls/rm/2001/4304.htm> (accessed 8 February 2005).
56 US Department of State, 'Dealing with North Korea's nuclear programs'. Statement by James A. Kelly, Assistant Secretary for East Asian and Pacific Affairs, to the Senate Foreign Relations Committee, 15 July 2004, available HTTP: <http://www.state.gov/ p/eap/rls/rm/2004/34395.htm> (accessed 8 February 2005).
57 US Department of State, 'The Six-Party Talks and the North Korean nuclear issue', statement by Christopher R. Hill, Assistant Secretary for East Asian and Pacific Affairs, before the House International Relations Committee, 6 October 2005, available HTTP: <http://www.state.gov/p/eap/rls/rm/2005/54430.htm> (accessed 26 October 2005).
58 Center for Nonproliferation Studies, 'Proliferation Security Initiative', last updated 18 August 2004, available HTTP: <http://cns.miis.edu/pubs/inven/pdfs/psi.pdf> (accessed 18 November 2005). As of June 2005, over 60 countries had joined the PSI, including the United States, Japan, the United Kingdom, France, Germany, Italy, Australia, the Netherlands, Poland, Portugal, Spain, Canada, Norway, Singapore, Argentina and Russia.
59 In December 2002 a Spanish naval ship in Operation Enduring Freedom intercepted a Cambodian-flagged vessel (manned with a North Korean crew) carrying an export cargo of short-range ballistic missiles to Yemen. This led to the launching of the Proliferation Security Initiative (PSI) by US President George W. Bush in May 2003.
60 Center for Nonproliferation Studies, 'Proliferation Security Initiative'.
61 *Yomiuri Shimbun*, 4 August 2004.
62 *Kyodo News*, 7 August 2004.
63 US Department of State, 'An overview of U.S.–East Asia policy', Testimony by James A. Kelly, Assistant Secretary of State for East Asian and Pacific Affairs, before the House International Relations Committee, 2 June 2004, available HTTP: <http://www.state.gov/p/eap/rls/rm/2004/33064.htm> (accessed 26 October 2005).

64   *Yomiuri Shimbun*, 15 August 2005.
65   US Department of State, 'The Proliferation Security Initiative (PSI): A record of success'. Testimony by Stephen G. Rademaker, Assistant Secretary of State for Arms Control, before the House International Relations Committee, Subcommittee on International Terrorism and Nonproliferation, 9 June 2005, available HTTP: <http://www.state.gov/t/ac/rls/rm/47715.htm> (accessed 26 October 2005).
66   David Fouse and Yoichiro Sato, 'Enhancing basic governance: Japan's comprehensive counterterrorism assistance to Southeast Asia', Asia–Pacific Center for Security Studies, February 2006, available HTTP: <http://www.apcss.org/Publications/APSSS/Japan%20CT%20Cooperation.pdf>.
67   US Department of State, 15 July 2004; and US Department of State, 'Northeast Asia: A region of vital concern to the United States', Testimony by Christopher R. Hill, Assistant Secretary for East Asian and Pacific Affairs, before the House Committee on International Relations, Subcommittee on Asia and the Pacific, 26 May 2005, available HTTP: <http://www.state.gov/p/eap/rls/rm/2005/46827.htm> (accessed 26 October 2005).
68   US Department of State, 'The Bush administration and non-proliferation policy: Successes and future challenges', Testimony by John Bolton, Under Secretary for Arms Control and International Security, in a hearing of the House Committee on International Relations, 30 March 2004, available HTTP: <http://www.state.gov/t/us/rm/31029.htm> (accessed 26 October 2005).
69   US Department of State, 2 June 2004.
70   US Department of State, 10 February 2005.
71   US Department of State, 'Dealing with North Korea's nuclear programs', Statement by Christopher R. Hill, Assistant Secretary for East Asian and Pacific Affairs, to the Senate Foreign Relations Committee, 14 June 2005, available HTTP: <http://www.state.gov/p/eap/rls/rm/2005/47875.htm> (accessed 26 October 2005); italics added.
72   US Department of State, 6 October 2005.
73   US Department of State, 6 October 2005.
74   *Asahi Shimbun*, 12 November 2005.
75   David Fouse, 'Japan gets serious about missile defence: North Korean crisis pushes debate', *Asia–Pacific Security Studies*, 2/4, June 2003, pp. 1–4, available HTTP: <http://www.apcss.org>.
76   Yoichiro Sato, 'Japan's naval dispatch plans expand the envelope', *PacNet Newsletter* 04A, 24 January 2003, available HTTP: <http://www.csis.org/pacfor/pac0304A.htm>; and Yoichiro Sato, 'Japan's security policies during OEF and OIF: Incremental reactions meet great expectations', *Asia–Pacific Security Studies*, 2/6, August 2003, pp. 1–4, available HTTP: <http://www.apcss.org>.
77   Sato, 'Japan's naval dispatch plans expand the envelope'; and Sato, 'Japan's security policies during OEF and OIF'.
78   Sato, 'Will the US–Japan alliance continue?'; and Yoichiro Sato, 'Comprehensive security of Japan and the US–Japan alliance in Northeast Asia', in Rouben Azizian (ed.), *Strategic and Economic Dynamics of Northeast Asia: Global, Regional and New Zealand Perspectives*, Wellington: Centre for Strategic Studies, Victoria University of Wellington and Auckland: Department of Political Studies, University of Auckland, 1999, p. 64.
79   Funabashi, *Alliance Adrift*, pp. 280–90; and Christopher W. Hughes and Akiko Fukushima, 'US–Japan security relations: Toward bilateralism plus', in Ellis Krauss and T. J. Pempel (eds), *Beyond Bilateralism: US–Japan Relations in the New Asia–Pacific*, Stanford, Calif.: Stanford University Press, 2004, p. 68.
80   Hughes and Fukushima, 'US–Japan security relations', pp. 74–6.
81   Sato, 'Japan's naval dispatch plans expand the envelope'; and Sato, 'Japan's security policies during OEF and OIF'.
82   Yoichiro Sato, 'The GSDF will go to Iraq without a blue helmet', *PacNet Newsletter*, 32, 31 July 2003, available HTTP: <http://www.csis.org/pacfor/pac0332.htm>; and Sato, 'Japan's security policies during OEF and OIF'.

5 Chinese North Korea policy: a secondary role for Japan

Quansheng Zhao

This chapter analyses Chinese foreign policy towards the Korean Peninsula, focusing on the North Korean nuclear crisis which has captured the world's attention in recent years. China has been one of the key players in dealing with the regime in Pyongyang, being a host for the much-publicized Six-Party Talks, which started in August 2003 and include China, the USA, North and South Korea, Russia and Japan. Although this chapter focuses on Chinese foreign policy towards North Korea in terms of its nuclear programme and other international concerns along the lines of the Six-Party Talks, it will also discuss Sino-Japanese coordination, and the linkage between Chinese North Korea policy and the ups and downs of the relationship between Beijing and Tokyo.

Although Beijing's primary concerns are with the two major players of the game – the USA and North Korea – the other parties, Japan, Russia and South Korea, are also necessary factors which Chinese policy makers take into consideration in deliberating their policies towards the Korean Peninsula. This chapter analyses the Japan factor in order to provide a better understanding of the overall picture of the Six-Party Talks, as well as the specific circumstances in which they are taking place. Take China and Japan, for example. The two countries are more likely to cooperate when there are overlapping national interests. At the same time, different concerns over their respective problems (such as the issue of North Korean refugees for China, and the issue of the abductions of Japanese citizens for Japan) may severely inhibit further collaboration, as will be analysed in the latter part of this chapter. Overall, the governments of China and Japan have performed different functions in the process of settling the North Korean nuclear crisis because of the differences between them in their degree of influence (a rising power versus a declining power[1]). It is nevertheless important to investigate the ways the two governments have cooperated over this issue, despite the significant downturn in their relations over the period in which the Six-Party Talks have been going on. It is therefore worthwhile for us to examine the concrete steps the governments of China and Japan have taken in coordinating their North Korea policies, as well as the circumstances and the mechanisms they have employed.

The Chinese effort in leading the Six-Party Talks can be called a game of policy coordination along three dimensions. First, Beijing has to clarify its own policy priorities along the lines of its perceived national interests. Second, it has to coordinate with each of the other five parties in terms of each country's political, security and economic interests. Third, in the negotiations, it has to use its diplomatic skills to coordinate the policy priorities with each party's different interests. In conclusion, this chapter will argue that, to understand better the dynamics of Beijing's role in this game of policy coordination, represented by the Six-Party Talks, it has to be put into the context of both domestic considerations and the international environment in the Asia–Pacific. To illuminate the complicated nature of this policy coordination, Beijing's coordination with Tokyo on its Korea policy will be analysed in the latter part of this chapter.

It has long been clear that there is a consensus among the four major powers in the North-East Asian region – China, the United States, Russia and Japan – that all oppose nuclear proliferation in the region in general, and prefer a nuclear-free Korean Peninsula in particular, and all must put stability and peace as their top policy priorities. The Chinese government has certainly gone along with this consensus, which became one of the foundations for the Six-Party Talks. From initially dealing with the North Korea issue passively to actively hosting the Six-Party Talks, Beijing has gone through a major shift in its policy orientation over the past few years. In doing so, it has conducted a highly visible and unprecedented shuttle diplomacy to ensure that the North Korean regime comes to the negotiating table.

The evolution of Chinese foreign policy towards the Korean Peninsula

Beijing's vital interest in the Korean Peninsula has long been demonstrated by its dilemma with regard to North Korea and South Korea, as well as its sensitivity towards the changing of great power relations in the peninsula. When examining the foreign policy of the People's Republic of China (PRC) on the Korean Peninsula, one needs to first look at historical, and then at strategic and geographical factors. Historically, China and Korea have shared complex and intimate relations, which were symbolized by a hierarchical tributary system. As Chae-Jin Lee points out, 'Korea's tributary relations with China began as early as the fifth century, were regularized during the Koryo dynasty (918–1392), and became fully institutionalized during the Yi dynasty (1392–1910)'.[2] There were many significant interactions between the two countries down the centuries. Each ruler of China – whether the leader of a dynasty or of a republic – has more or less regarded Korea as one of the prominent students of traditional Confucian Chinese culture, making Korea an important component of what may be called East Asian civilization. Moreover, Korea often served as a buffer between China and far-away countries, of which Japan is the prime example.[3]

The Japan factor is not new in the long history of international relations around the Korea Peninsula, and it has therefore long been considered as a key element in Chinese policy towards Korea. In Korea's early history, for example, the peninsula was divided into three kingdoms, Silla, Koguryo and Paekche.

In the seventh century, Silla, the kingdom in the south, entered into a political and military alliance with China's Tang dynasty, and in AD 668 unified the Korean Peninsula into a single country. During the unification process, the Chinese and the Silla state also repulsed a Japanese expedition sent to aid Paekche. From that time on, Korea remained a unified country, with only occasional and relatively brief periods of political division. The tributary relations between China and Korea came to an end when China was defeated in the Sino-Japanese war of 1894–5 and was forced to sign the treaty of Shimonoseki with Japan. At the same treaty, the Qing government was forced to cede Taiwan to Japan. In 1910, Korea became a colony of Japan, and remained so until 1945, after the Japanese defeat in World War II. In 1945 the peninsula was once again divided as a result of the beginning of the cold war between the two superpowers, the United States and the Soviet Union.

The Korean War[4] of 1950–3 served as another historical reminder to the Beijing leadership of the need to be fully aware of the importance of Korea to its national security. The Chinese re-entry into the Korean Peninsula began in October 1950, when the new leadership in Beijing made the momentous decision to cross the Yalu River and enter the Korean War, thereby placing itself in direct military confrontation with the United States. This conflict was to end in a military stalemate three years later. The casualties on both sides (estimates vary) were tremendous. Japan was not directly involved in the war but still played a significant role in terms of providing logistical support to the US military. The US–Japanese security treaty signed in 1951 has also provided a solid foundation for the US armed forces to function in the Asia–Pacific from the time of the Korean War, through the post-cold war era and up to the present.

The Korean War had other lasting consequences for the Asia–Pacific region. Most significantly, it left the Korean Peninsula with the long-term legacy of the division between North and South, which became a symbol of the East–West division during the cold war era in the Asia–Pacific. The war, therefore, had strategic implications in East Asian international relations; that is, Korea historically has been known as a place of *bingjia bizheng* (meaning a strategic stronghold for military conflict) among major powers. This strategic importance is still essential today.

All four major powers in East Asia – China, Japan, Russia and the United States – have their own vital stakes in the dynamics of the Korean Peninsula.[5] Whereas the United States and China are the two leading external players in this complicated diplomatic game in Korean affairs, Japan has not played a leading role since World War II, but is nevertheless an important player which cannot be ignored by either the USA or China. After all, Japan is not only historically important to the Korean Peninsula; it is still the second largest economy in the world, despite the economic slowdown it has suffered since the early 1990s. Furthermore, Japan is the most important US military ally in the region. Any settlement of the Korea issue will definitely require positive Japanese participation (although the leadership role will be provided by China and the USA, which have growing influence in both global and regional affairs in the post-cold war era).

Modernization has played a leading role in the shift of Chinese policy on the two Koreas. Economic development was one main incentive for the normalization of Sino-South Korean relations. China's modernization programmes cannot be realized without extensive external support and exchange from industrialized countries that can provide advanced technology, capital, markets and managerial skills. South Korea is a nearby supplier of these resources.

Since the normalization of relations between South Korea and China in 1992, China has become one of the most important destinations for Korea's overseas investment.[6] In addition, South Korea has become increasingly important as a trading partner for China. In 2004, for the first time, China became South Korea's largest trading partner: the value of their bilateral trade reached 79.3 billion US dollars (USD), surpassing South Korean trade with the United States (71.6 billion) and with Japan (67.8 billion USD). This momentum continued in 2005, when the total value of the trade between South Korea and China reached 100.5 billion USD, far bigger than the trade with Japan (72.4 billion USD) and the USA (71.9 billion USD).[7]

Thus, China's relations with the Korean Peninsula have followed a zig-zag path over the past half-century. This relationship may provide an excellent illustration of an old belief in international relations – that there are no permanent enemies and no permanent friends. The dynamics of and the ups and downs in the relations between Beijing, Pyongyang and Seoul have fully demonstrated the truth in this saying.

Turning to developments in the period since 11 September 2001, there are four major developments related to Chinese policy towards the Korean Peninsula.

First, the 11 September 2001 attacks on New York and Washington were the catalyst for a major shift in US foreign policy priorities. A convenient, yet legitimate, reason for the US government to shift its foreign policy priority is the need for anti-terrorist coalition-building. This war against terrorism has naturally become a centrepiece of US foreign policy. As a result, other considerations such as ideology, including anti-communism and the promotion of human rights, have been relegated to a secondary position. Geographically, the Middle East, namely Iraq, has become the top priority as there are several hundred thousand US troops stationed there, and East Asia has remained a concern, but secondary to the Middle East. There is therefore a growing desire in Washington for anti-terrorism coalition-building. And China has fulfilled this role as a partner in the US-led coalition against terror. Hence, Washington's perception of Beijing has shifted from that of a rival or competitor to that of a cooperative partner.

Second, attention to North Korea has intensified since the revelation of its nuclear project and since President George W. Bush labelled the country a member of the 'axis of evil'. The need for cooperation between Beijing and Washington in order to deal with the North Korean nuclear crisis has become central. Third, during the same period, China–Taiwan relations have deteriorated in general, partly because the independence-oriented Democratic Progressive Party (DPP) came to power in 2000, indicating a regime shift in Taiwan. In order to get help in stemming this movement towards independence, Beijing hopes to convince Washington of its good intentions by showing goodwill on the Korean front. Finally, there has been a movement towards East Asia community-building, starting on the economic end, including ASEAN 10+1, ASEAN 10+3, and a number of free trade agreements which are under way. At the same time, increasing discussion of the security dimension has brought an unprecedented possibility – a regional security framework that would include all the major powers, such as the USA, China, Japan, Russia and South Korea. This mood of coordination on the security front has also provided a foundation for China's shift of foreign policy towards the Korean Peninsula, mainly from a passive role to a more active position.

China's role in the Six-Party Talks

The fifth round of the Six-Party Talks was concluded on 11 November 2005. According to the chairman's statement, read by the head of the Chinese delegation, Wu Dawei, 'the parties have reaffirmed that they would fully implement the joint statement in line with the principle of "commitment for commitment, action for action", so as to realize the verifiable denuclearization of the Korean Peninsula'.[8] The parties also 'emphasized that they are willing to comprehensively implement the Joint Statement through confidence-building, carry out all commitments in different areas, commence and conclude the process in a timely and coordinated manner and achieve balanced interest and win-win result cooperation'.[9] The implementation measures include suggestions for 'setting up a standing team of experts from the six participating countries',[10] as well as an agreement between the United States and North Korea to 'hold bilateral talks' to resolve disputed issues.[11]

The Chinese government's active role in the Six-Party Talks is in accordance with its new security framework developed for the twenty-first century, also known as the 'new security concept'. This notion was elaborated by Chinese Vice Foreign Minister Wang Yi as a 'comprehensive, common and cooperative' security framework.[12] Under the new guidelines, China emphasizes gentler and friendlier relations with its neighbouring countries, as well as more accommodating policies on multilateral security arrangements in the region.

In addition to the new security concept, one must also examine the four broader factors that influenced its decision to host the Six-Party Talks.

First, Beijing's foreign policy priority continued to be ensuring a stable and peaceful international environment so that it can concentrate on economic modernization. A nuclear North Korea would not be conducive to this development. Second, a North Korea that was actively developing nuclear weapons would almost inevitably stimulate a new arms race in North-East Asia, prompting the governments of both South Korea and Japan to consider their own nuclear options. With Sino-Japanese relations at a low point, Beijing would definitely not want to see Tokyo move in this direction. Third, Chinese national interests and foreign policy headaches around the issue of Taiwan require close coordination between China and the United States in order to curb a possible shift in the latter's Taiwan policy. One incentive for the US government to support China on the Taiwan issue is Beijing's cooperation on the North Korean nuclear issue. Beijing's move from being a passive to an active player demonstrates its cooperative goodwill towards Washington. Finally, with these highly visible Six-Party Talks, China has portrayed itself as a responsible major power that can take the lead in handling difficult international issues, which has in turn raised its international standing. Indeed, the Chinese government has received broad praise from the international community for its leadership role in the Six-Party Talks. US Secretary of State Condoleezza Rice, for example, on her visit to Beijing in July 2005, applauded Beijing's role after meeting Chinese President Hu Jintao[13] (although others feel that it has not done enough in this regard)[14].

Beijing long ago dropped its view of North Korea as a close ally, although it still occasionally uses the expression 'as close as lips and teeth' to describe its relationship with the country. This policy shift was completed over a decade ago after Beijing established formal diplomatic relations with Seoul in 1992. For the past few years, although there is still a close relationship between the two countries, Beijing has been willing to put pressure on North Korea from time to time to indicate its displeasure with the latter's development of nuclear weapons. In addition to political pressure, Beijing also has economic means of exerting pressure: as is well known, China is the chief provider of energy and food for North Korea. At the same time, the Chinese government has further enhanced its ties to the North Korean regime in a substantial way. During the Six-Party Talks, China and North Korea have exchanged frequent visits, both at state and at working levels. One instance of this occurred in late October 2005 when Chinese President Hu Jintao visited Pyongyang in preparation for the talks and held lengthy meetings with North Korean President Kim Jong-Il.[15] The Japanese Chief Cabinet Secretary, Hiroyuki Hosoda, openly praised this visit, saying 'We believe there will be a good impact' on the forthcoming Six-Party Talks.[16] In turn, Kim Jong-Il visited China in January 2006, travelling not just to Beijing but also to cities in southern China. This visit is believed to have been made in the name of economic reform and aid from China, as well as in preparation for the next round of the Six-Party Talks.[17]

On the other hand, it has to be recognized that there are limits to the Chinese influence over North Korea. Pyongyang has certainly enjoyed its own independent foreign policy and autonomous decision making. It can even be suspected of having enjoyed using the nuclear issue as a bargaining chip to play with its long-time rival, the United States. Furthermore, increasing nationalistic sentiment in North Korea has also greatly counterbalanced China's potential influence, and Beijing has been keenly aware of this limitation and has thus behaved cautiously. For example, in the autumn of 2005 the Beijing leadership was pressured by Pyongyang to shut down an influential policy-oriented journal, *Zhanlie Yu Guanli* [Strategy and management] after the journal published an article that was highly critical of the North Korean regime, making suggestions that China should shift its policy towards North Korea in a more balanced direction.[18] This has further demonstrated the sensitive nature of the issues between Beijing and Pyongyang. It therefore cannot be assumed that the North Korean government will easily fall into line with China's stance, or that dialogues between the two countries will be smooth and continue to move forward.

The Six-Party Talks and Chinese foreign policy towards the Korean Peninsula can also be analysed from a regional viewpoint in terms of the balance of power and community-building process. The relevance to China of the regional balance of power could be seen in the PRC's decision in the early 1950s, inspired by the perceived threat of the invasion of Western imperialism, to provide substantial military support to North Korea in its war with the South. The Korean War resulted in direct military confrontation between China and the United States. There is no doubt that strategic and political calculations dominated Chinese Korea policy. Chinese leaders also learned several lessons from the war. In terms of casualties and the political implications for Chinese foreign policy and the evolution of East Asian international relations, the war proved very costly for China.

With the changing international and domestic environment, Beijing made substantial adjustments in its Korea policy. As the host of the Six-Party Talks, China has become a focal point whenever there are new developments in the North Korean nuclear crisis. The primary focus of Chinese diplomatic coordination is to find a compromise point between the two chief rivals – the United States and North Korea. On 12 February 2005, for example, Chinese Foreign Minister Li Zhaoxing had a telephone conversation with Secretary of State Condoleezza Rice to discuss how to handle the latest development in the North Korea nuclear crisis. Two days earlier, on 10 February, Pyongyang had made the announcement that North Korea now possessed nuclear weapons and was withdrawing from the Six-Party Talks. In this conversation, the two ministers agreed that the governments of both China and the United States wished to seek peace and stability on the Korean Peninsula and that the Six-Party Talks should be restored as soon as possible. Chinese displeasure over the North Korean announcement could be seen in the uncensored criticism of the action that appeared in the Chinese news media and on Internet discussion boards (previously, similar discussions were often removed from the Internet by the Chinese authorities).[19]

The Chinese efforts paid off when all parties agreed to resume the Six-Party Talks, which began in late July 2005. The fourth round of the talks proved to be long and difficult, yet relatively successful. The joint statement issued on 19 September 2005 clearly indicated that 'the six parties unanimously reaffirm that the goal of the six-party talks is the verifiable denuclearization of the Korea peninsula in a peaceful manner'. It then brought together the key positions of North Korea and the United States by stating that 'the DPRK is committed to abandoning all nuclear weapons and existing nuclear programs'; and the United States 'affirmed that it has no nuclear weapons on the Korean peninsula and has no intention to attack or invade the DPRK with nuclear or conventional weapons'. An interesting development is related to the North Korean demand for the right to peaceful uses of nuclear energy: the joint statement said that the other parties 'agreed to discuss at an appropriate time the subject of the provision of light-water reactor(s) to the DPRK'.[20]

It is interesting to note that Chinese leaders have indeed made some skilful behind-the-scenes efforts to bridge the gap between Pyongyang and Washington. In order to persuade the US government to be flexible on the North Korean demand for a light-water reactor in return for its commitment to abandon nuclear weapons, Chinese leaders sent a number of messages to their counterparts indicating that if the USA refused to compromise the Six-Party Talks would likely fail – an undesirable result for all parties, including Washington. Thus, on the night of 18 September Chinese Deputy Foreign Minister Dai Bingguo invited the leaders of all parties' delegations to participate in an autumn festival banquet, a traditional Chinese holiday, to enjoy the beauty of the full moon. During this 'moon banquet' it was clear that the USA would have to bear the blame if the Six-Party Talks failed the next day, at the scheduled closing for this round of talks. The banquet lasted from 8:00 pm to midnight, providing ample opportunity for delegation leaders to conduct last-minute informal negotiations. Agreement was reached at 1:00 pm the next day, 19 September, with the joint statement mentioned above.[21]

From this discussion of China's role in the Six-Party Talks regional security and economic arrangements, it can be seen that China holds one of the keys to the security interests of the USA and Japan in the area – a core issue of North-East Asian security configurations.

China's coordination with Japan on Korea policy

During the not-too-long course of the Six-Party Talks since August 2003, it has been clear that the governments of the USA, China and North Korea are the major players in the sense that the Washington and Pyongyang are the chief negotiators, and Beijing plays the role of host and mediator. Thus, Tokyo and Moscow, although important, have played only minor roles, while Seoul has performed a special function in terms of facilitating dialogue between North Korea and the USA. Beijing's main energies, therefore, are being devoted to bringing the US and North Korean negotiators to the table. The next tier of effort will be to coordinate with negotiators from Japan, Russia and South Korea. In this sense, Sino-Japanese coordination can be regarded as a secondary effort in its shuttle diplomacy.

A foundation upon which all major powers can sit down and negotiate with North Korea is the common interests that they share, including the governments of China and Japan.

Common ground

There is much common ground between Beijing and Tokyo in terms of the North Korea nuclear crisis. First, in their own national interests both governments would prefer a peaceful and stable international environment, and they do not want to see a military confrontation on the Korean Peninsula. As mentioned above, Beijing's top priority in its strategic goals for the new century will continue to be economic modernization, which requires a peaceful environment. Moreover, of the two flashpoints in the Asia–Pacific – Taiwan and the Korean Peninsula – the former is clearly more at the heart of core Chinese national interests (although Korea is also important). The Chinese government would therefore prefer to focus its energy and resources on the settlement of the Taiwan issue and not let a potential military confrontation on the Korean Peninsula jeopardize its position regarding Taiwan, as happened during the Korean War in the 1950s.

Second, both insist on a nuclear-free Korean Peninsula. For Beijing, even though it may not be very concerned about a nuclear threat to its own security, given the close relationship with Pyongyang, it may nevertheless be concerned that a nuclear North Korea could cause the development of Japanese nuclear weapons. Tokyo, on the other hand, has genuine security concerns about a possible nuclear attack from North Korea, given the long hostile relationship between the two countries. Thus, for their own reasons, neither Chinese leaders nor the Japanese leaders want an arms race to begin on the Korean Peninsula.

Third, both countries' governments view the Six-Party Talks as an excellent vehicle not only for raising their international profile in the region but also for providing mechanisms to solve their individual problems by simultaneously conducting bilateral negotiations with Pyongyang as well. For example, immediately before the fifth round of the Six-Party Talks, Japanese and North Korean negotiators conducted bilateral talks in Beijing on 3–4 November 2005, focusing on three key issues in bilateral relations: the issue of the abductions of Japanese citizens; nuclear missile and security issues; and negotiations over historical problems. In preparation for the talks in late October 2005, President Hu Jintao visited Pyongyang and held lengthy meetings with Kim Jong-Il.

Fourth, both governments have recognized the special role of the United States in the region as a stabilizer. Because of this, they are both willing to cooperate with it, albeit to different degrees. In other words, neither country wants to challenge the US position in the region or withhold cooperation as long as the US stance is in accordance with its own interests. Furthermore, all participating parties have clearly recognized that the format of the Six-Party Talks is the only multilateral security forum led by both Washington and Beijing, and that it may evolve into a new security framework (this is discussed in detail below). It is therefore only natural that Tokyo has also had a positive attitude towards this new framework. In virtually all opening statements from the Japanese government, its attitude has been very positive. After the three-day talks of the fifth round in November 2005, for example, Japanese delegation leader Kenichiro Sasae spoke highly of the statement issued by the Chinese delegation leader who also served as chairman as 'taking into account all parties' interests'.[22]

Different concerns

It has to be noted, however, that the Chinese and Japanese concerns differ on certain points. First, the two governments have different views of strategic goals with regard to the issue of regime change. Beijing is much less inclined to agree with the USA's position – that the ultimate goal may be a regime shift in Pyongyang – as a way to completely solve the problem. The hardliners in Washington, particularly within the Department of Defense, have long believed that the ultimate way to solve the North Korea problem is to facilitate regime change, as the US armed forces did in Iraq (although there have been constant warnings about the war option with North Korea). Beijing, however, has made it clear that it does not favour a quick regime change, which could lead to the total collapse of the government in Pyongyang. For one thing, this kind of collapse would enable a sizeable US military presence to move to the Chinese border along the Yalu River. Tokyo is more or less in agreement with Washington in this regard, although their rhetoric may be different. Over the course of the Six-Party Talks, it appeared that there are two different stances towards North Korea: the 'soft approach' favoured by the governments of China and South Korea, and the 'hard line' taken by those of the United States and Japan.[23]

Second, the Chinese government has its own security concerns over the possible collapse of the regime in North Korea, which would push even more refugees across the border into China. The refugee issue has already become a burden to the Chinese. As a result of the widespread famine in North Korea since the late 1990s, North Koreans have been crossing illegally into China.[24] According to the Seoul-based humanitarian group Good Friends, the estimated number of North Korean 'food refugees' in China reportedly reached 300,000 in 1999 – a number that is at odds with the official estimate of 1,500.[25] Hundreds of North Koreans have already made their way over the Sino-Korean border either by swimming along the coast of the Yellow Sea or by walking over the mountains. The flow of refugees has been so great that the South Korean consulates in Beijing and Hong Kong have been swamped with requests for asylum. Many more refugees were caught by the Chinese and returned to North Korea, where severe punishment awaited them.[26] Unfortunately, the refugees have little legal protection, and allegations of widespread abuse are common. Beijing therefore does not want to see the further deterioration of this situation, which is what would happen following a regime collapse. Thus, for the time being, Beijing may prefer the Pyongyang regime to continue to exist and serve as a buffer between Chinese and US military forces.

The refugee issue has caused problems for China's foreign relations, including those with Japan. On 8 May 2002, five North Korean asylum seekers tried to rush into the Japanese consulate in Shenyang, China, and were arrested inside the consulate gate by Chinese police. The incident created diplomatic tension between the governments of China and Japan.[27] Similar previous attempts by North Koreans also took place in Beijing with the embassy compounds of the United States, Germany, Canada and Spain.[28] The unhappy episode of the Shenyang incident indicated that, even if Beijing and Tokyo share common interests in dealing with Pyongyang, unexpected incidents like this can jeopardize Sino-Japanese relations in a sensational way time and again.

Tokyo, on the other hand, has its own grievances with Pyongyang, namely the issue of North Korean abduction of Japanese citizens over the past few decades, an issue that caused outrage in Japan and made a hard-line policy towards Pyongyang quite popular. Japanese leaders and diplomats have repeatedly raised this issue whenever they have an opportunity to meet representatives from North Korea, either within or outside the negotiating forum of the Six-Party Talks. Obviously, the abduction issue has no direct linkage with Chinese interests, and Beijing has not hidden its disapproval of Tokyo's attempts to bring the issue to the Six-Party Talks. In Chinese newspapers, for example, one finds such headlines as 'No role for Japan at Six-Party Talks – Pyongyang'. Although this headline refers to a North Korean statement, China's negative attitude towards Japan's attempts to bring the abduction issue to the talks is clear.[29]

Third, there are also different policy preferences in the sense that the Chinese negotiators prefer to rely more on 'carrots', whereas the Japanese negotiators tend to lean towards the use of 'sticks'. Beijing has advocated a more patient policy with North Korea, providing more incentives for it to change its policy. Tokyo, in contrast, would more often than not prefer to show its solidarity with Washington, including in its North Korea policy. This does not mean that the Japanese government falls into line with every US proposal, but rather that, as mentioned earlier, it is seen as joining Washington in taking a hard line vis-à-vis North Korea.

Fourth, it is obvious that the governments of China and Japan carry different weights in terms of their political and economic influence over North Korea. In addition to being a long-time ally with relations rooted back in the Korean War, Beijing has enjoyed much economic leverage over North Korea. As a chief provider of energy and food, it is able to use economic means to indicate its policy preferences, as already mentioned. Japan, historically a colonizer on the Korean Peninsula, has time and time again been an easy scapegoat for North Korean propaganda. Whenever there is something that requires someone on whom to pin the blame, Japan has proved an easy scapegoat. It is nevertheless expected that the importance of Japan will increase if and when it begins to provide official development assistance (ODA) to North Korea.

Despite these differences, there is every reason to believe that the common interests between the two powers will prevail and the four factors behind the Chinese decision to host the Six-Party Talks will remain.

Coordination between China and Japan

There is naturally frequent coordination between the six parties. Beijing's shuttle diplomacy has been helpful in bringing different parties together. As one can imagine, the Six-Party Talks, even in a technical sense, are not an easy task in terms of interpretation. Interpreters for five languages – Chinese, English, Korean, Russian and Japanese – are needed. But perhaps even more difficult now is coordinating different positions, stances and concerns. In the case of China and Japan, the same applies. Fortunately the common ground is large enough to overcome the differences so that all parties concerned have been relatively well coordinated by the Chinese.

There are at least five ways to coordinate between China and Japan. First, there are frequent enough gatherings and discussions among the leaders of the five countries, including China and Japan, to give them opportunities to adjust their policy towards North Korea. Although there have been no state visits between Japan and China over the past few years due to Japanese Prime Minister Junichiro Koizumi's repeated visits to the Yasukuni shrine, the two countries' leaders have met from time to time in international settings, such as the annual meetings of the Asia–Pacific Economic Forum (APEC) and ASEAN + 3.[30] The issue of Korea crisis management is among the topics discussed at such meetings. In addition, leading politicians and leaders other than the heads of state do visit each other and take these opportunities to discuss the issue of North Korea.

Second, Beijing has fully utilized its shuttle diplomacy to coordinate different parties' positions. Its envoys have paid periodic visits to Tokyo to brief the Japanese Ministry of Foreign Affairs and to make preparations.

Third, the Chinese government has recently proposed the setting up of a strategic dialogue between China and Japan at the deputy foreign minister level.[31] General security issues, including North Korea, will be among the major points discussed. In May 2005, for example, Japanese Vice Foreign Minister Shotaro Yachi held 15 hours of talks with his Chinese counterpart Dai Bingguo. Although the dialogue was primarily about the anti-Japanese riots that had taken place in several Chinese cities a month before, other issues of mutual concern were also discussed. Both sides agreed that the 'dialogue was positive and helpful' and 'should be carried on'.[32]

Fourth, frequent information exchanges through diplomatic channels have taken place, primarily between the Japanese Embassy in Beijing and the Chinese Embassy in Tokyo. For example, in November 2005, before the fifth round of the Six-Party Talks, Li Bin, the Chinese ambassador for Korean Peninsula affairs, and Akitaka Saiki, deputy head of the Japanese Foreign Ministry's Asian and Oceanian Affairs Bureau, exchanged views in Beijing. They also promised that the two countries 'will continue to closely cooperate' in future talks.[33]

Fifth, frequent working discussions at the lower level of the government hierarchy have also taken place between the two countries' diplomats.

Among the five channels discussed above, the most noteworthy recent development is the forthcoming regular security and strategic dialogue at the deputy foreign minister level, which will certainly provide a new, high-level forum to discuss issues of mutual concern, with North Korea certainly included.

Bargaining chips?

It is well known that the current status of Sino-Japanese relations is known as *jinre zhengleng*, meaning 'economically hot, but politically cold'. For example, in 2004, the value of the bilateral trade between China and Japan reached 213 billion USD, for the first time passing Japan's trade with the USA (of 197 billion USD in 2004).[34] Increasingly, debate in Japan takes the view that China must be regarded as an opportunity for development. At the same time, however, the political relations between the governments of China and Japan have reached a new low. Their mutual perceptions have declined noticeably and in each of their respective capitals the question of how to deal with the other has become a major foreign policy problem.

Antagonistic political relations may promote hostile security policy. The best example in this regard is China's Japan policy. The Japanese government has long been cautious not to offend the Chinese government by openly including Taiwan in its military alliance with the United States, not only because of Japan's past colonial history, but also in recognition of Taiwan as a key Chinese national interest and a desire not to antagonize the Chinese leadership. However, beginning with a state visit by Chinese President Jiang Zemin to Japan in 1998, bilateral relations have declined significantly. On the one hand, Tokyo has received the message telling of Beijing's unease about Japan's treatment of historical issues, but on the other hand, Japanese leaders may now feel that they have a free hand not to care so much about the Chinese reaction. Since relations are at such a low point already, then an additional complication (such as Beijing's refusal to hold annual meetings between the two countries' leaders due to the Japanese prime minister's visits to Yasukuni shrine) adds little urgency to the situation. In addition, in the Japanese perspective, the Chinese unease seems almost inevitable or a permanent state of affairs, and this has resulted in making the Japanese less diplomatic.

In February 2005, a 'two plus two' meeting took place in Washington, including Secretary of State Rice and Secretary of Defense Donald Rumsfeld from the USA, and Foreign Minister Nobutaka Machimura and Defense Agency Director Yoshinori Ono from Japan. The meeting issued a statement on 19 February indicating that the countries had produced a 'revised US–Japanese strategic understanding' which for the first time included security in the area around Taiwan as a 'common strategic objective'.[35] In fact, it is reported that an informal anti-Chinese submarine alliance of the governments of the United States, Japan and Taiwan had been formed. This was revealed after the intrusion of a Chinese submarine into Japanese waters in late 2004.[36] A follow-up US–Japan meeting between Secretary of State Rice and Foreign Minister Machimura in September 2005 further confirmed security and military cooperation between Washington and Tokyo, including implementation strategies for future actions.[37]

It is natural, considering the complicated nature of Sino-Japanese relations, that people have begun to speculate that Beijing may use its advantageous position as host of the Six-Party Talks as a bargaining chip in its relations with Tokyo. For example, it may appear less warm towards Japanese participation in the talks in order to induce a change in the Japanese attitude towards China. This has so far not yet materialized, for the following three reasons.

First, it is indeed in the common interests of Beijing and Tokyo to resolve the North Korean issue, and North Korea is not only a Japanese problem, but a Chinese one as well. Beijing does need Tokyo's cooperation. In the case of a settlement of the North Korea problem, Beijing has few bargaining chips over Tokyo that it can use without damaging cooperation between the two. Second, the

Six-Party Talks themselves are an on-and-off matter and have not yet been fully institutionalized. The future development of the talks themselves is therefore uncertain, making it difficult for participants (except for North Korea) to use them as a bargaining chip. Third, the main powers that provide leadership in the Six-Party Talks are China and the United States, whereas Japan has only played a marginal role. For the time being, therefore, there is not much Beijing can do to use this issue as a bargaining chip with Tokyo.

Conclusions: a constructive mechanism for China–Japan dialogue

The significance of the Six-Party Talks is twofold. First, they have dealt forcefully with – and hopefully resolved – one of the biggest threats in the Asia–Pacific – the North Korean nuclear challenge. Although the drama is still unfolding, it has been moving in a constructive and positive direction. Second, in the long run, the Six-Party Talks may evolve into a new security framework in the Asia–Pacific. They have already brought four major powers – China, the USA, Japan and Russia – into this framework. More importantly, this is the first multilateral forum jointly led by the governments of the United States and China. Thus, it has provided necessary forums and mechanisms for all related parties to resolve their security concerns in a collective, collaborative and constructive spirit. Given the deterioration of Sino-Japanese relations, particularly in the current Koizumi era, the Six-Party Talks provide a more meaningful framework than any other forum for substantive dialogue between China and Japan. The talks may also prove helpful in future in that they may ultimately prevent the escalation of tension (or, in a remote scenario, military confrontation) between China and Japan. It is therefore very helpful at this point to discuss the future directions of a possible new and more inclusive security framework in the region.

Although the Six-Party Talks have experienced ups and downs since they started in 2003, including frustrations over periodic North Korean threats to withdraw from the multilateral negotiations, such as those made in the spring of 2005, some observers are optimistic about their future. In the long run, the Six-Party Talks may not only bring the parties concerned to the table to work together on a peaceful solution for the region, but also present the possibility of institutionalizing a new security framework in the Asia–Pacific. Considering the tension present in relations between China and Japan, this would be a very important development.

Beijing's main concern is the United States, and Japan is its second. It is known that there are hardliners and softliners within the US foreign policy apparatus.[38] In Washington, there have been advocates of a 'soft landing' in Korea – a gradual process of unification in which neither side is swallowed up by the other and the US government helps its North Korean counterparts to achieve China-style economic reform.[39] Beijing is deeply suspicious about the role played by Washington. It does not believe that the US government truly wants to solve the Korean problem.[40] But, as a China specialist points out, 'China cannot change the U.S. forward deployment or its web of alliances in Asia in the foresee-able future. Working with the US has become not a choice but a necessity'.[41] Beijing, nevertheless, would not want to see a US military presence in a unified Korea along the China–Korea border. Consequently, it is necessary for the two governments to further develop confidence-building measures and to coordinate routine consultations between themselves over the issue of Korea.

The same considerations can be applied to the Sino-Japanese relationship in terms of confidence-building measures, given that the two countries' territorial disputes, disputes over offshore oil exploration and production, and animosity over historical issues have increased. These mechanisms are extremely important to the relationship between the governments of China and Japan as well. Indeed, over the course of the Six-Party Talks Chinese and Japanese negotiators have held numerous bilateral consultations in preparation for the talks.

In sum, the evolution of Chinese foreign policy towards the Korean Peninsula has a rich historical background and dynamic interactions between its domestic considerations and international environments. The understanding of this process will provide a solid foundation for full comprehension of the active Chinese role in the Six-Party Talks at present. Although Beijing's role has been as chief coordinator and facilitator, focusing primarily on the two major rivals, the United States and North Korea, its coordination with other (and secondary) players such as Japan also deserves attention. The Six-Party Talks, which may lead to a new and more inclusive multilateral security framework, will not only provide a powerful forum to deal with the North Korean nuclear crisis and to ensure stability and security in the region, but will also provide more effective mechanisms for Sino–Japanese coordination as well as a channel for Beijing and Tokyo to conduct useful dialogue to resolve issues of mutual concern.

Notes

1 For an analysis of the 'two ups and two downs' structure in East Asian international relations in the post-cold war era, see Quansheng Zhao, 'The shift in power distribution and the change of major power relations', *Journal of Strategic Studies*, 24/4, December 2001, pp. 49–78.

2 Chae-Jin Lee, *China and Korea: Dynamic Relations*, Stanford, Calif.: Hoover Institution, 1996, p. 1.

3 Among many excellent analyses of the historical legacy of Chinese security concerns over Japan, see Thomas J. Christensen, 'China, the U.S.–Japan alliance, and the security dilemma in East Asia', *International Security*, 23/4, spring 1999, pp. 49–80.

4 There are many studies analysing the Korean War. See e.g. Allen Whiting, *China Crosses the Yalu: The Decision to Enter the Korean War*, New York: Macmillan, 1960; Bruce Cumings, *The Origins of the Korean War*, Princeton, NJ: Princeton University Press, 1981 and 1990; Sergei Goncharov, John W. Lewis and Xue Litai, *Uncertain Partners: Stalin, Mao, and the Korean War*, Stanford, Calif.: Stanford University Press, 1993; and Jian Chen, *China's Road to the Korean War*, New York: Columbia University Press, 1994.

5 For an excellent account of the importance of the Korean Peninsula, see Robert Scalapino, 'The changing order in Northeast Asia and the prospects for U.S.–Japan–China–Korea relations'. Paper presented at joint East–West Center/Pacific Forum Seminar held in Honolulu, 13–28 August 1998.

6 For a detailed analysis of economic relations between China and Korea see Chae-Jin Lee, *China and Korea*, in particular Chapter 5, 'Economic relations'.
7 Korea Customs Service, 'Trade statistics 2004 and 2005', available HTTP: <http://english.customs.go.kr/kcshome/jsp/eng/PGAS301.jsp>.
8 'Full Text of chairman's statement of first phase', *China Daily*, 11 November 2005. Available at <http:www.chinadaily.cn/english/doc/2005-11/15/content_494856.htm>.
9 Ibid.
10 [China chief negotiator proposes six-party experts club], *Chosun Ilbo*, 10 November 2005.
11 'Chinese "experts" cited on six-way talks', BBC Monitoring Asia Pacific, 11 November 2005.
12 Michael Vatikiotis and Murray Hiebert, 'How China is building an empire', *Far Eastern Economic Review*, 20 November 2003, pp. 30–3.
13 'Rice applauds China's role in Korean nuclear talks', Xinhua News Agency, 11 July 2005.
14 Bill Gertz, 'Report hits China over N. Korea role', *Washington Times*, 10 November 2005.
15 During this visit President Hu Jintao also visited a new Chinese-financed glass factory in Pyongyang. See Anthony Faiola, 'N. Korea gains aid despite arms standoff', *Washington Post*, 16 November 2005, p. A14.
16 'Japan expects Hu's Pyongyang visit to move nuclear talks forward', Agence France-Presse, 21 October 2005 (in English).
17 'Kim's China visit a "detour" around US sanctions experts', Global News Wire, 10 January 2006.
18 John J. Tkacik, Jr, 'China's "S&M" journal goes too far on Korea', *Asia Times*, 2 September 2004, available HTTP: <http://www.asiatimes.com>.
19 Anthony Faiola and Philip P. Pan, 'N. Korea declaration draws world concern', *Washington Post*, 11 February 2005, p. A1.
20 'Full text of six-nation statement on North Korea', Nautilus Institute, 20 September 2005, available HTTP: <http://www.nautilus.org/napsnet/sr/2005/0577Agreement.html>.
21 'The inside story of the fourth round of Six-Party talks on the North Korea nuclear crisis', *Sino-American Times*, 29 September–5 October 2005, p. C5.
22 'Japan delegation head praises six-way talks statement', BBC Monitoring Asia Pacific, 11 November 2005.
23 Peter Baker and Anthony Faiola, 'US, S. Korea find unity against North's nuclear arms program', *Washington Post*, 17 November 2005, p. A20.
24 Kim Ji-ho, 'N.K. "food refugees" in northern China suffer abuses without legal protection', *Korea Herald*, 7 September 1999, available HTTP: <http://www.koreaherald.co.kr/news/1999/09/__11/19990907_1140.htm>.
25 'Human rights of N.K. refugees', *Korea Herald*, 6 September 1999, available HTTP: <http://www.koreaherald.co.kr/news/1999/09/__03/19990906_0318.htm>.
26 Mary Jordan, 'Fearing deluge, political fallout, China spurns fleeing N. Koreans', *Washington Post*, 14 April 1997, p. A14.
27 David Kruger, 'Diplomatic chaos', *Far Eastern Economic Review*, 23 May 2002, p. 11.
28 'Korean refugees', *Far Eastern Economic Review*, 9 May 2002, p. 24.
29 'No role for Japan at six-party talks – Pyongyang', *China Daily*, available HTTP: <http://www.chinadaily.com.cn/english/doc/2005-2007/20/content_461843.htm>.
30 However, Chinese Prime Minister Wen Jiabao refused to meet Koizumi during the East Asia summit in Kuala Lumpur in December 2005 because of the latter's repeated visits to the Yasukuni shrine.
31 *Asahi Shimbun*, 8 February 2005, p. 2.
32 'Japan–China talks fail to settle April vandalism', *Japan Times*, 16 May 2005.
33 'China, Japan reaffirm cooperation over 6-way talks', *Japan Economic Newswire*, 2 November 2005.

34 Paul Blustein, 'China passes U.S. in trade with Japan', *Washington Post*, 27 January 2005, p. E1.
35 Edward Cody, 'China protests U.S.–Japan accord', *Washington Post*, 21 February 2005, p. A24. See also *Shijie Ribao* [World journal], 19 February 2005, p. 1.
36 'Anti-submarine alliance among U.S., Japan, and Taiwan triangle against PLA', *Qiao Bao* [China Press] 3 December 2004, p. B4.
37 'Joint statement: Strategic development alliance', 17 September 2005, on the web site of the Japanese Ministry of Foreign Affairs, available HTTP: <http://www.mofa.go.jp/region/n_america/us/joint0509.html>.
38 For a detailed analysis and discussion of US foreign policy towards North Korea, see Victor D. Cha and David C. Kang, 'The debate over North Korea', *Political Science Quarterly*, 119/2, 2004, pp. 229–54.
39 Selig Harrison, 'Promoting a soft landing in Korea', *Foreign Policy*, 106, spring 1997.
40 Yu Meihua, 'Xin shiqi mei ri er dui chaoxian bandao zhengce tedian jiqi zoushi' [The Korea policies of the United States, Japan and Russia in the new era and future direction], *Contemporary International Relations*, January 1997, p. 33.
41 Suisheng Zhao, 'China's periphery policy and its Asian neighbors', *Security Dialogue*, 30/3, September 1999, p. 345.

6 Russian North Korea policy: old conflicts obstacle for Russo-Japanese cooperation

Alexander Zhebin

A Russian proverb says: 'You can't throw out words from the song' (in English, 'A leopard cannot change its spots'). The proverb can be applied to illustrate the stances taken by the governments of Russia and Japan in their bilateral relations today and their unfortunate tendency to refer back to their military conflicts in the last century. Japan is the only country in East Asia that Russia was at war with several times in the twentieth century. Twice Russia had to conduct large-scale operations in Korea against Japan, in 1904–5, and in 1945. There were also limited military engagements between the USSR and Japan at the end of the 1930s, during the Japanese expansion in North-East Asia. Both countries participated in the Korean War of 1950–3, although Japan's participation was quite limited.

The heritage of these conflicts remains, both in the bilateral relations between the two countries and in the system of international relations in North-East Asia, and it is one of the main obstacles to the development of political and economic cooperation between Russia and Japan. It also affects the Russo-Japanese interaction on the international scene, including in North-East Asia. The formulation and implementation of coordinated measures by the governments of Russia and Japan aimed at transforming North-East Asia into a zone of peace and prosperity for all the states in the region look especially urgent in the light of the current situation regarding the nuclear programmes of the Democratic People's Republic of Korea (DPRK, North Korea).

The Russian government of today realizes this. As the threat of global nuclear conflict has receded into the past, other global challenges have assumed centre stage – international terrorism, the proliferation of weapons of mass destruction (WMD), organized crime involving drugs, the trafficking in human beings, the illegal arms trade, illegal migration, illegal financial transactions, and threats to the environment and health.[1]

At the same time the Russian government has stated that only a multilateral search for solutions to the problems facing the world community can be successful. This will of course require serious efforts to harmonize interests and work out a common strategy for dealing with international problems. The new world order should be based on the broadest kind of multilateral cooperation. The long-term objectives of countering the global threats and challenges objectively outweigh the unilateral approaches, which are in any case often based on ad hoc tactical interests.[2]

Exactly the same approach is used by the Russian government in its cooperation with other countries, including Japan, in the search for a resolution of the nuclear and other problems on the Korean Peninsula.

At the beginning of the 2000s the Russian government had basically completed formulating a policy on Korea, a process which took almost ten years. The new policy takes into account both social and economic changes in Russia and the geopolitical realities on the international arena. The new Russian foreign policy, including that for the Korean Peninsula, is characterized by the total disappearance of the ideological factor and by greater pragmatism in defining approaches to current global and regional problems.

According to my analysis, the new Russian Korea policy includes the following four major approaches:

1   Moscow is strongly in favour of the denuclearized status of the Korean Peninsula. It is impossible to achieve relaxation of the tensions on the peninsula without ensuring non-proliferation of WMD in the world in general, and on the Korean Peninsula especially. Moscow is ready to contribute to that cause.
2   The peace process and cooperation between North Korea and South Korea (the Republic of Korea (ROK)) should be developed on the basis of the principles agreed upon by the two Koreas and their leaders themselves, without interference from others.
3   All problems should be solved only by peaceful, diplomatic means, according to the spirit of the Joint Declaration of North Korea and South Korea of 15 June 2000.
4   Moscow will welcome a process of the establishment of a peaceful united Korean state which is friendly to Russia and other countries.

The nuclear problem in North Korea and Russia

The explosive situation on the Korean Peninsula is subject to close Russian scrutiny, as the peninsula borders on the Russian Far East. It is in the Russian government's interests, as well as those that of other governments to preserve the denuclearized status of the peninsula and develop peaceful cooperation in North-East Asia with direct Russian participation.

Shortly after the beginning of the current nuclear crisis in Korea, a lively discussion broke out in Russia on how the Russia government should handle the situation. From the very outbreak of the crisis in January 2003, when Pyongyang withdrew from the 1968 Treaty on the Non-proliferation of Nuclear Weapons (NPT), there was a tendency to approach the situation as mainly a bilateral dispute between the governments of the USA and North Korea.[3] At the same time, a number of observers argued that the Russian position on the matter should be determined by the country's global responsibility as both a nuclear power and a depositary state of the NPT.[4]

Some experts even expressed opinions in favour of the creation of a united front with the USA and its allies to demonstrate a 'collective firmness' towards Pyongyang in order to put an end to its nuclear ambitions.[5] Opponents of such an approach pointed out that the Russian government would in that case be retreating to the type of diplomacy it had exercised in Korea during the first half of the 1990s, which had resulted in the loss of Pyongyang's trust in Moscow, the drastic decline of Russian influence in South Korea, and the Western neglect of Russian opinion on the Korea issue.[6]

The Russian stance is that the nuclear problem needs to be resolved by taking all its aspects into consideration. On the one hand, it is important to secure North Korea's return to the NPT and generally to ensure the nuclear-free status of the Korean Peninsula. On the other hand, it is necessary to provide the North Korean leadership with security guarantees, and to ensure more active participation by the international community in helping Pyongyang resolve its complex economic problems.

As for the various side issues raised by the other countries involved in the Korean negotiations, the Russian government believes that it would be desirable in the course of the negotiations to concentrate on the most important matter: the major challenge is how to handle the crisis around the nuclear problem and to provide conditions for its resolution once and for all. The remaining issues, including the North Korean abduction of Japanese citizens, which currently clouds Japan and North Korea, should be discussed but as part of additional contacts and nego-tiations specifically for this purpose.[7]

It is worth noting that Moscow did not hesitate to express its displeasure with North Korea's decision to withdraw from the NPT. The Russian Ministry of Foreign Affairs said in a statement on 10 January 2003 that the North Korean move 'can only exacerbate the already tense situation around the Korean Peninsula and inflict substantial harm upon the universal international legal instruments for ensuring global and regional security'.[8]

On 10 February 2005, the North Korean government declared that it had suspended its participation in the Six-Party Talks and made a formal announce-ment concerning its possession of nuclear weapons. On the same day, the Russian Ministry of Foreign Affairs issued a statement saying that Russia:

> cannot but regret the DPRK's decision on an 'indefinite suspension' of its participation in the six-party talks and the public announcement of an intention to build up its nuclear potential … [s]uch an approach is inconsistent with the striving expressed by Pyongyang for the denuclearization of the Korean Peninsula. [Moscow] treats with respect and attention the DPRK's security concerns, but at the same time considers that a solution of this problem should lie in the mainstream of the talks and not on the path of building up the arms race, especially nuclear.[9]

Two weeks after the North Korean announcement, Russian Foreign Minister Sergei Lavrov discussed the issue with his counterparts from the USA, China,

South Korea and a number of other countries. It is a regrettable fact that Japan was the last country on the list. The two countries' foreign ministers spoke on the subject only on 4 March 2005.[10] Clearly, both sides have a great deal to do to ensure stable and fully fledged cooperation on the nuclear problem. Another conclusion to be drawn from this fact is that the gap between the governments of Russia and Japan on outstanding bilateral issues, such as the territorial claims, is so serious that it hinders them from cooperating on a number of international issues which are of great importance to both of them and to the rest of the world.

The situation is in apparent contrast to the handling of the nuclear issue in relations between Russia and the USA. Russian President Vladimir Putin stated that the positions of Russia and the United States on problems of WMD non-proliferation 'are closer than they may seem'. Because of his close relationship with the North Korean leader, Kim Jong-Il, Putin avoided mentioning North Korea by name until the Russian–US summit meeting in Bratislava in February 2005. However, the Russian approach to Iran could be easily extrapolated to embrace North Korea. According to Putin, the Russian leadership 'doesn't need to be persuaded that WMD must not spread and proliferate across the planet. This concerns not only Iran, but also other regions of the world'.[11]

Pyongyang expressed a negative attitude towards the declaration adopted at the summit meeting of the Group of Eight industrialized countries (G8) in Evian, France, in June 2003, and towards the G8 Action Plan on Non-proliferation endorsed at the Sea Island (USA) G8 summit in June 2004, thus indicating its displeasure at the Russian government's signing of both documents.[12] The spokesman for the North Korean Foreign Ministry characterized the Declaration of the Evian summit as 'an expression of mean flattery' of those countries that 'favour the US' arbitrary practice'.[13] Pyongyang expressed the same negative attitude towards the Action Plan on Non-proliferation, claiming that the part of the document dealing with North Korea 'was prompted by the US intention to force its unilateral will on the DPRK in violation of the principle of justice, equality and impartiality in international relations'.[14] Since both documents were signed by the Russian government, it was clear that the North Korean criticism included Russia, too.

It was reported that President Putin and US President George W. Bush, at the Russian–US summit held in Bratislava, Slovakia, on 24 February 2005, agreed that neither Iran nor North Korea should possess nuclear weapons. At the same time, however, a quite distinct gap remained between the Russian and US positions on how to settle the problem. When Putin met Bush in Washington, DC on 16 September 2005, he emphasized that 'the potential of diplomatic solutions to all these questions is far from being exhausted, and we'll undertake all the steps necessary to settle all these problems and issues, not to aggravate them, not to bring them to extremities'.[15]

Russia and the reunification of Korea

Moscow's position on the inter-Korean rapprochement and its possible results is determined by the Russian national interests, which can only benefit from the elimination of the hot spot right next door to the Russian Far East and from the founding in the long term of a unified Korea that is capable of maintaining relations of friendship and cooperation with Russia.

Thus, for both security and economic reasons, the Russian government is vitally interested in peace, reconciliation and the unification of Korea. This conclusion is especially salient in view of the continuing attempts by some experts to convince public opinion that none of the neighbouring countries, including Russia, is interested in Korean unification.

At the same time, there is no doubt that Moscow's priority task, if any unification scenario is to be realized, remains the maintenance of peace and stability on the peninsula. The contents of the Pyongyang and Moscow declarations of 2000 and 2001, respectively, signed by President Putin and North Korean Leader Kim Jong-Il (in his capacity as chairman of the North Korean National Defence Committee), and also the joint statements on the results of the Russian–South Korean summits in 2001 and 2004, speak quite clearly to that effect.[16]

It is also important for Moscow to ensure the greatest possible predictability for the final results of the unification process. A high degree of uncertainty concerning the character of the foreign policy of a united Korea, about a united Korea's possible participation in military–political alliances with other states, and about the orientations of such alliances, compels the Russian government to take a more cautious position towards the prospect of unification, while welcoming inter-Korean détente.

The same could be said about the other major countries' approaches to Korean unification. For example, in the context of the unresolved Taiwan problem, the Chinese leadership appears to fear the advance of US troops along the almost 1,400 km-long Korean–Chinese border. However, it seems that the US government will be compelled to put an end to its military presence in South Korea if Korea is reunified. Tokyo views a future unified Korea as a strong competitor, obsessed with the desire for historic revenge for past humiliations suffered during its colonial past.

Moscow can hardly welcome a new neighbour with a 70 million population that was very much under US influence and with US troops on its territory. It would be the equivalent to the emergence of an Asian clone of NATO. Some prominent Russian experts consider that the stationing of US troops in South Korea is an anachronistic relic of the cold war period.[17] They consider it necessary to put an end to foreign military presence in Korea after its reunification, since foreign troops can be directed against Russia, as well as China. Even more so, any US troops on the Korean Peninsula would be almost certain to be included in the Theater Missile Defense (TMD) established by the USA in the region.

Generally, especially in view of its present capabilities, the real task for the Russian government is not to establish positions in Korea but to prevent a situation where Korea would be placed under the influence of another state, especially one unfriendly to Russia.[18] Under the present balance of power in North-East Asia, and in the light of Russia's economic position, the possibility of such a scenario cannot be completely excluded. The existence of North Korea as a friendly sovereign state that acts as a buffer for US geopolitical ambitions in this region is therefore favourable to Moscow. In view of all these factors, the North Korean unification formula, calling for the creation of a neutral non-aligned state on the peninsula, is more attractive to Russian security interests than the South Korean commitment to the US military presence even after reunification.

The Russian government's firm conviction is that there is no alternative to the inter-Korean dialogue and cooperation, which has become more active since the signing of the Joint Declaration in 2000. The North and South Korean partners have expressed interest in a continued active role for Moscow in assisting this dialogue. According to President Putin, it is 'in Russia's interests that the Korean peninsula becomes the peninsula of peace, stability and prosperity'.[19]

The stabilization of the situation on the Korean Peninsula is completely in line with the Russian national interest. The tensions that arise from time to time between North and South Korea obviously do not promote the realization of joint economic projects, such as linking the Russian Trans-Siberian Mainline to the Trans-Korean Railways. This project is extremely important, as President Putin has remarked, as its 'realization will not only open new opportunities for business cooperation and economic integration on the Eurasian continent, but will also serve to strengthen confidence, peace and security in the Asia–Pacific region'.[20] The normalization of relations between North Korea and South Korea, and the eventual reunification of the two parts of the peninsula, are expected to provide better opportunities for the development of trade and economic cooperation between the Russian Federation and both parts of the unified Korean state. Undoubtedly this would also open up new opportunities for the economic development of the Russian Far East and for the linking of its economy to the integration processes under way in the Asia–Pacific region.

Some Russian experts believe that a reunified Korea would be a good alternative to Japan as a political and economic partner, especially in view of the latter's reluctance to make large-scale investments in Russia and its obvious inability to play a more independent role in international affairs.[21]

Opportunities for Russo-Japanese cooperation on the Korean Peninsula

The above-mentioned Russian priorities for the Korean Peninsula mean that one could identify the following similar, or even identical, goals for Russia and Japan in Korea:

- preventing the presence of nuclear weapons on the Korean Peninsula to ensure the non-proliferation of WMD and their means of delivery; and
- preventing a new military confrontation in Korea, since such a conflict would inevitably threaten the security of both Russia and Japan, as well as other neighbouring states.

Here it has to be noted that Tokyo quite often prefers not to notice the Russian interests on the Korean Peninsula and not to consider Russia as an important player in the region. Japanese scholars when discussing issues of multilateral cooperation in resolving the nuclear and other security problems on the Korean Peninsula as a rule even forget to mention Russia as partner for Japan to cooperate with. Even less do they mention it as a partner whose interests should be taken into account.[22] However, at key moments, such as immediately after the North Korean missile launch in 1998, or immediately before Japanese Prime Minister Junichiro Koizumi's first visit to North Korea in September 2002, the Japanese side quickly recollects the Russian presence and starts to besiege Moscow with requests and even demands, including demands for Russia to put pressure on Pyongyang.[23]

It has to be accepted that initially some of the plans for interaction between Russia and Japan regarding the Korean Peninsula were poorly deliberated at an expert level; the plans looked a little idealistic, and appeared to be more declaratory than practical. Among them was the idea of a joint visit by Russian and Japanese politicians to North Korea. The idea, according to Dmitrii Rogozin, then chairman of the International Affairs Committee of the Russian State Duma, was proposed by a high-ranking Japanese diplomat to the delegation of the State Duma during its visit to Japan in December 2000.[24]

One could also place the idea of North Korean participation in multilateral exercises to improve search and rescue operations in the Pacific Ocean in the same category. This idea was reportedly proposed by the Japanese side at talks in Tokyo between Russian Defence Minister Igor Sergeev and officials of the Japan Self-Defense Forces.[25] Another idea, that of the North Korean border guard services participating in cooperation between border guards in the region, mainly in the struggle against transnational crimes at sea, hardly had any chance of being realized. It was proposed by the director of the Russian Federal Border Guard Service, Colonel-General Konstantin Totsky, at a meeting in Tokyo in December 2000 of the representatives of the relevant services from the USA, China, Japan and South Korea.[26]

Later, however, the efforts of Prime Minister Koizumi in 2002–2004 to normalize relations with North Korea met with the public and fairly active support of the Russian government, and the personal support of President Putin. This is clear proof of the fact that the Russian government considers Japan as a desired and important partner in the efforts towards the normalization of relations on the Korean Peninsula.

Two weeks prior to his visit to North Korea, on 5 September 2002, Koizumi called Putin. Putin welcomed Koizumi's intention to visit Pyongyang, and underlined the Russian interest in the normalization of relations between Japan and North Korea. Upon Koizumi's request, Putin explained the results of his recent meeting with Kim Jong-Il in Vladivostok. Putin and Koizumi exchanged opinions on the situation in the Korean Peninsula and prospects for an inter-Korean settlement. It was stressed that the improvement of the situation in North-East Asia would promote the development of economic cooperation and the realization of large-scale projects such as the reconstruction of the Trans-Korean Railways, and its subsequent connection to the Trans-Siberian Mainline.[27]

After returning from Pyongyang, Koizumi again called Putin and, continuing the theme begun in the course of the previous telephone conversation, described the results of his visit to North Korea. Putin congratulated Koizumi on the successful completion of the first Japanese–North Korean summit, noting the importance of normalizing and developing relations between the two countries to ensure security and stability in the region. Both leaders spoke in favour of building up cooperation with a view to assisting the process of inter-Korean settlement. They promised that the governments of Russia and Japan would continue their consultations on this issue, both bilaterally and multilaterally.[28]

Putin and Koizumi stressed the great importance of the ceremonies held in Korea to mark the start of work on restoring the rail link between North and South Korea, the Trans-Korean Railways, and connecting it in the long term to the Trans-Siberian Mainline. They noted the need for the active participation of interested countries in the realization of this project, which has enormous significance for an inter-Korean settlement and regional economic cooperation. Later Putin confirmed his position concerning the Japanese prime minister's visit at the summit meeting with Koizumi in Moscow in October 2002.[29]

Moscow appears to have emphasized the importance of Koizumi's visit in the hope of attracting Japanese investment in an international fund-raising consortium to be established. Speaking at an international conference held to launch the consortium in Vladivostok in July 2002, the Russian Minister of Railways, Yuri Fadeev, reported that 'a number of countries have expressed their interest including Japan, China and the Central Asian countries'.[30]

In Russia, Prime Minister Koizumi's visit has been seen as a continuation of the process of 'opening up' North Korea to the outside world, important from both a political and an economic point of view. Russian expectations for the railway project were high – so much so that at the Baikal economic forum in September 2002 Russian Deputy Minister of Railways Vladimir Yakunin, who was recently appointed chairman of the Russian Railways Joint Stock Company, let it be known that the exploitation of the international transport corridor using the Trans-Siberian Mainline will earn Russia up to 1 billion US dollars (USD) annually.[31]

Besides its interest in securing Japanese participation in the realization of multilateral economic projects with itself and both Koreas, Moscow hopes that Japanese–North Korean reconciliation will bring about the relaxation of tension in North-East Asia and help put the negotiations on Korea back on track.

Koizumi's visit to Pyongyang was seen in Moscow as proof that interest in the settlement of the region's accumulated problems is stronger than 'ideological postulates' such as the 'axis of evil'. The Kremlin has concluded that 'even Washington's closest allies show the artificiality of such postulates by their actions'.[32] In effect, in the context of earlier North Korean contacts with the governments of Russia, China and South Korea, the Japanese prime minister's visit to Pyongyang signalled that, in contrast to the Bush administration's policy of isolating North Korea, the countries of the region have made a choice in favour of a policy of engagement towards North Korea.

According to informed sources in the Kremlin, Koizumi's visit to North Korea became possible partly 'thanks to the active diplomacy of Russia'. The source believed that President Putin's contacts with Kim Jong-Il had brought about a breakthrough in North Korea's relations with the world and strengthened international and regional security. 'Pragmatic politicians, especially from neighboring countries, have also taken advantage of this circumstance', the source added.[33] Moscow was interested in Japanese–North Korean reconciliation since (a) it would clearly lead to a weakening of the Bush administration's attempts to achieve a regime change in North Korea, and (b) it hoped to ensure Japanese participation in the implementation of the multilateral gas, oil and transport projects in North-East Asia, including those on the Korean Peninsula.

Some experts, analysing the Six-Party Talks, noted that Tokyo failed to support Washington on some questions. They commented that in North-East Asia Japan could take a position similar to that taken by Turkey during the Iraq War, when Turkey, while remaining a US ally, actually refused to allow US troops to deliver strikes against Iraq from Turkish soil.[34]

The Russian Foreign Minister at the time, Igor Ivanov, was quoted as saying that Moscow's opinion on the situation on the Korean Peninsula was important for Japan. According to Ivanov, Moscow had always supported an active dialogue between North and South Korea, and that of North Korea with Japan and the USA. Ivanov added that it was important that the development of such contacts promoted an atmosphere of confidence and cooperation on the Korean Peninsula. He also stated that Japanese Foreign Minister Yuriko Kawaguchi had told him that Koizumi had very much appreciated the offer made by President Putin in their telephone conversation on the eve of the former's visit to Pyongyang. As Ivanov noted, it was important for the Japanese side to hear Moscow's position on the visit to Pyongyang.[35]

The Russian government expected that the expansion of dialogue and contacts between the North Korean government and those of neighbouring countries, primarily South Korea and Japan, and also the USA, would lead to a more active search for a solution to the problems of grave concern.[36] For this reason Moscow welcomed the results of Koizumi's visit to Pyongyang, which have allowed the commencement of meaningful dialogue between the governments of Japan and North Korea. Ivanov pledged to provide all the assistance needed to renew such dialogue in order to avoid an aggravation of the situation on the Korean Peninsula. He called on both Tokyo and Pyongyang to take all necessary steps to prevent such developments, and stated that Russia, as the country with friendly relations with North Korea, and active contacts with Japan, would try to use its political potential to promote the renewal of meaningful dialogue.[37]

Toyohisa Kozuki, the director of Japan's Foreign Ministry department in charge of relations with Russia, also expressed a positive estimation of the constructive role played by the Russian government in arranging the Japanese–North Korean dialogue. Kozuki, a diplomat, particularly valued the advice given by President Putin to Prime Minister Koizumi on the eve of the latter's visit to Pyongyang in September 2002, and emphasized that Russia 'plays an important role for a rapprochement of the positions of all parties in our region'.[38]

Commenting on Koizumi's trip, some Russian experts explained that the North Korean decision to start rapprochement with Japan was just a tactical move, part of the North Korean diplomatic strategy designed to take advantage of the inconsistencies in the policies of the other big countries towards itself: North Korea makes overtures to each country separately to get unilateral benefits and expand the international dialogue in order to prevent the 'Iraq script' being replayed on the Korean Peninsula.[39]

In the initial stages of the Japanese–North Korean rapprochement, Russian authorities maintained regular contact with their Japanese counterparts concerning North Korea's nuclear programmes. In a telephone conversation with his Japanese counterpart, Yuriko Kawaguchi, on 24 December 2002, Foreign Minister Ivanov called on all parties concerned to display restraint, to fulfil their respective obligations, and to continue the dialogue with the purpose of negotiating the settlement of all problems causing concern.[40]

Regrettably, the positive trend in the Russo-Japanese cooperation on Korean affairs was drastically reduced by the time of Prime Minister Koizumi's second visit to North Korea, in May 2004. One clear indication of this decline was the absence of top-level contacts between the Russian and Japanese leaders. Compared to September 2002, when Putin and Koizumi spoke on the matter twice, in May 2004, the information was passed on only at the foreign ministers' level.

On 22 May 2004, Japanese Foreign Minister Kawaguchi informed Sergei Lavrov, her new Russian counterpart, of the results of Prime Minister Koizumi's second visit to North Korea. From the Russian side the hope was expressed that the results of the second summit would be an important step along the way towards the normalization and development of relations between Japan and North Korea, and would contribute to security and stability in the region. Both sides welcomed the settlement in Pyongyang of some humanitarian problems existing between Japan and North Korea. Lavrov and Kawaguchi spoke in favour of building up cooperation in order to make a contribution to the progress of the Six-Party Talks on the settlement of the North Korean nuclear programme.[41]

However, initial Russian optimism was rather quickly followed by disappointment; among other things, the Japanese government's persistence regarding the issue of the abduction of Japanese citizens by North Korea hindered progress in all other areas. The impasse appreciably devalued the Russian government's contribution as one of the major initiators and intermediaries in the normalization process between Japan and North Korea. Meanwhile some observers in Russia predicted that, once Tokyo had received apologies from Kim Jong-Il for the abductions, it would forget about the necessity of carrying out its own promises given to North Korea in September 2002.[42]

Economic priorities for Russia and Japan on the Korean Peninsula

According to some Russian experts, such as Valentin Fedorov, former governor of Sakhalin Island, or Gennady Chufrin, deputy director of the Russian think tank the Institute of World Economy and International Relations (IMEMO), Moscow's bargaining chip in its dialogue with Tokyo is the prospect of regional integration in North-East Asia, including some of the richest resources in Siberia and the

Far East.[43] The prospects for economic development of those Russian regions are connected to the realization of some large-scale international projects. The implementation of almost all these projects depends on the level and extent of Russo-Japanese cooperation.

The largest and most promising project is the construction of a transport corridor between North-East Asia and Europe through Russian territory, by linking the Trans-Korean Railways to the Trans-Siberian Mainline. The realization of this project can not only bring major economic gains but also have substantial political consequences. Its success will depend on the situation of North–South relations, but the project can in turn have a positive influence on these relations. The modernization and development of a transport infrastructure in North-East Asia could give a powerful impulse to the integration process, which is of interest not only to Moscow but to the governments of all neighbouring countries.

Cooperation between Moscow and other countries of the region in the development of the energy resources of Siberia and the Russian Far East, and their transport to the participating countries, plays an important role in the integration processes in North-East Asia. Central to this system are the long-distance pipelines from Eastern Siberia up to the Russian Pacific coast.

In January 2005 the chief executive of Gazprom, Alexei Miller, visited North Korea. His visit showed that the Russian and North Korean sides are both interested in the realization of a gas pipeline from Russia through North Korea to South Korea. It came at a time of intensifying Russian energy politics directed towards a gas-starved Asia, and talk of a Russian pipeline through North Korea. The Gazprom statement said that Miller had met North Korean Premier Pak Pong-Ju, as well as industry and oil ministers, to discuss cooperation in the oil and gas sectors. Gazprom had been mulling over various routes for pipeline options to supply South Korea and Japan with oil and gas, including a route through North Korea. The visit suggested that if the appropriate political conditions for the project were created it might be implemented in the not-too-distant future.[44]

The start-up of the Bureiskaya hydroelectric power plant has opened up real prospects for the export of electric power from Russia to North Korea. North Korea's problems with its electricity supply, which began in the late 1980s, have proved to be one of the underlying causes for the economic and humanitarian crises in the country, posing a threat to security and stability in the entire region. The construction of an electric power transmission line from Russia to North Korea could be one of the most realistic solutions to North Korea's energy problem. Its cost is estimated at around 160–180 million USD.

Among the priority projects aimed at normalizing the electric power supply in North Korea, experts have cited the completion of the second part of the East Pyongyang thermal power plant (TPP), with an expected cost of about 50 million USD, as calculated by Russian specialists, and the reconstruction of the Pyongyang TPP (150 million USD) and the Bukchan TPP (110 million USD). Moscow would be able to implement all the projects in cooperation with the governments of Japan and South Korea, as well as with international financial organizations.[45] Considering the political sensitivity of the projects for the North Koreans, a leading role for Russia in the reconstruction is perhaps the only option acceptable to Pyongyang. For both national security and practical reasons, the North Korean leadership will find it very difficult, if not impossible, to let the Japanese into its energy sector; all North Korean specialists in the field have received Russian training and have worked almost exclusively with Russian-made equipment.

The construction of energy transmission lines to North Korea, and the modernization of the country's thermal power plants, will provide North Korea with non-nuclear energy, and can thus become an important bargaining chip in any future talks on the nuclear problem.

Some Japanese experts also express the opinion that economic assistance to North Korea should play a key role in the process of settling the North Korean nuclear problem. According to Satoshi Saito, the matter of providing such aid to North Korea should become the central issue at the Six-Party Talks, with Moscow and Washington taking the lead.[46] There are also ideas for establishing an International Emergency Assistance Fund for North Korea which could coordinate efforts in this area, similar to the post-World War II Marshall Plan which was used to rebuild Western Europe, with the participation of the governments of Japan, China, Russia and other interested countries.

In this context, the qualitative change of the situation on the Korean Peninsula and the transformation of this area from an arena of confrontation into a zone of cooperation are the major and essential elements of the regional development and economic integration in North-East Asia which are vital for the prosperity of all the states in the region in the twenty-first century.[47]

In turn, the processes of economic integration and globalization in North-East Asia provide new opportunities and prospects for the settlement of such chronic problems as the Korean one. It is highly likely that active North Korean involvement in those processes can produce a positive change in Pyongyang's behaviour on the international scene. Only this course can convince the North Koreans that the international community is interested in the peaceful integration of North Korea into the existing international political and economic structures, instead of forcing a regime change scenario on the country.

Obstacles to partnership

At the same time there are quite a number of factors that essentially limit the opportunities for Russo-Japanese cooperation on the Korean Peninsula. They are the result both of the delicate situation in the bilateral relations between Moscow and Tokyo and of the countries' respective policies towards the Korean Peninsula and North-East Asia. Among them are the following main factors.

1   The first is the unsettled state of bilateral relations between Russia and Japan in general and the unresolved territorial disputes in particular. Moscow sees in the Japanese position a desire to solve political problems on its own terms, exploiting the Russian interest in economic cooperation with Japan for the sake of the economic development of the Russian Far East.[48]

Moscow gave a fairly negative reception to the Japanese attempts to internation-alize the territorial dispute by mentioning it in the Common Strategic Objectives adopted on 19 February 2005 at the Japan–US 'two plus two' meeting, involv-ing their respective foreign and defence ministers. The mention of the question of normalizing Russo-Japanese relations by resolving the Northern Territories issue caused bewilderment in Moscow. 'We have already stated our view more than once regarding attempts to internationalize the problem of a peace treaty with Japan, which pertains entirely to the domain of bilateral relations. This kind of "prompting", with the enlistment of a third party, can hardly exert a favorable influence on the dialogue on such a complex and delicate matter', the statement from the Russian Ministry of Foreign Affairs read.[49]

Tokyo has territorial disputes with China and South Korea as well. Moscow is striving to maintain friendly relations with those two countries and has no territorial problems with them. It is therefore likely to be more inclined to sympathize with their positions in their disputes with Japan. Thus on Russian maps, for example, the island of Dokto (or Takeshima in Japanese), which is claimed by both Japan and South Korea, is marked as belonging to South Korea.

2   Both Russian politicians and the Russian public express concern about the ongo-ing process of strengthening the US–Japanese military–political alliance and its orientation. Neither Moscow nor Beijing has any enthusiasm for the US creation of a TMD system in North-East Asia, with Japanese participation. There are fears that TMD will result in a sharp change in the strategic balance in the region, thus giving impetus to a new arms race and ultimately leading to the emergence of new lines of division and discord in North-East Asia. These concerns, which were expressed by Moscow at the end of the 1990s, are still valid, as the Russian ambassador to Japan, Alexander Losëkov, recently confirmed.[50]

'Tokyo prepares for war' was a typical headline in the Russian media when they reported on the Japanese government's decision on missile interception last year.[51] Some Russian observers consider the decision of the ruling Liberal Democratic Party (LDP) to revise the Japanese constitution in such a way as to allow *de jure* use of the Japanese armed forces outside the country as an 'unprecedented turn'. The change has in fact already been implemented *de facto,* through the Japanese participation in the Iraq War.[52] In November 2005, the influential Russian daily *Nezavisimaya gazeta* openly accused Prime Minister Koizumi of being 'the initiator of an arms race' in the region, and of attempting to subordinate Japan's growing military power to the USA's plans to build a military fence around China and the Russian Far East, too.[53] The joint Russo-Chinese military exercise held in autumn 2005 is the first, and certainly not the last, response to these developments.

3   There are fears in Russia, as well as in the international community, about the transformation of Japan's nuclear policy. They are caused both by Japan's technical capabilities and its stocks of plutonium, and by statements made by some Japanese politicians. Since the 1960s politicians such as former

prime ministers Eisaku Sato and Yasuhiro Nakasone, and some others, including members of the current Japanese Cabinet, have spoken of the opportunities for Japan to possess nuclear weapons and the conditions under which it might possess them. Among the most revealing statements to this effect are: an interview given by Shingo Nishimura, deputy director-general of the Japanese Defense Agency, in 1999; the warning which Ichiro Ozawa, former secretary-general of the LDP and then leader of the Liberal Party, addressed to China in April 2002, about Japan's ability to produce 'from 3,000 to 4,000 nuclear warheads'; and, finally, in May 2002, Chief Cabinet Secretary Yasuo Fukuda's claim that there was no constitutional limitation on Japan's possessing nuclear weapons, which received immediate endorsement by the governor of Tokyo, Shintaro Ishihara.[54] It is possible that, given a certain combination of domestic and international factors, Tokyo may reconsider its existing nuclear policy.

4   Russian readiness to cooperate with Japan on the Korean problem will also depend on the Japanese position concerning possible Russian participation in political–economic and trading bodies, such as the East Asian summit or the free trade agreement (FTA) between the governments of China, South Korea and Japan. Attempts to leave Russia outside the new regional organizations, while giving it the role of supplier of cheap energy for the new economic initiatives being undertaken by the members of these unions, will not meet with understanding in Moscow.

5   Moscow and Tokyo have different visions for the future role of the united Korea in the regional and global systems of international relations. Tokyo sees a united Korea within the framework of a tripartite alliance with the USA and itself.[55] Such an approach can hardly satisfy the governments of Russia or China, both of whom are likely to perceive such an alliance as a mechanism of containment or even deterrence against themselves. The continued presence of foreign troops on the Korean Peninsula even after reunification will also be interpreted in a similar manner.

6   In contrast to Tokyo, which has so far failed to establish diplomatic relations with North Korea, Moscow maintains diplomatic relations with both Koreas. Moreover, Russia and North Korea have a long history of friendship and cooperation in several spheres. In 2000 they signed the new Treaty on Friendship, Good Neighbourliness and Cooperation. Because of the treaty, Russia cannot discuss sanctions or preventive hostile strikes against North Korea, even should Japan wish to do so.

7   The Russian government does not entertain the same fears as the Japanese government does concerning North Korea's nuclear weapons. It is highly unlikely that Pyongyang will ever use its nuclear weapons against either Russia or China. However, most experts agree that they could be used against the US bases in Japan in the event of an attack aimed at North Korea. The Russian government sympathizes with the Japanese concerns in this area, but at the same time believes that a solution to the problem is not to be found by threatening to impose sanctions, building up the military, preparing to use the

Self-Defense Forces for emergency situations on the Korean Peninsula, and other similar moves recently made by Tokyo.[56]

8   Moscow and Tokyo have different approaches to the methods to be used to solve the nuclear problems on the Korean Peninsula. Their disagreements include the scope of the nuclear programme, how much of it should be eliminated (only the military part, or all of it, including the generation of nuclear power for civilian use), the scale and scope of forthcoming inspections, the conditions and character of security guarantees, and any economic assistance which North Korea could be given.

9   Moscow sympathizes with Tokyo's efforts to find a resolution of the issue of the abductions of Japanese citizens. According to the Japanese media, Russian Foreign Minister Lavrov has declared that Russia was ready to exert its influence on North Korea for the resolution of this problem.[57] At the same time Moscow believes that the search for a settlement of the problem should not hinder the achievement of the ultimate objective of the Six-Party Talks, namely, to ensure non-nuclear status for the Korean Peninsula. It seems that the priority Tokyo has unwaveringly given to the abduction issue deprives its foreign policy of the flexibility which is so necessary in the present highly complex circumstances. Japanese Korean policy itself has become a hostage of the abduction issue. Because it has only very limited room for manoeuvre on the abduction issue, Japan's value as partner in any talks with Pyongyang has been drastically reduced. Moscow has therefore welcomed the resumption of Japan–North Korean normalization talks.

10   Some Russian experts regard Japanese North Korea policy as rather inconsistent.[58] Tokyo officially declares its desire to ensure the opening up of North Korea and advocates North Korean engagement with the international community, but in practice Tokyo, along with Washington, has for several years been blocking North Korean participation even as an observer in the Asia Development Bank.[59]

Certainly, the opportunities for Russo-Japanese cooperation aimed at the maintenance of peace and stability in North-East Asia and on the Korean Peninsula are far from being exhausted. There are still new fields to explore. This was demonstrated during the joint exercise conducted by the Russian and Japanese navies in September 2004 in the waters around Tsushima Island. The official purpose of the exercise was to provide joint training for military rescuers on the evacuation of crew from ships suffering a disaster at sea. In addition, the Russian and Japanese ships carried out a joint search of a mock-enemy submarine with the help of deck helicopters. The Russian press reported that these exercises were undertaken within the framework of a joint struggle against piracy and terrorism.

At the same time, some newspapers expressed bewilderment about the anti-submarine training. From time to time, Tokyo expresses its concern over the intrusion of unknown ships and submarines into its territorial waters. In the light of the fact that the most recent such incidents were connected with North Korea and China, such joint operations could hardly be welcomed in these countries.[60]

Conclusion

Under President Putin, Russia has taken a rather active and, what is more important, quite independent position in the process of settling the nuclear problem on the Korean Peninsula, and on other aspects of the Korean settlement. The 'Korean theme' has become one of the major topics in Russia's top-level contacts with the governments of the two Koreas, China, the USA and Japan.

However, any Russo-Japanese cooperation on the Korean problem will be more limited than the cooperation between Moscow and the governments of other neighbouring countries because of the unresolved territorial issue between Russia and Japan, and Moscow's growing suspicions concerning the future of the US–Japanese military alliance.[61]

The Russian government has drawn one major conclusion from its experience of handling the Korean nuclear issue for the past five years, namely that it is unproductive and even dangerous to make abrupt movements and statements, especially attacking or offending this or that participant in the negotiating process. The use of labels with negative connotations and the application of excessive pressure on North Korea delayed the fourth round of the Six-Party Talks for more than a year, and routinely interrupted the Japan–North Korea normalization talks. These delays have vividly demonstrated the negative consequences of such an approach for the resolution of the Korean nuclear issue. It is also particularly important to bear in mind that in East Asia a 'face-saving' resolution of a dispute is generally considered a much more important and acceptable outcome than outright victory for one side.

Moscow has its own interests on the Korean Peninsula. These interests, as shown above, are similar to or coincide with those of Japan and other countries involved in the Korean nuclear issue. However, Moscow will hardly pull other people's chestnuts out of the fire only to please them. Russia has its own history of dealing with North Korea, as well as a fairly advanced legal framework for bilateral relations, such as the Basic Treaty of 2000, the two Joint Declarations adopted as a result of the Russian–North Korean summits of 2000 and 2001, and last, but not least, the confidential political high-level contacts that have been re-established since 2000. Moscow is using these opportunities, which are far from being exhausted, to secure Russian interests on the Korean Peninsula.

At the same time Moscow has recently demonstrated its readiness to take into consideration the legitimate interests of all other countries concerned, to have close and regular consultations with them, and to work together in the search for a mutually acceptable solution of the problems which can endanger peace and security in North-East Asia. Tokyo is quite aware of this change in the Russian approach – hence its seeking to consult with Moscow urgently at the critical moments of Japanese–North Korean relations.

Notes

1 Sergei Lavrov (Russian Minister of Foreign Affairs), 'Democracy, international governance and a future world pattern', *Russia in Global Politics*, 6, 27 December 2004, available HTTP: <http://www.mid.ru>.

2 Ibid.
3 *Kommersant*, 16 January 2003.
4 *Vremya novostei*, 14 October 2003.
5 Ibid.
6 *Rossiiskaya gazeta*, 27 August 2003.
7 'Russian Deputy Minister of Foreign Affairs Yuri Fedotov answers questions from Japanese NHK television company', 6 August 2003, available HTTP: <http://www.mid.ru>.
8 Statement by the Ministry of Foreign Affairs of the Russian Federation [Regarding the DPRK's intention to withdraw from the Treaty on the Non-proliferation of Nuclear Weapons], Moscow, 10 January 2003, available HTTP: <http://www.mid.ru> (in Russian).
9 'Statement by Alexander Yakovenko, the spokesman of Russia's Ministry of Foreign Affairs, regarding DPRK's decision to suspend its participation in Six-Party talks indefinitely', Moscow, 10 February 2005, available HTTP: <http://www.mid.ru>.
10 [Russia and Japan foreign ministers talk by telephone], Moscow, 4 March 2005, available HTTP: <http://www.mid.ru> (in Russian).
11 'Russian President Vladimir Putin joint press conference with US President George W. Bush', St Petersburg, 1 June 2003, available HTTP: <http://www.mid.ru>.
12 'Statement by spokesman for DPRK Foreign Ministry on the declaration adopted at G-8 summit', KCNA, Pyongyang, 6 June 2003; and *Rodong Sinmun*, 21 June 2004.
13 'Statement by spokesman for DPRK Foreign Ministry on the declaration adopted at G-8 summit', ibid.
14 *Rodong Sinmun* 21 June 2004.
15 'Remarks by President Bush and President Putin of the Russian Federation in a joint press availability' (distributed by the Bureau of International Information Programs, US Department of State, 16 September 2005, available HTTP: <http://usinfo.state.gov>).
16 Alexander Z. Zhebin, 'Inter-Korean relations: A view from Russia', *Far Eastern Affairs* (Moscow) 2, 2002, p. 77.
17 Valery I. Denisov, [Inter-Korean settlement and Russia's interests], [*International Affairs*] (Moscow) 1, 2002, p. 59 (in Russian).
18 Vadim P. Tkachenko, *Koreiskii poloustrov i interesy Rossii* [The Korean Peninsula and Russia's interests], Moscow: Orient Literature Publishing House, 2000, p. 165.
19 'On Russian President Vladimir Putin's message to President Kim Dae-Jung of the Republic of Korea', publication of the Ministry of Foreign Affairs of the Russian Federation, 26 July 2002, available HTTP: <http://www.president.kremlin.ru>.
20 [On Russian President Vladimir Putin's welcome address to participants of 'Korean–Russian Friendship Train–2002,], publication of the Ministry of Foreign Affairs of the Russian Federation, 29 July 2002, available HTTP: <http://www.president. kremlin.ru> (in Russian).
21 See Mikhail L. Titarenko, [The Korean Peninsula and security in North-East Asia: A view from Russia], in Vadim P. Tkachenko (ed.), [*Urgent Problems of the Korean Peninsula*: Collection of articles], Moscow: Institute of Far Eastern Studies, 1996, p. 193 (in Russian); and Vladimir D. Andrianov, [Current conditions and prospects for the development of trade and economic cooperation between Russia and the Republic of Korea], in [*Russia and Korea: Modernization, Reforms and International Relations*], Moscow: Vostochnaya Literatura Publishing House, 1997, p. 60 (in Russian).
22 See Hisahiko Okazaki, 'Thoughts on the North Korean nuclear issue', *Korean Journal of National Unification* (Seoul), special edn, 1993, pp. 23–30; Yosihde Soeya, 'Japan's multilateral diplomacy in the Asia–Pacific and its implications for the Korean Peninsula', *Asian Perspective* (Seoul and Portland, Or. (USA)) 192/2, 1995, pp. 223–42; Hajime Izumi, 'The present North Korean situation and its implication for Japan', *Korean Journal of National Unification* (Seoul) 6, 1997, pp. 63–76; Masako Ikegami, 'Anatomy of North Korean nuclear crisis'. Paper presented at the 54th Pugwash Conference, Seoul, 4–9 October 2004; and Hideki Yamaji, 'Policy recommendations

for Japan: Unification of the Korean Peninsula', Washington, DC: Brookings Institution, July 2004.

23 [Korea in search of peace and prosperity], IFES RAS (Moscow), 2004, p. 163 (in Russian).

24 ITAR-TASS, 18 December 2000.

25 ITAR-TASS, 19 November 2000.

26 ITAR-TASS, 19 December 2000.

27 [Russian President Vladimir Putin speaks to Japanese Prime Minister Junichiro Koizumi by telephone], Moscow, 5 September 2002, available HTTP: <http://www.president.kremlin.ru> (in Russian).

28 'Russian President Vladimir Putin speaks to Japanese Prime Minister Junichiro Koizumi by telephone', ibid.

29 Available online at <http://www.strana.ru/news/2002/10/14>.

30 *Moscow Times*, 4 October 2002.

31 *Vremya-MN*, 18 September 2002.

32 ITAR-TASS, 17 September 2002.

33 Ibid.

34 Information and Analytical Agency MiK, 13 January 2005.

35 [Interview of Minister for Foreign Affairs of Russia Igor Ivanov to Japanese Telebroadcasting corporation NHK], Tokyo, 19 December 2002, available HTTP: <http://www.mid.ru> (in Russian).

36 'Igor Ivanov: It is important for Japan to know Moscow's opinion on the situation on the Korean Peninsula', available HTTP: <http://www.strana.ru/news/2002/09/16>.

37 Available HTTP: <http://www.strana.ru/news/2002/09/19>.

38 *Vremya novostei*, 19 November 2002.

39 *Vremya novostei*, 17 September 2002.

40 [Telephone conversation of Minister of Foreign Affairs of Russia Igor Ivanov with Minister for Foreign Affairs of Japan Yuriko Kawaguchi], Moscow, 24 December 2002, available HTTP: <http://www.mid.ru> (in Russian).

41 'Telephone conversation of Minister of Foreign Affairs of Russia Igor Ivanov with Minister for Foreign Affairs of Japan Yuriko Kawaguchi', ibid.

42 Available online at <http://www.gazeta.ru/print/2002/09/17/kimotkryldve/shtml> (in Russian).

43 Interview with Valentine Fedorov, Marketing and Consulting Information–Analytical News Agency, 20 July 2005; and Gennady Chufrin, [Russia in North-East Asia], [*Asia and Africa Today*] (Moscow) 3, 2003, p. 6 (in Russian).

44 ITAR-TASS, 21 January 2005 (in Russian).

45 *The Korean Problem and Integration Processes in Northeast Asia*, Moscow: Gorbachev Foundation, 2005, p. 27.

46 Satoshi Saito, 'Urgent problems of Six-Party economic negotiations'. Paper presented at the 2nd Russian–Japanese Conference on Development and Stability in Northeast Asia, Moscow, MGIMO(U) of the Ministry of Foreign Affairs of the Russian Federation, 10–11 September 2004.

47 [*Russia and Inter-Korean Relations*] Moscow, Gorbachev Foundation, 2003, p. 69 (in Russian).

48 *Vremya novostei*, 21 January 2005.

49 'Russian MFA Information and Press Department commentary regarding a question from ITAR-TASS News Agency concerning the mention of Russia in a recently adopted Japan–US document, Common Strategic Objectives', Moscow, 24 February 2005, available HTTP: <http://www.mid.ru>.

50 *Nezavisimaya gazeta*, 26 March 1999; and Interfax News Agency, 5 March 2004.

51 See, e.g., <http://www.vip.lenta.ru/news/2004/12/03/japan/>.

52 *Nezavisimaya gazeta*, 1 November 2005.

53 Ibid.

54 On Nishimura's remarks see *The Guardian* 21 October 1999; on Ozawa's statement see *Japan Times*, 17 April 2002.
55 Hideki Yamaji, 'Policy recommendations for Japan: Unification of the Korean Peninsula', Brookings Institution, July 2004, p. 6.
56 Interfax News Agency, 5 March 2004.
57 *Nihon Keizai*, 15 May 2004.
58 'Tendencies of development of situation on the Korean Peninsula and possible alternatives for Russian policy', Moscow, IFES RAS, 1999, p. 72.
59 *Korea Times*, 30 April 2004.
60 *Novye izvestiya*, 8 September 2004.
61 *Nezavisimaya gazeta*, 1 November 2005.

7 The EU's North Korea policy: no trace of Japanese influence

Rüdiger Frank

The European Union (EU) and Japan are economic giants but, unlike the United States, their political influence lags behind their economic power. Closely linked by economic exchanges and through cooperation in various international organizations, in their capacity as civilian powers (defined as states dependent on economic cooperation, supranational structures, and primarily economic rather than military means of defending their national interest)[1] both share a sense of responsibility for global political developments. Moreover, Japan has supported the stabilization and rebuilding of the former Yugoslavia. The Japanese commitments for assistance to Kosovo ranked third among all bilateral sources,[2] which was highly appreciated in Europe. Could it now be the EU's turn to assist Japan in the case of North Korea? Does it have its own interests in that region? What is the EU's North Korea policy, and how does this policy relate to Japan? Is there bilateral cooperation between the EU and Japan on the various North Korean issues, such as weapons of mass destruction, humanitarian aid, human rights, and economic reforms? If so, how intense is this cooperation? Is it based on a convergence of interests? Does North Korea policy represent a particular area of bilateral cooperation between the EU and Japan?

The European Union consists of intergovernmental as well as supranational institutions, which makes a clear, one-dimensional usage of the term 'EU' difficult. For the purpose of this chapter, the bulk of European activities are relevant, and numbers have an indicative, qualitative function. Accordingly, the term 'EU' will be used to describe the aggregate of EU member states including – and often represented by – the European Commission as the EU's supranational executive organ or the Council of the European Union as the main decision-making body of the EU consisting of the single member states' ministers, without explicitly and in detail stating this in every instance. It has to be noted that some discrepancies might occur concerning the standards for quantitative data. Usually, bilateral contributions of single member states for purposes such as food aid or energy assistance are channelled through EU organizations such as ECHO (the European Community Humanitarian Office), the European Atomic Energy Community, and so on. However, the same contributions are often also separately listed as bilateral transfers; this is correct, but easily leads to confusion. A less acute conceptual problem exists for trade; the EU as a trading partner of course consists exclusively of its single member states; trade regulations and quotas, however, are issued by the combination of these member states, represented by the European Commission. 'EU trade' with a given country therefore is not the EC's trade, but the aggregate of the single members. On the other hand, despite the fact that the Common Foreign and Security Policy is one of the three pillars of the Union, when 'the EU' opens diplomatic relations with a country, this refers to the European Commission and does not necessarily mean that these relations have been established with every single member state. It must be noted that this unique structure provides the EU with the option of 'multilateral bilateralism'[3] – one EU can, though its members states, to a certain degree pursue different policies. This offers interesting options that are not available to the other involved parties, but it also weakens the weight of the EU aggregate and limits the potential role Europe can play.

North Korea policy: Europe and Japan

In the traditional relationship between Europe and North Korea, a great asset is the absence of any unpleasant past such as a history of colonialism or war. On the contrary – among the less well-known chapters of history is the economically and psychologically significant support that East European countries which are now members of the EU rendered to North Korea (the Democratic People's Republic of Korea, DPRK) during and after the Korean War. This includes the forgotten story of the reconstruction of the totally destroyed city of Hamheung, the second-largest in North Korea, a provincial capital and the centre of North Korea's chemical industry, by the German Democratic Republic (East Germany) between 1955 and 1962,[4] and other important projects by Poland, Czechoslovakia and Hungary. This work created not only a positive image of Europe, but also a huge and up to now largely untapped resource of practical, long-term experience with aid and development assistance to North Korea. It is also of great relevance to the EU and Japan, since, as the leaders emphasized at the 11th EU–Japan summit meeting, the EU, the EU member states and Japan taken together account for approximately three-quarters of the total funds available for development assistance worldwide.[5]

Of more recent significance for the development of relations are the events after the 1994 Agreed Framework, and especially the diplomatic normalization between Europe and North Korea which started with a political dialogue meeting in December 1998, while such normalization of relations is still outstanding between North Korea and its neighbour to the East.

Tokyo, like Brussels, initially embarked on a cautious rapprochement with North Korea in the early 1990s, although this was interrupted by the 1998 missile crisis, when a North Korean long-range missile flew over Japan and landed in the Pacific Ocean.[6] The underlying motivations for the North Korean government's readiness to talk to the Japanese government are difficult to assess. Pyongyang would of course like to receive Japanese capital and technology, but it is questionable whether this economic benefit would compensate for the loss of a long-standing concept of the enemy that forms one of the very foundations of the country's political system. This ideological concern is even more crucial given the rising pan-Korean nationalism, especially since the first North–South summit meeting of 2000.[7] Unless the North Korean ideological groundwork is changed – which would be risky and difficult – Pyongyang needs at least one external threat to sharpen its nationalist *juche* profile and to keep up what Selig Harrison has called the 'permanent siege mentality'.[8] Since South Korea is becoming increasingly unsuitable for the role of the 'enemy', only the USA and Japan remain. Although both emphasize their uncompromising attitude,[9] a significant improvement of relations with Washington appears to be unavoidable if Pyongyang wants to move beyond the current limits on its development. This would turn Japan into Pyongyang's last and pivotal enemy and make a true normalization very unlikely.

Tokyo, too, stands both to lose and to gain from normalization. Normalization could ease the concerns over North Korea's military capabilities.[10] This is particularly true since the significant improvement of Pyongyang's relations with Seoul has made an attack on the South less likely, while the remaining arch-enemy, the USA, is simply out of range. However, the Japanese situation is much more complex; the alliance with the United States and the relationship with China are issues that have great relevance for Japanese defence policy, too, although they are much less present in the public debate. Normalization with North Korea would necessitate a new justification for further enhancing Japan's diplomatic and military standing. Hughes suggests that the latter will take place within the context of the current alliance with the United States.[11] However, Tokyo appears to be looking for a more independent position within this alliance. To complicate the issue, the Japanese government itself seems to be divided over how to appraise the North Korean attempts to develop nuclear weapons. The diplomats perceive this as a tactical gamble, while the military sees a real threat.[12]

The EU's record of engagement of North Korea is significantly longer than that of Tokyo. This can be explained by absence of normal Japanese–North Korean diplomatic relations and the presence of serious disagreements. One can only speculate whether Brussels has deliberately utilized the benefit of its less complicated position to do what Tokyo could not. Whatever the underlying motivation, the EU has in recent years significantly contributed to stabilizing the situation in North Korea and to integrating the country into networks of international cooperation and dialogue.

The EU has provided humanitarian support to North Korea through the ECHO since 1995, first in the form of food deliveries, and since 1997 also in the form of 'food security', that is, fertilizers, agriculture-related know-how and machinery. Since 2003, more attention has been given to the reconstruction of water and sanitation facilities and various measures in the health sector. Assistance has also been provided bilaterally, via the United Nations' World Food Programme (WFP) and European non-governmental organizations (NGOs). As of October 2005, the latest – and, in the light of the North Korean decision to stop accepting humanitarian aid, probably also the last – instance of EU aid was a 10.7 million euros (EUR) plan to support the North Korean health sector in summer 2005.[13] (See Table 7.1.)

Table 7.1 EU Humanitarian aid to North Korea, 1995–2004

Year	1995	1996	1997	1998	1999	2000	2001	2002	2003	2004	Total
Aid	0.29	0.5	77.6	59.9	34.8	33.4	27.9	41.1	26	65	366.49

Source: Delegation of the European Commission in Korea, 'European Commission humanitarian assistance to North Korea', available HTTP: <http://www.delkor.cec.eu.int/en/eukorea/humanitarian.htm> (accessed 11 September 2005).

Figures are in million EUR.

This amounts to 0.10 EUR per capita for the 'EU 15' – the 15 member states before the enlargement of May 2004 (383 million citizens[14]). To put this in perspective, the total amount of aid provided to the North by South Korea during the same period was about 3.5 billion US dollars (USD),[15] or about 7.30 USD per capita, reflecting the difference in the priority given to North Korea. In per capita terms, Seoul has transferred over 70 times more funds to North Korea than the Europeans. From 1996 until 2004, Tokyo delivered about 1.25 million metric tons of food to North Korea, with a value of about 420 million USD.[16] This is about 0.34 USD per capita – more than three times higher than the deliveries by the EU.

A similar picture is presented by the activities related to the now dissolved Korean Peninsula Energy Development Organization (KEDO). On 19 September 1997 the EU, represented by the European Atomic Energy Community, entered KEDO as an executive board member – to join, among others, Japan. The EU's contribution to KEDO amounted to only 2 per cent of the total finance. After the second nuclear crisis broke out in October 2002, KEDO's oil shipments were suspended in December 2002 and work on the reactor project was stopped one year later. In late 2005, KEDO decided to end the project and dissolve itself.

The EU's input has been an overall amount of about 121 million USD, while Tokyo has contributed over 480 million USD (see Table 7.2). Per citizen, the contributions over the period from March 1995 until December 2004 amounted to 0.36 USD for the EU and 3.84 USD for Japan. Assuming that preferences

Table 7.2 Financial support for KEDO by country, March 1995–December 2004: Contributions of 1 million USD or higher

Country	Amount	Country	Amount
Australia	14,444,400	New Zealand	2,539,460
Canada	4,683,664	South Korea	1,364,428,695
European Atomic Energy Community	121,377,723	Singapore	1,600,000
Germany	1,011,485	United Kingdom	1,000,000
Italy	1,821,429	United States	405,106,000
Japan	480,898,610		

Source: KEDO.

Figures are in USD.

find their expression in the willingness to pay, this shows that North Korea is indeed of significantly greater relevance in Japan than in Europe.

Annual rounds of political dialogue with North Korea at the level of senior officials have been held since 2 December 1998. EU Council decisions have called for a more coordinated approach towards the Korean Peninsula, and for the EU's assistance efforts to be expanded in a measured way, that is, linked to Pyongyang's response to international concerns in regard to progress in inter-Korean reconciliation, non-proliferation issues, respect for human rights and economic structural reform in North Korea.[17] Delegations of the European Parliament have visited North Korea several times. The Stockholm European Council of March 2001 agreed to enhance the role of the EU in support of peace, security and freedom on the Korean Peninsula by deciding on what can be seen as the indisputable highlight of relations between the EU and North Korea so far – the visit of a high-ranking EU delegation to Pyongyang in May 2001, including Swedish Prime Minister Göran Persson, who at that time held the EU Presidency, External Relations Commissioner Chris Patten, and High Representative for the Common Foreign and Security Policy Javier Solana.

A few days later the European Commission, in consultation with the member states, decided to establish diplomatic relations with North Korea 'to facilitate the European Community's efforts in support of reconciliation on the Korean Peninsula, and in particular in support of economic reform and easing of the acute food and health problems in the DPRK'.[18] Subsequently, the first explanatory talks between Pyongyang and Brussels on human rights started on 13 June 2001. So far, with the exception of France and Estonia, all 25 EU member states have established diplomatic relations, although only a few (including the Czech Republic, Germany, Poland, Sweden and the United Kingdom (UK)) maintain resident embassies in Pyongyang.

Several EU member states have a long history of trade with North Korea. The major exports of the EU countries to North Korea are agricultural machinery, cars, steel, electronics and electrical supplies, measuring instruments, medical supplies and rough diamonds. The major imports of the EU countries from North Korea are clothes, electronic and electrical products, jewellery, machinery, plastic products and salt. The value of North Korea's trade with the EU countries in 2003 amounted to 2.4 billion USD, with imports of 1.6 billion USD and exports worth 777 million USD.[19] North Korea's major trading partners in 2003 were China, Japan, Thailand, India and Russia. North Korean trade with the EU area in 2001 amounted to slightly over 311 million USD, or 13.7 per cent of the total for that year.[20] Within the EU, Germany has the strongest economic ties with North Korea, distantly followed by France, Spain and the UK. On the individual firm level, out of consideration for investors, economic relations with North Korea are usually not publicized too enthusiastically, as the recently 'revealed' case of British American Tobacco showed: the world's second-largest cigarette company was said to have been secretly operating a factory in North Korea for the past four years.[21] In addition to security and ethical considerations, the unresolved issue of North Korea's outstanding debts – in the case of Germany about 260 million EUR – seriously complicates the expansion of economic exchanges.

The EU has been very active in terms of technical assistance in recent years. A first fact-finding mission was sent to North Korea in February 2001 'to assess technical assistance needs and identify areas in which the Commission could ... launch pilot projects'.[22] It presented its results at a meeting of donors consisting of EU member states, representatives of the international financial institutions, the USA, Japan, South Korea and others in Brussels in March 2001, with the participation of officials from North Korea. As a result, it appeared that the European Commission would be 'the only substantial donor of technical assistance to the DPRK for the time being'.[23]

The North Korean priority needs were defined as training in regard to institution-building, basic technical advice on the energy system, rural development and transport.[24] The first two points are considered to be essential. Efforts were made to initiate a training programme for officials from key ministries, such as Foreign Affairs, Finance, and Foreign Trade. A North Korean delegation headed by Foreign Trade Minister Ri Gwan Gun visited Brussels, Rome, Stockholm and London between 4 and 16 March 2002 with the declared aim of becoming acquainted with European economic policy models.

It is attributable to this and similar missions that North Korean institutions such as the Ministry of Foreign Affairs, the Ministry of Finance, the Ministry of Foreign Trade, the Foreign Trade Bank, the University of National Economy, and the Kim Il-Sung University's Faculty of Political Economy could define their priority needs for training and identify the following: principles of international trade; the settlement of trade disputes; multi- and bilateral treaties; the economic and social structures of EU economies; international financial institutions; free market economy principles; international accounting standards; international debt management; corporate management training; trade information research; loans, credits and clearing systems; sovereign credit rating; sovereign risk management; insurance and reinsurance; the relationship between government and the private sector; international law; EU institutions; the promotion of foreign direct investment; marketing; commercial contacts; intellectual property; standards; finance; export credit insurance; letters of credit; foreign exchange dealing; e-commerce; the principles of taxation; corporate governance; stock market operations; and double-entry bookkeeping.[25]

Considering the geographical distance of North Korea from Europe and the generally low level of international exchange with North Korea, this is an impressive record for Europe, with a clearly rising trend in technical assistance and other contacts over the past decade. However, under the impact of the revelations in October 2002 that Pyongyang had continued to pursue a nuclear programme, EU–North Korean relations were dealt a severe blow in November 2002, when the Council decided that:

> ...the future of North Korea's relations with the international community is conditioned on Pyongyang's prompt and verifiable actions to dismantle

the programme... The Council requested, in light of North Korea's nuclear weapons programme, that the Commission and Member States review their activities regarding North Korea, including technical assistance and trade measures, based on an inventory of all means at their disposal. Humanitarian and food assistance to the population of North Korea remains in place.[26]

This was the beginning of the end to a remarkable and very dynamic development. Although EU–North Korean relations recovered slowly in 2003 in connection with hope for progress of the Six-Party Talks, it would be too early to say that they have reached the former level. In 2003, the European Council confirmed its position: it reiterated that 'enhancing the EU's cooperation with the DPRK will be possible only when the DPRK fully complies with its international non-proliferation obligations'.[27] As of 2005, EU assistance to North Korea is still 'limited to the humanitarian field, particularly in the form of food aid, support for agricultural rehabilitation and non-food humanitarian assistance'.[28]

There have been a few signs that some EU member states could be more ready than others to pursue their own, independent policy in East Asia. The recent commissioning of reports on North Korea by the Ministry of Defence of France and the Ministry of Foreign Affairs of Denmark (in 2004) indicates a growing interest in independent information about North Korea. Very importantly, various European institutions such as the German Friedrich Naumann Foundation[29] have held training seminars in North Korea, among them the First Workshop on Economic Reform and the Development of Economic Relations Between the EU and the DPRK in September 2004, and the second such workshop in October 2005; the writer of this chapter participated in both and witnessed the great interest of the North Korean side in such exchanges. The governments of other countries, such as Spain, Italy, The Netherlands and Poland, have shown a keen interest in active engagement.

The North Korean side has been at times quite active in lobbying the European Union. Ford and Kwon in their analysis of the Korean Workers' Party's newspaper *Rodong Sinmun* provide striking proof of the North Korean attempts to please the EU and to use it in the old game of playing one foreign power off against the other: 'Of 128 EU-related articles between 2001 and 2004, a majority praised Europe's independent counter-US stance, emphasized its increasing economic power and influence, and heralded its autonomous regional integration. *Rodong Sinmun* portrays the EU as the only superpower that can check and balance US hegemony and the USA's unilateral exercise of military power'.[30]

It is surprising that the Chinese potential as a superpower is neglected, according to the quotation above. In fact, this hints at a propagandistic – in the sense of a self-fulfilling prophecy – rather than a realistic assessment of the situation. Despite the disagreements over the 'war on terror', it would be naive to expect Europe to be ready to take a stance that runs openly counter to US policies. Brussels clearly and explicitly prefers a peaceful resolution of the nuclear issue and has strong concerns for the humanitarian situation in North Korea – a view shared with Washington. Differences exist about the way to achieve these goals, but not on the principal aim. This now seems to be under-stood in Pyongyang. However, the North Korean leadership still attempts to gain from asymmetrical treatment of its counterparts. This is exemplified by its reaction to the UN human rights resolution, which was initiated by the EU and adopted by the General Assembly on 21 November 2005. It is not the EU that Pyongyang blames for the resolution, but the UK (which had the EU presidency at the time); according to diplomatic insiders, other European countries are met with stubborn resistance when they try to explain that they support the reso-lution, too. In general terms, the United States is attacked for using the human rights card to stifle North Korea, not the EU.[31]

As Brussels' country strategy paper makes clear, the EU recognizes the need to provide assistance that has lasting effects, mainly in the areas of institutional support and capacity-building, sustainable management and use of natural resources, and a reliable and sustainable transport sector.[32] This corresponds with the wishes of the North Korean side, as expressed repeatedly; the latest such instance, in late September 2005, was the official request that aid-providing NGOs leave the country by the end of 2005. However, the North Korean prefer-ence for development assistance collides with the 2002 European Council decision. Various EU representatives have expressed very clearly that they do not intend to violate the letter of this document. Hence, the future of EU–North Korean cooperation, as well as its scope and scale, remains insecure and depends on developments regarding the nuclear issue, as well as on an improvement of relations between the USA and North Korea.

Europe's relations with Japan

The history of European relations with Japan is very complex. The relationship has switched between conflict and cooperation ever since the Portuguese and the Dutch established trade relations and sent their missionaries. In World War I, Japan joined the alliance against Germany, but it was one of the Axis powers in World War II. While Europe was a model for Japanese reforms in the nineteenth and early twentieth century, since the latter half of the twentieth century the European business community in particular has increasingly discovered the benefit of learning from the Japanese example. The present relations are based on the 1991 Political Declaration between Japan and the European Community, which was issued at the First EC–Japan Summit.[33] These summits have since then taken place on a yearly basis. Both sides emphasize their shared attachment to the core values of democracy, the freedom of peoples, and their respect for the rule of law and for the protection of human rights.

Today, Japan and Europe as developed industrial societies face the same domestic and external challenges, such as demographic change, environmental issues, the demand to streamline their administrations, and security concerns, and they have established a number of networks to cooperate or to exchange views on how to meet these challenges. As indicated above, both are also confronted with a great asymmetry of their 'soft'[34] and 'hard' power.

A major issue in foreign policy for both Brussels and Tokyo is the definition of their relationship with Washington, and increasingly also with Beijing. Both sides have relied since World War II on a close alliance with the USA to guarantee their security, and put a priority on their economic and social development. The end of the cold war has led to a rethinking of those arrangements and to attempts to increase the capacities for a more independent position – or at least for more equality in the alliance with the USA.

Although Europe and Japan share similar challenges and goals, and despite the similarities in their nature as civilian powers, this does not automatically lead to close cooperation. The case of UN reform is very interesting in this respect. The governments of both Japan and Germany aim for improved status in the context of the UN Security Council and hope to gain permanent representation there. In the first round, Brussels and Tokyo supported each other. In January 2006, however, the Japanese government decided against sponsoring the latest bid by Brazil, Germany and India to reform the Security Council, and instead started searching for its own way to gain US support for a permanent seat for itself. The German media[35] speculated that Japan might 'beat' Germany in the 'race' for a permanent Security Council seat. The emergence of a possible competitive situation could influence the EU's readiness to support the Japanese position on North Korea.

The focus of EU–Japan cooperation has so far clearly been on economic exchanges. Trade between them amounted to about 117 billion EUR in 2004. This is less than the EU's continuously increasing trade with China (175 billion EUR in 2004); however, Japan still has a much larger gross domestic product (GDP) than China (as compared with 3.7 trillion EUR, 1.3 trillion EUR), and its direct investments in the EU are also higher, at 4.7 billion EUR as compared to 3.1 billion EUR by China.[36] This creates a strong incentive for a cooperative political relationship, including over issues such as North Korea.

The numbers above hint at another possible source of cooperation. Japan and the EU as established global economic powers have to develop a strategy for coping with the rise of China, both in economic and in political terms. Again, North Korea policy is closely linked to this issue. Depending on the approach chosen *vis-à-vis* Beijing, this could lead to increased coordination of Japanese and EU policies *vis-à-vis* Pyongyang.

Against this background, both Brussels and Tokyo are interested in global stability and peaceful international relations as a necessary condition for economic prosperity. These common goals are directly affected by the North Korean question. The humanitarian aid for vulnerable groups in North Korea, the concern over the human rights situation in that country, and of course the security threat emerging from the North Korean nuclear programme, not forgetting the risk of nuclear proliferation, are topics that we should expect to bring leaders in Japan and the EU closer to each other in attempts to resolve these problems. On the other hand, differences in the nature of the alliance with the USA, in the relationship with China, and in the geopolitical situation, combined with the ongoing transformation of Japan and probably Europe from civilian powers to players with a new perspective on military power, could lead to a divergence of interests and weaken their cooperation on North Korea.

North Korea in EU–Japan relations

A brief analysis of the available joint statements issued at the annual EU–Japan summit meetings is useful in helping to trace the absence, emergence, submergence and re-emergence of North Korea as a topic of discussion between both sides.

The Joint Declaration of 1991, the first document of its kind in EU–Japan relations, does not mention North Korea at all. This is no surprise; at that time, although it was of some interest to Japan, North Korea played almost no role for Europe. What is more difficult to comprehend is that the Joint Declaration issued at the summit meeting of 1995 does not mention the country either, although less than one year before, in the autumn of 1994, the conclusion of the Agreed Framework was only able at the last minute to prevent the outbreak of an open conflict over the North Korean nuclear programme. Instead, economic issues such as improved access for European exporters to the Japanese market and various points related to the General Agreement on Tariffs and Trade (GATT) (later to become the World Trade Organization, WTO) still dominated the cooperation. In 1996, Korea is mentioned only in one brief sentence, putting the EU's contribution to KEDO in the perspective of Japan's economic support for reconstruction in the former Yugoslavia, and supporting the EU's readiness to join KEDO.

In 1997, Korea for the first time occupies a whole paragraph in the joint declaration. The document stresses the need to proceed with the Four-Party Talks and to find a guarantee for non-proliferation, and lauds the EU's cooperation in the context of KEDO. In 1998, in addition to those points, inter-Korean cooperation is encouraged. The joint statement of 1999 contains a shorter paragraph on North Korea, but now explicitly emphasizes a policy of engagement towards the country.

The EU–Japan summit meeting of July 2000 took place under the strong impact of the first ever North–South Korean summit one month before, an event of such significance and so acclaimed internationally that a few months later it earned South Korean President Kim Dae-Jung the Nobel Peace Prize. Accordingly, North Korea is even more prominently mentioned in the July 2000 statement, repeating most of the points made in previous years and adding the regional dialogue in the context of existing structures, such as the Asia–Europe Meeting (ASEM).

After this, the most extensive reference to North Korea up to that point, it comes as somewhat of a surprise that the 2001 joint statement does not refer to Korea. Nor does the 25-page Joint Action Plan adopted at the 2001 summit.[37] Significant economic matters obviously caught the full attention of the policy makers. In April 2001, a Mutual Recognition Agreement (MRA), a framework which enables certain procedures required in the importing country to be undertaken in the exporting country, was signed after six years of consultations.[38] It was the first such agreement for Japan. The Japanese minister of foreign affairs stated on the occasion of the signing of the agreement that 'The significance of further developing Japan–Europe economic relations, which constitutes the two of the triple poles of the world economy, cannot be overemphasized'.[39]

The absence of a reference to North Korea in the 2001 joint statement could also be interpreted as a sign of a certain optimism regarding future progress towards the peaceful resolution of the issues previously discussed – an optimism that led to a reduced perception of urgency. If this is true, then it would present an interesting explanation for the allegedly irrational and spontaneous North Korean foreign policy behaviour. If a low level of tension leads to a lower level of recognition, then moves to increase tension suddenly appear to be much less irrational and unmotivated than many observers would think. The converse could also be true: if tension is too high and the readiness of international players to react decisively and boldly increases, then a sudden extension of olive branches has to be expected. Pyongyang's behavioural options in foreign policy seem to oscillate between a maximum and a minimum level of tension.

The events of 11 September 2001 and the US choice of a military response prompted a mixed reaction on the part of Tokyo and Brussels. They issued their Joint Declaration on Terrorism, in which they expressed 'firm support for the military operations undertaken by the United States and other countries'.[40] However, there was also concern that there was too little emphasis on peaceful engagement in the US position. This is reflected in the bilateral diplomatic activities between Brussels and Pyongyang described in the previous section and the visit of Japanese Prime Minister Junichiro Koizumi to Pyongyang in September 2002. The joint press statement of the 11th Japan–EU summit in July 2002 preceded this visit, but it is not coincidental that it takes North Korea up again and encourages Pyongyang to continue its dialogue with the administrations of South Korea, the United States, Japan and the EU. Furthermore, the statement suggests economic reforms to assist the North Korean engagement with the international community – a step that was indeed taken in July 2002, although certainly not as a direct reaction to these suggestions:

> We encourage the DPRK to move further toward dialogue with the [Republic of Korea], the US, Japan and the EU and share the expectation that this will create tangible results in securing peace and security on the Korean Peninsula and in the region. It is now important to make progress on various issues of concern to the international community including security, humanitarian issues and human rights. We share the view that economic reform in the DPRK will also assist its engagement with the international community.[41]

The statement of the 12th EU–Japan summit in 2003, containing the most extensive passage on North Korea so far, reflects the dramatic change in the situation after October 2002. On 16 October 2002, the US government revealed that the North Korean regime had continued to work on a nuclear programme in violation of the spirit of the 1994 Framework Agreement. Koizumi's September 2002 visit to Pyongyang did not bring the anticipated success; instead, the Japanese public reacted in an unexpectedly angry way at North Korea's admission that it had indeed abducted Japanese citizens. The admission and the subsequent release to Japan of a handful of survivors did not put an end to the issue, but rather fanned suspicions that other allegations that had previously been denied were also true. Instead of supporting normalization with North Korea, as policy makers on both sides had obviously expected, the Japanese public demanded a thorough examination of the open cases first and strongly opposed any normalization until the open issues were completely resolved.

There are no sources that would indicate that Japan had informed the EU of the 2002 Koizumi–Kim Jong-Il summit in advance. Later, in the 2003 joint statement, Tokyo and Brussels pledged to cooperate to find a multilateral solution to the North Korean issue.

In 2004, the Six-Party Talks are mentioned, although no explanation is given as to why the EU is not a member of those talks. The EU nevertheless 'underlined its readiness to support international efforts to find a comprehensive solution to the nuclear and other issues'.[42] The statement also repeats the preferred US term for a solution at that time – CVID (complete, verifiable and irreversible dismantlement).

The latest, May 2005, summit produced a joint statement that silently dropped the demand for irreversibility, implying a possible support for another freeze of North Korea's nuclear programme:

> Summit leaders reiterated their commitment to a peaceful resolution of the DPRK nuclear issue. They urged the DPRK to completely dismantle its nuclear programmes subject to credible international verification and, to that end, return to the Six-Party Talks process expeditiously and without preconditions. Both parties encouraged the DPRK to take further steps in modernising its economy and promoting the welfare of its population.[43]

The Japan factor in Europe's North Korea policy

As shown above, the cooperation between the EU and Japan reflects the position of both sides as strong international economic powers and relatively weak political players. The nuclear issue, as well as the war on terror, prompted the inclusion of passages related to North Korea in the cooperation agenda. Opportunities for cooperation, such as KEDO, were used, but neither side saw the need to form an alliance to tackle the issues at hand. They preferred to remain within their established networks of cooperation. Pierre Jacquet observes that 'Even though the "triad" (USA, Europe, Asia) clearly dominates geostrategic considerations of the late 20th and early 21st centuries, attention is mostly paid to either transatlantic or transpacific relations'.[44] He further stresses that 'Asia–Europe affairs… remain mostly undervalued, if not ignored at all, which is especially true for political efforts going beyond trade and investment'. This can only to a certain degree be explained by the ignorance of observers. More likely, the reason is that there is in fact not much to pay attention to.

The EU's North Korea policy was almost non-existent until the wave of humanitarian aid prompted by the growing evidence on the 1995–7 famine. The fact that the EU is not a member of the Six-Party Talks limits the options for EU–Japan cooperation on North Korea. Whereas Brussels generally seems to be greatly concerned with the humanitarian and human rights situation in North Korea, there is a clear asymmetry between Tokyo and Brussels with regard to the intensity of the perception of the security threat and the abduction issue. Some observers even see the EU and Japan standing on opposite sides of the fence in North East Asia:

> The problem is with Japan and the U.S. In Japan, opinion is split by hard-liners in the Liberal Democratic Party who view problems with North Korea as a convenient excuse to justify the abandonment of the Peace Constitution. They don't want a quick solution until crisis has catalyzed the transformation of Japan into what advocates call a 'normal' country. The U.S. expects an EU financial commitment, but not EU participation. The neocons believe that EU participation would change the balance of forces within the talks inexorably toward critical engagement rather than confrontation.[45]

This statement indicates that the US–Japan alliance is very different from the EU's ties with the United States. From a neo-realist perspective, despite repeated denials, there is clearly a zero-sum power game going on in North-East Asia between Beijing on one side and Tokyo and Washington on the other, with North Korea right in the middle as the 'bone of contention'. South Korea has a complicated and contradictory constellation of interests, and so far is not sure which side to join. Accordingly, Seoul is attempting to remain neutral, as President Roh's remarks in March 2005 on the desired role of his country as a regional 'balancer' indicate.[46] The EU, as outlined above, is not a regional power and sees no reason to jeopardize its relationship with such an important economic and global power as China. Here we find a significant difference between Japanese and EU interests, despite their common nature as civilian powers.

Apart from the political readiness to act or not to act, the scope of the EU's North Korea policy itself appears to be quite limited. Among the few active and independent efforts are training measures and support for economic reforms. Here, Brussels is taking advantage of its reputation as a relatively unconcerned power, although it would be naive to expect that Pyongyang would accept the EU as a neutral broker. The transatlantic relationship has suffered since 2001, but it is still strong and driven by a number of very powerful common interests. A similar statement can be made for Japan. The close relationship with the USA represents a limitation for individual actions *vis-à-vis* North Korea, because these actions affect US interests and both the EU and Japan will always be inclined to consider these American interests: 'A strong and robust alliance with the U.S. continues to be a pillar of Japan's foreign and security policies'.[47] Furthermore, the EU does not play any significant role in a number of questions of great importance to Japan, such as the abduction issue or national security. This greatly reduces the utility of the EU from Tokyo's perspective and explains the relatively harmonious, but rather general, tone of the joint statements analysed above.

A minor but nevertheless notable issue is the difference between Brussels and Tokyo in terms of political culture. Yuki Tatsumi argues that Japanese foreign policy depends to a great extent on a working policy coordination mechanism, which 'although criticized as opaque and driven by parochial factional rather than national interests... allowed factions to broker deals behind the scenes. As unseemly as this process was, it worked'.[48] This lack of transparency makes close cooperation on foreign policy not impossible, but certainly more complicated. Against this background, it comes as no surprise that little more than verbal expressions of support for Japan's concerns has been issued by the EU.

Although it cannot be denied that the EU does consider Japan in its political decisions, in particular with regard to Japan's neighbour North Korea, it would be too much to say that there is a significant role for the 'Japan factor' in the EU's North Korea policy. This is also due to the fact that this policy, as described above, is not over-intensive, either regarding its scope or regarding its scale. EU–Japan relations seem to reflect the general feature of Europe–Asia relations, where politics often lag behind economic exchanges.

The future of North Korea policy

If we want to determine whether North Korea policy could be a major field of relations between Brussels and Tokyo, in addition to the strategic considerations as outlined above, we must assess the possible future developments in and around North Korea itself. In other words, what will the object of such cooperation look like?

The record of the EU and Japan as civilian powers suggests that not the nuclear issue but the question of development assistance will be of the greatest relevance in this respect. Cases such as that of South Korea have shown that a military dictatorship can be transformed into a democratic society through economic development.[49] There are hopes that the North Korean regime, too, can embark on a gradual path of development and transformation.

The current (as of late 2005) official North Korean position indicates a readiness to accept foreign development assistance. The aim is the stabilization of the current system, not its transformation; however, the cases of China and Vietnam have shown that the intentions of economic policy do not always determine its outcome.[50] Improved conditions for foreign investors, an expanding legal base for investment, and successful examples such as the Gaeseong Industrial Zone can be considered as hopeful signs.

The prospects for development assistance to North Korea are indeed manifold. The last decade has shown a remarkable development in the country, in particular in economic terms, but also in ideological terms. Despite continued fears of a collapse of the regime, as happened in Eastern Europe, an increasingly pragmatic attitude is developing. The economic changes in North Korea were inspired by the Chinese example after 1979, and prompted by the economic consequences of the collapse of the socialist bloc in the late 1980s and early 1990s. They were catalysed by the transition of power from Kim Il-Sung to Kim Jong-Il (1994–7), and were given a strong boost by the famine of 1995–7. Significant changes have taken place in the last few years which we only partially understand. Among them are the introduction of a new ideology (the Military First Policy of 1997) and an amended constitution (1998), as well as the economic adjustment measures of July 2002, and the opening of a number of special economic zones (most notably the Geumgangsan tourism project and the Gaeseong Industrial Zone) after the North–South summit in 2000. In addition to these major events, there have been a number of minor yet significant changes, such as the removal of limitations on the nature of goods allowed to be traded legally on non-state markets in 2003, the monetization of the economy, the fact that there is now inflation, the scrapping of the custom of having special 'foreign exchange certificates' as a parallel currency for foreigners, and so on.[51]

Inflation seems to be the biggest short-term problem for North Korea's economic policy makers and the major motivation for a shift in economic policy that opens the doors to outside assistance, including from the EU and Japan. After the deliberate inflationary push of the July 2002 price reforms, prices have kept rising at breathtaking speed. The present author's own calculations suggest an annual inflation rate of about 215 per cent since 2002.[52] One reason could be the predominantly industrial structure of the North Korean economy, where only about 30 per cent of the population earn their income in agriculture. Accordingly, the government in late 2005 was forced to reintroduce public distribution of basic food and to ban the trading of staple foodstuffs on the free market in order to get inflation under control.[53]

Against this background, the North Korean shift in late 2005 to ask for development assistance instead of food aid can be understood as an attempt to do what the principle of comparative advantage would suggest – to accept the basically unfavourable natural conditions for agriculture,[54] use the cheap, disciplined and well-educated workforce as well as the industrial base which has existed in the country for decades, and focus economic efforts on manufacturing and services.

In such a setting, development assistance would focus on modernization, not industrialization. The latter has already been done during the Japanese colonial occupation and later with support from the Soviet Union.[55] International isolation and the lack of technology, capital and most of all energy are the biggest problems, and can only be resolved with external assistance.

From the perspective of a possible engagement of Tokyo and Brussels in modernizing the North Korean economy, a resolution of the nuclear issue must be the first step. In addition to the nuclear problem, providing development assistance beyond humanitarian aid faces a number of other serious obstacles. From a legal perspective, the fact that North Korea is on the United States' list of 'state sponsors of terrorism' precludes the delivery of a wide range of goods to that country, as the restrictions listed in Box 7.1 indicate.

Box 7.1   Implications of the status as a state sponsor of terrorism

1   A ban on arms-related exports and sales.
2   A requirement for notification to Congress of any license issued for exports that could make a significant contribution to the state sponsor's military potential or could enhance their ability to support acts of international terrorism.
3   Prohibitions on foreign assistance.
4   Miscellaneous financial and other restrictions, including:
   • US opposition to loans by the World Bank and other international financial institutions.
   • Providing an exception to sovereign immunity to allow families of terrorist victims to file civil lawsuits in US courts.
   • Restrictions on tax credits for income earned in state sponsor countries.
   • Denial of duty-free treatment of goods exported to the United States.
   • Prohibition of certain Defense Department contracts with companies controlled by state sponsors.

Source: US Department of State, *Country Reports on Terrorism 2004*, Washington, DC: US Department of State, April 2005, p. 88, available HTTP: <http://www.state.gov/documents/organization/45313.pdf> (accessed 19 October 2005).

Moreover, the issue of outstanding debts is another stumbling block. In particular from the Japanese perspective, the still not satisfactorily resolved issue of the abductions limits the scale and scope of assistance and cooperation. Last but not least, there is the ideological and ethical problem of the totalitarian political system in North Korea and the serious concerns over human rights. In the case of China, similar reservations were overridden by the prospect of access to the gigantic market of 1.3 billion consumers. North Korea with its 23 million people does not have the same benefits to offer. However, with South Korea, it now seems to have a strong and respected advocate, in particular since both the current president, Roh Moo-Hyun, and his predecessor, Kim Dae-Jung, are active supporters of a policy of peaceful engagement.

Any significant development assistance depends on whether the international community can find ways of resolving the issues mentioned above. Can Tokyo and Brussels become driving forces of such a process? And once the obstacles are removed, will they cooperate closely in modernizing the North Korean economy?

Conclusions

The history of cooperation between the European Union and Japan and the constellation of interests as outlined in this chapter send mixed signals. Despite many similarities with regard to their position in international relations, this chapter has shown that their approaches are different. Both must find a way to maintain a cooperative relationship with the United States. However, beyond this common issue, the EU is primarily concerned with community-building, while

Japan is struggling to find a proper response to the Chinese challenge. North Korea is therefore of much greater significance for Japan than for the EU. Expectations of reciprocity – the EU would support Japan's policy in North Korea in exchange for the help in rebuilding the former Yugoslavia – cannot be satisfactorily confirmed. There are no explicit official statements to that effect, and the EU's actual engagement can be explained by other considerations. Furthermore, no explicit traces of Japanese influence on the EU's policy-making process could be found. With the dissolution of KEDO, the only official forum for concrete cooperation on North Korea between Japan and the EU has disappeared. While multilateral and track-II institutions[56] remain, it is not expected that they will produce results other than those the annual bilateral EU–Japan summit meetings produce.

Even if all the obstacles that have been mentioned could be removed, we might witness competition rather than cooperation over development assistance to North Korea. Tokyo would engage in enhanced development assistance with strategic considerations in mind, and the issue would immediately become highly political given Korean and Chinese memories of a similar Japanese economic initiative in the late nineteenth century. The EU, on the other hand, would assist North Korea for humanitarian reasons and in order to support the policy of its allies. The latter, however, include South Korea and China, not only Japan. At the micro level, European companies will try to sell their products such as railways, telecommunications systems and so on, and inevitably compete with Japanese and other enterprises.

To conclude, the interests of Brussels and Tokyo in North Korea are characterized by great diversity, regarding both their scale and their scope. Tokyo and Brussels cooperate to a certain degree on the basis of their economic interdependence and as civilian actors of considerable weight in international relations. Their respective North Korea policies are formulated in this context. However, the research for this chapter did not find sufficient proof of cooperation that goes beyond what can be expected from this general setting.

Notes

1 See Hanns W. Maull, 'Germany and Japan: The new civilian powers', *Foreign Affairs*, winter 1990/91.
2 See United Nations Development Programme (UNDP), 'The government of Japan and UNDP cooperation in Kosovo', available HTTP: <http://www.undp.or.jp/news/Kosovo05Sep.htm> (accessed 28 October 2005).
3 I am indebted to my friend and colleague Maurizio Martellini for sharing this term with me.
4 See Rüdiger Frank, [*The GDR and North Korea: The Reconstruction of Hamhùng 1954–1962*], Aachen: Shaker, 1996 (in German).
5 Japanese Ministry of Foreign Affairs (MOFA), '11th Japan–EU Summit: Joint press statement', 8 July 2002, available HTTP: <http://www.mofa.go.jp/region/europe/eu/summit/joint0207.html> (accessed 15 September 2005).
6 BBC News, 1 September 1998.
7 Yong-Chool Ha, 'South Korea in 2000: A summit and the search for new institutional identity', *Asia Survey*, 41/1, January/February 2001, pp. 30–9.

148   *Rüdiger Frank*

8 Selig S. Harrison, *Korean Endgame: A Strategy for Reunification and US Disengagement*, Princeton, NJ and Oxford: Princeton University Press, 2002.
9 See Balbina Hwang, 'Cautious optimism for the Six-Party Talks', WebMemo #850, 2005, The Heritage Foundation, available HTTP: <http://www.heritage.org/Research/AsiaandthePacific/wm850.cfm> (accessed 19 October 2005).
10 Japan Defense Agency (JDA), *Japan Defense White Paper 2005*, Tokyo: Japan Defence Agency, 2004, available HTTP: <http://www.jda.go.jp/e/publications/wp2005/index.html>.
11 Christopher Hughes, *Japan's Re-emergence as a 'Normal' Military Power?*, Adelphi Paper no. 368, Oxford: Oxford University Press, 2004.
12 David Fouse, *Japan's Post-Cold War North Korea Policy: Hedging Toward Autonomy?* Asia Pacific Center for Security Studies Occasional Paper no. 11, February 2004, available HTTP: <http://www.apcss.org> (accessed 19 September 2005).
13 European Commission, Joint Declaration on Relations between the European Community and its Member States and Japan, 2005, available HTTP: <http://europa.eu.int/comm/external_relations/japan/intro/joint_pol_decl.htm> (accessed 15 September 2005).
14 Source: Eurostat.
15 *Chosun Ilbo*, 21 June 2005.
16 Mark Manyin, 'Foreign assistance to North Korea', CRS Report for Congress, 26 May 2005, available HTTP: <http://www.nautilus.org/napsnet/sr/2005/0550ACRS.pdf>.
17 European Union, *The EU's Relations with the Democratic People's Republic of Korea*, 2002, available HTTP: <http://europa.eu.int/comm/external_relations/north_korea/intro> (accessed 25 October 2002).
18 Ibid.
19 M. A. Cho, *North Korea's 2003 Foreign Trade*, Seoul: KOTRA, 2004, available HTTP: <http://www.kotra.or.kr> (accessed 7 January 2005).
20 Woo-Suk Nam, *North Korea's Foreign Trade in 2001*, 2002, available HTTP: <http://www.kotra.or.kr/main/info/nk/eng/main.php3> (accessed 25 October 2002).
21 *JoongAng Ilbo*, 18 October 2005.
22 European Union, 'The EC–Democratic People's Republic of Korea (DPRK) country strategy paper 2001–2004', 2002, available HTTP: <http://europa.eu.int/comm/external_relations/north_korea/csp/01_04_en.pdf> (accessed 25 October 2002), p. 20.
23 Ibid., p. 21.
24 Ibid., p. 21.
25 EU–DPRK Pilot Project in Institutional Support; annex II: Terms of Reference, appendix 1.
26 European Union, General Affairs and External Relations Council (GAERC), 'The EU's relations with the Democratic People's Republic of Korea', Brussels: GAERC, 2002, available HTTP: <http://europa.eu.int/comm/external_relations/north_korea/intro/gac.htm#nk19110> (accessed 11 September 2005).
27 European Council, 'Presidency conclusions, 12–13 December 2003', available HTTP: <http://ue.eu.int/ueDocs/cms_Data/docs/pressData/en/ec/78364.pdf> (accessed 11 September 2005), pp. 22.
28 Europeaid, 'Programmes and projects: Asia: North Korea', 2005, available HTTP: <http://europa.eu.int/comm/europeaid/projects/asia/northkorea_en.htm> (accessed 12 January 2005).
29 See <http://www.fnfkorea.org>.
30 Glyn Ford and Soyoung Kwon, 'Can Europe help break the North Korea impasse?', *Japan Focus*, 20 March 2005, available HTTP: <http://japanfocus.org/article.asp?id=239> (accessed 3 October 2005).
31 KCNA, 19 December 2005.
32 European Union, 'The EC–Democratic People's Republic of Korea (DPRK) country strategy paper', p. 3.

33 For the full text, see European Commission, Joint Declaration on Relations between the European Community and its Member States and Japan.

34 Joseph S. Nye, *Soft Power: The Means to Success in World Politics*, New York: Public Affairs, 2004.

35 *Deutsche Welle*, 6 January 2006.

36 Source: Eurostat.

37 For the full text, see European Union, 'Shaping our common future: An action plan for EU–Japan cooperation', 2001, available HTTP: <http://europa.eu.int/comm/ external_relations/japan/summit_12_01/actionplan.pdf> (accessed 11 September 2005).

38 Japanese Ministry of Foreign Affairs (MOFA), 'Japan–EC Mutual Recognition Agreement (MRA)', 2001, available HTTP: <http://www.mofa.go.jp/region/europe/eu/ agreement.html> (accessed 15 September 2005).

39 Japanese Ministry of Foreign Affairs (MOFA), 'Statement by Mr Yohei Kono, Minister for Foreign Affairs, on the signing of the Agreement on Mutual Recognition between Japan and the European Community (EC)', 4 April 2001, available HTTP: <http:// www.mofa.go.jp/announce/announce/2001/4/0404.html> (accessed 15 September 2005).

40 For the full text, see Japanese Ministry of Foreign Affairs (MOFA), 'EU–Japan Joint Declaration on Terrorism', 8 December 2001, available HTTP: <http://www.mofa.go.jp/ region/europe/eu/summit/terro0112.html> (accessed 15 September 2005).

41 Japanese Ministry of Foreign Affairs (MOFA), '11th Japan–EU summit: Joint press statement', 8 July 2002.

42 Japanese Ministry of Foreign Affairs (MOFA), '13th Japan–EU summit: Joint press statement', 22 June 2004, available HTTP: <http://www.mofa.go.jp/region/europe/ eu/summit/joint0406.pdf> (accessed 15 September 2005).

43 Japanese Ministry of Foreign Affairs (MOFA), '14th Japan–EU summit: Joint press statement', 2 May 2005, available HTTP: <http://www.mofa.go.jp/region/europe/ eu/summit/joint0505.pdf> (accessed 15 September 2005).

44 Pierre Jacquet, 'The third leg of the triad', *NIRA Review*, autumn 1996, available HTTP: <http://www.nira.go.jp/publ/review/96autumn/jac.html> (accessed 12 September 2002).

45 Ford and Kwon, 'Can Europe help break the North Korea impasse?'.

46 See Rüdiger Frank, 'A new foreign policy paradigm: Perspectives on the role of South Korea as a balancer', Nautilus Institute Policy Forum Online, 03-35 A, 25 April 2005, available HTTP: <http://www.nautilus.org/fora/security/0535AFrank.html> (accessed 11 September 2005).

47 Brad Glosserman, 'Koizumi declares war', *PacNet* 36, Honolulu: Center for Strategic and International Studies (CSIS), 25 August 2005, available HTTP: <http:// www.csis.org/pacfor/pac0536.pdf> (accessed 1 October 2005).

48 Yuki Tatsumi, 'Koizumi's gamble and its impact on the U.S.–Japan alliance', *PacNet* 36A, Honolulu: CSIS, 25 August 2005, available HTTP: <http://www.csis.org/ pacfor/pac0536a.pdf> (accessed 25 September 2005).

49 See Tat Yan Kong, *The Politics of Economic Reform in South Korea*, London and New York: Routledge, 2000; and Jung-En Woo, *Race to the Swift: State and Finance in Korean Industrialization*, New York: Columbia University Press, 1991.

50 See John McMillan and Barry Naughton, *Reforming Asian Socialism: The Growth of Market Institutions*, Ann Arbor, Mich.: University of Michigan Press, 1996.

51 For more details, see Rüdiger Frank, 'Economic reforms in North Korea (1998–2004): Systemic restrictions, quantitative analysis, ideological background', *Journal of the Asia Pacific Economy*, 10/3, 2005, pp. 278–311.

52 See Rüdiger Frank, 'International aid for North Korea: Sustainable effects or a waste of resources?', *Japan Focus*, 7 December 2005, available HTTP: <http:// www.japanfocus.org/article.asp?id=468>.

53 See Rüdiger Frank, 'Whither economic reforms in North Korea?', *Korea Herald*, 8 October 2005, p. 14.

54 For an excellent study, see Hermann Lautensach, *Korea: A Geography Based on the Author's Travels and Literature*, Berlin: Springer Verlag, 1945, repr. 1988.
55 See Gi-wook Shin and Michael Robinson (eds), *Colonial Modernity in Korea*, Cambridge, Mass.: Harvard University Press, 1999.
56 Track-II diplomacy represents an informal diplomacy where non-officials search for solutions to security and other issues.

8 Japan and multilateralism in the North Korean nuclear crisis: road map or dead end?

Christopher W. Hughes

Introduction: A multilateral future for North-East Asian security?

Since 2003, multilateral approaches to addressing the North Korean security issue have increasingly come to the fore. The most notable of these approaches has been the Six-Party Talks process. Hosted by China, it was first launched in August 2003, with further rounds held in February and June 2004, in July to September 2005, and with the fifth and latest round, as of the time of writing, in November 2005. The talks have involved the participation of the USA, Japan, China, Russia, and South and North Korea. They experienced an initial setback with Pyongyang's announcement in February 2005 of the indefinite suspension of its participation in the talks.[1] Nevertheless, US policy makers in particular, but also to varying degrees the policy makers of the other states involved, have remained committed to the Six-Party Talks and other multilateral approaches to dealing with North Korea's nuclear programmes and additional related security concerns. Japan for one has worked hard to back the US efforts to push forward the Six-Party Talks process, even though it has been constrained to some extent in its active participation by domestic pressures over the issue of the abduction of Japanese citizens (*rachi jiken*).

As of January 2006, US and Japanese policy makers' faith in the Six-Party Talks appears to have paid off, with the issuing of a Joint Statement at the September 2005 talks in which Pyongyang agreed that it would at an 'early date' abandon all its nuclear programmes, while Washington and the governments of other participating states agreed to respect North Korea's right to a peaceful nuclear programme, and to extend negative security guarantees and potential economic assistance.[2] In turn, the loose consensus among academic commentators has been to echo their policy-making counterparts in arguing for the need to pursue, and even loosely institutionalize, the Six-Party Talks and other multilateral approaches to the current North Korean nuclear crisis, and that these approaches may form a nascent framework for new multilateral security cooperation in the region.[3]

The September 2005 Joint Statement was clearly an important breakthrough, establishing a negotiating process and related principles, and thus a potential multilateral road map for resolving the North Korean security issue. However, it is also vital to note that 'the devil is the detail', or in fact lack of detail, of the Joint Statement. The issues of how to sequence the North Korean abandonment of its nuclear programme and the US and other states' provision of security guarantees and economic assistance, and the exact content of these incentives, are still to be negotiated, and only minimal progress on these issues was made at the November 2005 talks. Moreover, it is important to remember the troubled past of the talks, and the hiatus of over a year between 2004 and 2005, which suggest that future negotiations are likely to be equally difficult or could even fail.

Hence, in assessing the significance of the Six-Party Talks and other multilateral approaches to addressing the North Korean security issue, it is necessary to interrogate in a more robust way the emerging policy-maker and academic consensus concerning the value for North-East Asian regional security of the extant and evolving multilateral security frameworks.

This chapter takes issue with many assumptions of the current consensus. Based on a stronger conceptual understanding of multilateralism, it posits a more sceptical perspective on the long-term value of the Six-Party Talks' multilateralism and other current US-inspired varieties of multilateral frameworks, such as the Trilateral Coordination and Oversight Group (TCOG) and the Proliferation Security Initiative (PSI). It argues that many analysts have failed to read the significance of recent trends correctly because they have not examined carefully enough the types of multilateralism emerging and the implications for the perpetuation of the current power relations and tensions in the region. Specifically, the Six-Party Talks process, although it indicates some potential shifts away from the current US administration's penchant for unilateralism, has so far largely served to strengthen the USA's dominant position in the region and its bilateral alliance relationships, and to generate a particular form of hegemonic multilateralism, or 'pseudo-multilateralism',[4] rather than generating any new or lasting forms of multilateralism and a new security architecture that might have greater long-term and effective purchase in the region. Consequently, the Six-Party Talks may well yet go the way of their predecessors of the mid-1900s, the failed Four-Way Peace Talks. Moreover, in many cases it is possible to see the virtual death, under largely US direction, of other forms of multilateralism such as the Korean Peninsula Energy Development Organization (KEDO).

This chapter also argues that Tokyo has played an implicit part in many of these trends because of its support for the US-inspired format of the Six-Party Talks, and its participation in other multilateral frameworks such as the TCOG and the PSI, but also because of its simultaneous prioritizing of its bilateral alliance relationship with the USA, to the detriment of its interest in other non-US-inspired forms of multilateral frameworks.

Furthermore, the chapter questions whether multilateralism as presented in its current format is in fact the appropriate resolution to the Korean Peninsula security issue, and whether it is a diversion from other genuine resolutions that might be available. The overall conclusion is that, despite the current progress of the Six-Party Talks, a serious rethink of current multilateral approaches may be required, and that, if the Six-Party Talks are not in the end to prove a multilateral dead end, Japan and other states need to apply themselves more strenuously to a range of frameworks for resolving the nuclear issue.

Multilateral rationales?

The focus of policy makers from the USA and other states, as well as academic commentators, upon multilateral approaches towards North Korea (although in the US case seemingly ironic, given the inconsistent record of the current administration on adhering to multilateralism in the Korean Peninsula and other regions) appears to be derived from a range of at times overlapping rationales.

First, there is a sense in which the North Korean security issue is now entering a phase of such significance for regional and global security that it is forming the point of initiation for multilateral frameworks in greater numbers and in more durable fashion than has hitherto been possible. For, while the 'four-plus-two'-type formula of the Six-Party Talks is not a new one – its origins go back to cold war proposals for great-power coordination on the Korean Peninsula and the now increasingly forgotten Four-Party Peace Talks of 1997–9[5] – the implementation of this and other types of multilateral approaches has proved difficult and sporadic in the past. In contrast, since 2003 the second North Korean nuclear crisis has given fresh life to the USA–China–North Korea trilateral talks in April 2004, the Six-Party Talks, and the PSI, and has sustained the USA–Japan–South Korea TCOG and its more informal trilateral dialogue successor.

Second, policy makers and academics also share an apparent sense not only that the Korean Peninsula is serving as the site for the generation of long-mooted and new multilateral frameworks in greater numbers and of greater durability, but also that these frameworks represent a fresh approach for dealing with North Korea, and a break from the largely US-centred and bilateral dominant approaches that have mostly been prevalent until now. The current administration of President George W. Bush is fond of stating that multilateral approaches provide opportunities for regional states with a 'stake' in the nuclear issue to take increased responsibility for its eventual resolution.[6] Clearly, it is not advocating the weakening of the existing North-East Asian bilateral security frameworks and alliances, but it is arguing for multilateral approaches as complementary and as bringing added flexibility and innovation to dealing with North Korea.

Added to this sense of a degree of qualitative change in the approaches to North Korea, multilateralism is also argued to bring a greater degree of effectiveness. The Bush administration has concluded that previous bilateral approaches have allowed North Korea to abrogate agreements because doing so risked the condemnation of only one state, whereas agreements made within a multilateral forum would deny it this bilateral 'divide and rule' strategy.[7] At the same time, others have expressed the hope that multilateral frameworks would also serve to bind the USA to its own commitments regarding North Korea and prevent any repeat of the process of the collapse of the 1994 Agreed Framework.[8]

Finally, as well as qualitative change in terms of the nature and effectiveness of the response to the North Korean security issue, the growth of multilateralism around the Korean Peninsula is also hoped to have spin-off effects for a readjustment of the security architecture of North-East Asia as a whole. It has recently been argued that the Six-Party Talks, regardless of their ultimate outcome, could form the basis for an institutionalized five- or six-power grouping, or even organization, that would function to deal with future North Korean security and a range of other security issues across North-East Asia.[9]

Japan's new multilateral options?

Japan, as a major state actor with vital security interests on the Korean Peninsula, has also shown a strong degree of attachment to the pursuit of various multilateral approaches towards North Korea. It has contributed to their quantitative expansion as a participant in the Six-Party Talks, as a member of the TCOG, and as a sponsor of the 'Team Samurai' PSI interdiction exercise in Sagami Bay in October 2004. Japanese policy makers and academic commentators similarly view the Six-Party Talks as presenting opportunities for important qualitative change in approaches to the North Korean security issue and to regional security as a whole. Prime Minister Keizo Obuchi first put forward proposals for six-party dialogue in 1997, and Japan has strongly backed the current US-inspired format as a means to provide fresh impetus to and effectiveness for the region in dealing with North Korea – the USA and Japan in their joint foreign ministers' statement of 19 February 2005 agreeing that the best means for a peaceful resolution to the nuclear crisis was for North Korea to immediately re-engage in the Six-Party Talks.[10] The Japanese government also appears to share the conviction that the Six-Party Talks format will contribute to adjustments in the overall security architecture of North-East Asia. Japanese policy makers, in similar fashion to their counterparts in the USA, view the Six-Party Talks and other multilateral initiatives resulting from the North Korean security issue as complementary to the existing security structures of the US–Japan and other regional bilateral alliances, and as additional frameworks that can be assimilated into the Japanese concept of multi-layered security for North-East Asia and for the East Asia region as a whole.[11]

Japanese policy makers, moreover, perceive multilateral frameworks as an additional route by which to pursue their own state's particular diplomatic and security agenda *vis-à-vis* North Korea. The Japanese government's overall policy preference in dealing with the North Korean security issue has been one of engagement,[12] but it has also reserved the option of containment,[13] and this is an option that it has increasingly looked to as bilateral relations have deteriorated over the cases of the abductions. Japan's policy makers have attempted, with a mixed record of consistency and success, to pursue this self-declared policy of 'dialogue and pressure' (recently modified from the previous stance of 'dialogue and deterrence', so suggesting a more active stance in dealing with North Korea). Prime Minister Junichiro Koizumi's bilateral summit diplomacy with North Korea in September 2002 and May 2004 was clearly designed, while holding to the common bottom-line position with the USA that the North Korean nuclear programme must cease, to demonstrate to Washington the importance of persisting with diplomatic approaches.[14] At the same time this diplomacy has also been designed to make a start in tackling the abductions issue in order to free up the domestic constraints on Japan's own diplomacy and rehabilitate it as a more unitary and consistent state actor in Korean Peninsula diplomacy.[15] Simultaneously, Tokyo has ratcheted up its bilateral containment options through the passing of new legislation to enable the independent imposition of sanctions on North Korea, and this has been coupled with alterations in Japanese military security capabilities, including the 2004 revision of the National Defense Program Guidelines, the passing of national emergency legislation, and the decision to introduce ballistic missile defence (BMD).[16]

However, this pursuit of bilateral approaches towards North Korea is not without hazards and limitations. Japanese–North Korean bilateral summitry is clearly not sufficient either to restrain Washington or to put pressure on Pyongyang, and its own national military capabilities, given its lack of offensive or retaliatory weaponry, are clearly incapable of exerting pressure on the North. Indeed, exclusive reliance on bilateral summitry and any failure of this process, as well as the initiation of means to impose bilateral sanctions on North Korea, would pose hazards for Japanese policy makers. This is because it would exacerbate the preferences of some domestic constituencies and their ability to push for a hard-line stance over the abductions issue, regardless of the consequences for Japan's own and regional security.[17]

For the Japanese government, therefore, multilateral frameworks, in conjunction with bilateral ones, offer a potential means to broaden and juggle its options for 'dialogue and pressure' in dealing with North Korea. The Six-Party Talks provide Tokyo for the first time with a direct place at the table in negotiating on Korean Peninsula affairs, as well as a means to encourage Washington to persist with dialogue with North Korea. The talks also lend potential legitimacy to the government's engagement strategies, thereby providing a means for Japanese policy makers to persuade their own domestic constituencies of the need to keep open the option of engagement. For instance, the 2005 Joint Statement stressed the importance of Japan–North Korea bilateral normalization as coordinated with and underpinning the success of the Six-Party Talks process.[18] The TCOG serves a similar function, and the PSI offers a means to leverage Japan's military capabilities, restricted by constitutional prohibitions, in containing North Korean weapons of mass destruction (WMD) and ballistic missile programmes.

A triumph of multilateral form over substance?

From the perspective of the North-East Asian states, there exist persuasive arguments, which are especially strong in the case of the axis of the US–Japanese alliance, for initiating multilateral approaches towards North Korea. These would seem to explain and vindicate the growth in multilateralism since 2003. However, at the same time as these arguments may be influencing the preferences of policy makers in North-East Asia, there are also grounds for pausing to consider whether the arguments put forward to support multilateralism, especially from the US and Japanese side, are really so compelling in practice. It is important to remember that at the same time as the Bush administration urges the importance of the Six-Party Talks and multilateralism in facing down North Korea, it has also been in large part responsible for KEDO falling by the wayside (it was officially wound up from November 2005); that earlier attempts at multilateralism in the shape of the Four-Party Peace Talks failed; and that the Six-Party Talks have a record of stuttering progress, and have so far only made a start, since September 2005, in meeting their own stated objectives.

All this raises initial doubts over whether the arguments relating to the importance of the current forms of multilateralism in dealing with North Korea really are all they are cracked up to be, and raises the key questions that this chapter seeks to investigate. It asks: To what extent has the quantitative growth of multilateral frameworks surrounding the Korean Peninsula in recent years really been accompanied by a durable and fundamental qualitative shift towards multilateral approaches, and, concomitantly, to what extent are the types of multilateral frameworks now extant really capable, now or in the future, of delivering any significantly different approaches from the previous US-led bilateral efforts to deal with the North Korean security issue?

Conceptualizing typologies of multilateralism

Many types of multilateralism exist, all with differing implications for the nature of the cooperation among states that is generated. The most basic definition of multilateralism is the 'practice of coordinating national policies in groups of three or more states'.[19] However, as is well known, analysts of multilateralism have demonstrated that it is not just the existence of multilateral frameworks and the inclusion of a number of states within them that matters, but also the character and actual substance of the cooperation that results from them.[20]

As Figure 8.1 illustrates, and adapting a typology originally used to analyse multilateralism in the Asia–Pacific in the early post-cold war period,[21] four types of multilateralism can be broadly distinguished, depending on the pattern of interstate relations and the degree of institutionalization. The pattern of interstate relations can be assessed along a continuum that stretches from hierarchical to egalitarian, the former assuming that multilateral frameworks are dominated and organized by great powers primarily for their own ends, the latter assuming a more equal distribution of responsibilities among states for organizing the framework and its functions. The degree of institutionalization of cooperation is assessed along a continuum that stretches from the highly formal to the informal, the former assuming the establishment of more formal or routinized mechanisms and even institutions for interaction, and the latter assuming more informal rules and 'soft' institutions.

Hegemonic cooperation refers to a type of multilateralism which is dominated by a hegemonic state that possesses sufficient power to accord a place to other states within the framework, determine the mode of interaction among states, and

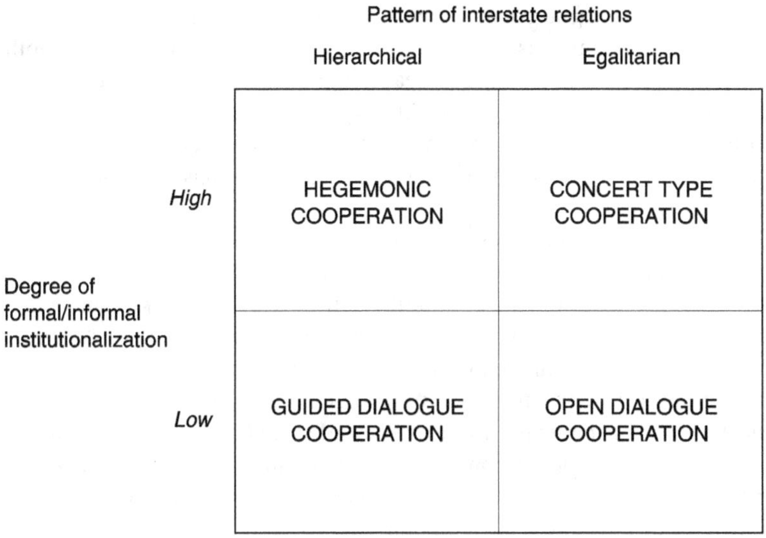

Pattern of interstate relations

	Hierarchical	Egalitarian
High	HEGEMONIC COOPERATION	CONCERT TYPE COOPERATION
Low	GUIDED DIALOGUE COOPERATION	OPEN DIALOGUE COOPERATION

Degree of formal/informal institutionalization

Figure 8.1 A typology of multilateralism in terms of the qualities of cooperation.
Source: Based on Jörn Dosch, 'Asia-Pacific multilateralism and the role of the United States', in Jörn Dosch and Manfred Mols (eds), *International Relations in the Asia–Pacific: New Patterns of Power, Interest and Cooperation*, New York: LIT and St Martin's Press, 2001.

impose the distribution of the costs and benefits upon other states.[22] An ideal type of framework for this is represented by the Warsaw Pact under Soviet domination during the cold war, or the collective self-defence framework of the North Atlantic Treaty Organization (NATO).[23]

Guided dialogue cooperation refers to multilateralism that is usually under the leadership of a great power. The degree of intrusion by the great power is less than it is under hegemonic cooperation. Nevertheless, the great power or hegemon may instigate guided cooperation dialogue in order to deepen its influence over a group of major and small powers in a region. Interaction is usually mediated via relatively tight diplomatic dialogue between the great power and others. An example of guided dialogue cooperation is the role of France and Germany in the very early stages of the formation of the European Union (EU).

Concert type cooperation is multilateralism that revolves around a group of states that perceive themselves to have a relatively equal standing in addressing security responsibilities in a particular issue area or region, and that coordinate their relations through concert diplomacy. The Concert of Europe in the nineteenth century is a historical example.[24] In the contemporary period, the Group of Eight industrialized countries (G8) and the United Nations (UN) Security Council aspire to this role at the global level. Hopes have also been expressed for this type of framework in East Asia.[25]

Finally, *open dialogue cooperation* is a form of multilateralism that is neither hierarchical nor highly institutionalized. All states, whatever their capabilities, are reluctant to be seen to exercise leadership over this type of multilateralism. The most apparent examples of this type are the multilateral cooperative security frameworks of the Organization for Co-operation and Security in Europe (OSCE) and the Association of Southeast Asian Nations (ASEAN) Regional Forum (ARF).

This typology now provides a conceptual toolbox that can be used to probe more effectively the claims of US and other regional policy makers and analysts concerning the development of multilateralism around the Korean Peninsula. It provides a means to gauge more exactly the types of frameworks that have existed around the Korean Peninsula in the past and the present; the continuities or discontinuities in patterns of multilateral interaction; the specific types of cooperation that accompany these frameworks; and the degree to which they are dominated by the great powers, and in particular the USA, in seeking their own security ends. This typology also enables a clearer understanding of the role that Japan has played in promoting multilateral frameworks in relation to North Korea.

Typologies of multilateralism around the Korean Peninsula

If this typology is now applied to the North Korean security issue, it reveals more clearly the characteristics of current developments in multilateralism. That there has been a quantitative growth in the number of frameworks is unchallengeable: at the start of the first Bush administration, the intergovernmental multilateral bodies consisted of KEDO and the TCOG, but since then there have been added the Six-Party Talks, the US–Chinese–North Korean trilateral dialogue, the PSI, the ARF, and increasingly the Asia–Pacific Economic Cooperation (APEC) forum, which have all addressed aspects of the North Korean security issues. This contrasts strongly with the previous history of Korean Peninsula multilateralism, which was largely non-existent, save for the role of the UN in legitimizing the US-led multinational military effort during the Korean War, and the failed Four-Party Peace Talks.

The Six-Party Talks

More revealing, though, is the position these frameworks occupy when plotted against different typologies of multilateralism, as in Figure 8.2.

At first sight, the Six-Party Talks would appear to equate to concert-type cooperation, involving as they do all the major powers of the region – namely, the USA, China, Japan and Russia – attempting to address an important security issue that originates from the insecurity of smaller powers – namely, North and South Korea. But if the actual substance of the Six-Party Talks is examined, then it is doubtful how far this multilateral format can really be ascribed concert-type characteristics.

Pattern of interstate relations

Hierarchical   Egalitarian

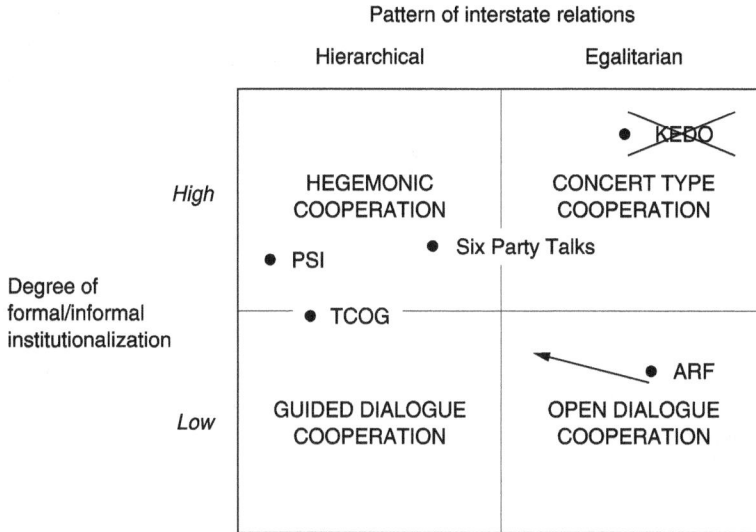

Figure 8.2 A typology of multilateralism in terms of the qualities of cooperation in East Asia since the second Bush administration and 11 September 2001.

Arguably, the Six-Party Talks, for most of their existence, have in fact been closer to a hegemonic form of cooperation. Washington was largely responsible for the inception of the talks, and it took the lead role in coaxing Beijing, and especially a reluctant Moscow, into the talks. Moreover, the impression, especially from the first three rounds of talks, was that the US government viewed them as just another format through which to pursue essentially the same approaches and agenda as it had pursued through previous channels towards Pyongyang, but to do so with a greater cloak of multilateral legitimacy. The Bush administration, as is its wont elsewhere in the region and globally, sought to lead a 'coalition' of states to confront North Korea in the Six-Party Talks,[26] and in particular sought to utilize its existing bilateral alliance ties with Tokyo and Seoul to form its own 'caucus' within the talks.[27] The US design also appears to have been to use the Six-Party Talks as a means to bring Beijing and Moscow on side in its objective of pressuring Pyongyang over its nuclear programme, while at the same time using the multilateral format to counter Chinese and Russian objections to US unilateralism. In terms of the agenda of the talks, Washington clearly dominated the direction of this also, and it has shown limited willingness to utilize the multilateral format of the talks to actually negotiate any significantly new approach towards resolving the nuclear issue. Indeed, it would appear that for most of the course of the first three rounds of talks the US negotiating team had only been empowered by the Bush administration to broach the same negotiating position that it intended to employ towards North Korea regardless of whether the negotiations were in a multilateral format or otherwise.[28]

The position of the other states in the Six-Party Talks would seem to reflect the fact that this is a framework that has often leaned more towards US hegemonic domination than towards concert-type cooperation. The Chinese government appears to have been sceptical of the USA's commitment and objectives to a multilateral approach following Beijing's sponsorship of trilateral talks with North Korea in April 2003, feeling that the USA had utilized this framework more as an attempt to engineer a face-saving formula to get around its previous position that it would not talk with the North Korean government bilaterally, rather than as an attempt to find a fundamentally new forum in which to engage in serious negotiations with Pyongyang over the nuclear issue.[29] The Chinese government saw considerable strategic value in its own role in sponsoring the Six-Party Talks in order to demonstrate its indispensable position as a peace-broker in North-East Asia. But it seems to have demonstrated further scepticism over US proposals for the Six-Party Talks format, and how far this was just another face-saving exercise and how far it was a genuinely new approach to negotiating with North Korea.[30] Nevertheless, Beijing has invested considerable diplomatic effort in attempting to make the Six-Party Talks function by leaning on North Korea to negotiate, trying to keep the process moving despite the hiatus after the third round, and seeking to persuade Washington to engage in genuine give-and-take negotiations. However, despite this investment of diplomatic credibility, Chinese policy makers have remained sceptical about the USA's intentions to utilize the legitimacy of the multilateral format in order to press its own unbending demands, and about how far Beijing and Moscow may be being used as diplomatic proxies for the US strategy towards North Korea.[31] The Russian government, for its part, despite its long-standing enthusiasm for a multilateral resolution to the nuclear issue and its involvement in it in order to re-establish its influence on the Korean Peninsula,[32] appears to be highly sceptical and somewhat detached from the current multilateral exercise.[33]

The above analysis suggests that the Six-Party Talks for much of their course have fallen more into the category of hegemonic cooperation, if not absolute hegemonic domination, than into any other category. The characteristics of the talks do not provide evidence of any significantly qualitatively different or more effective approach to addressing the North Korean nuclear issue. It might be argued that the Six-Party Talks in the first three rounds at the very least instituted a process which led to some gradual change in the positions of the states involved, including that of the USA, thereby mitigating the hegemonic nature of the interaction and bringing about the possibilities of more concert-type cooperation. Certainly, by the third round of the talks the US government had shifted its position in some ways as a result of interaction with other states in the talks, for example, avoiding the use of the term CVID (complete, verifiable and irreversible dismantlement) in the talks in order not to aggravate Pyongyang, and specifying to a greater extent than before the possible security and economic rewards that would be made available to North Korea for an end to its nuclear programme.[34] In this way, the talks were seen to be functioning to tie the USA into a less unilateral approach, and there may have been some satisfaction at this on the part of China and other powers. Similarly, the talks might have been seen to work in the fact that the North Korean regime at times appeared isolated by its own intransigence, especially after the first round, thereby making for a slightly softer approach by Pyongyang in subsequent rounds, and showing the value of multilateralism in moderating its security behaviour;[35] and this is certainly an argument that US policy makers have been fond of making.

Nevertheless, the general conclusion from the first three rounds of the Six-Party Talks has to be that their essential hegemonic, rather than true concert-type nature, hindered their ability to bring a new approach and effectiveness to dealing with North Korea. The governments of China and Russia – the parties that automatically found themselves on the other side of the negotiating divide within the talks, as a result of the fact that US policy makers brought their ready-made caucus to the talks – perceived relatively clearly the US attempt to use the unilateral format to exert its power, and thus were not prepared to go along with its intentions. Chinese policy makers have clearly been frustrated with their North Korean counterparts and willing to pressure them to desist from their nuclear programme, but Beijing may have been equally frustrated with the USA, and in the final calculation it is still not prepared to see Pyongyang coerced into a settlement that only satisfies the US agenda.[36] Hence, as long as the US policy makers attempted to run the Six-Party Talks in the main as a hegemonic multilateral framework to isolate and coerce North Korea, and with the offer of little real give-and-take in negotiations, then Beijing was unlikely to support the framework wholeheartedly. Russian policy makers appear to have similar concerns that the Six-Party Talks are an exercise in US power in the region.[37]

Meanwhile, North Korean negotiators have long perceived more clearly than anyone else that the Six-Party Talks have been a means for Washington to bring forward its same demands, but repackaged in a form of 'pseudo-multilateralism'.[38] It is not surprising that Pyongyang was not prepared to fall for the promises of the Six-Party Talks formula in the early rounds of talks.

Instead, it has only been since the fourth rounds of talks and related shifts in the US negotiating stance that there have been signs of the potential of the Six-Party Talks as more of a concert-type multilateral framework. The Bush administration in its second term, and in need of diplomatic successes given the debacle in Iraq, has adjusted its approach to the Six-Party Talks. The new negotiating team, led by Christopher Hill, Assistant Secretary of State for East Asian and Pacific Affairs, appears to have greater authority than its predecessor to cut a deal with Pyongyang, and has shown greater flexibility in its demands, for instance, dropping the previous US objections to recognizing the North's right to even a peaceful nuclear capacity, and agreeing to respect this right in the September 2005 Joint Statement; and increasing its willingness to meet with North Korean negotiators bilaterally within the Six-Party Talks. In part, this new stance has been brought about by pressure from the other partners of the USA in the Six-Party Talks, thus again supporting the argument that the framework can exercise some minimal multilateral traction on US unilateralism. But, equally importantly, the new US flexibility is the result of the pressures of Iraq, outside the region, which have eroded some of the US hegemonic dominance, rather than actual pressure from within the East Asia region itself or any increased hold of the other involved states on Washington through the Six-Party Talks process.

If Washington continues on this path of flexibility in the Six-Party Talks, then this framework may shift more towards concert-type cooperation, and the Six-Party Talks' purchase in resolving the nuclear issue and constraining the USA may increase. However, as pointed out earlier, the US concessions in the Joint Statement are still small-scale and the real negotiations still lie ahead. It remains to be seen whether the US shift of position within the Six-Party Talks is simply a short-term tactical one to generate some momentum in the negotiations before again reasserting its former negotiating line and hegemonic multilateralism, or whether this is a true cognitive conversion to concert-type multilateralism, learned from interaction with other states. The Bush administration's past record on multilateralism perhaps suggests the former more than the latter, and thus that the Six-Party Talks may once again stall.

Further doubts about the effectiveness of the Six-Party Talks formula arise from the fact that the entire exercise may have proved to be a major diversion from more direct means to negotiate with North Korea.[39]

The Bush administration spent the greater part of its first term attempting to find a coherent approach towards North Korea, and then devoted the remainder of it to initiating the Six-Party Talks as its preferred framework for negotiating with the North. As noted above, in part the multilateral approach may have been a face-saving exercise for the USA, regardless of the rationale of the need to prevent Pyongyang engaging in divide and rule tactics. However, the Six-Party Talks may have also been an exercise in time-wasting, given that it has taken the Bush administration so long to finally construct this approach and the opportunities this has given to the North Korean regime in the meantime to take the wraps off its nuclear programme. The Six-Party Talks may also prove to be a dangerous diversion of policy efforts. The diplomatic credibility that the USA has invested in the Six-Party Talks as its prime vehicle for negotiating with North Korea means that it will be reluctant to give up this format. The likely result is thus further deadlock. Meanwhile, alternative diplomatic formats for dealing with North Korea may remain unexplored, and the latter may be continuing its nuclear programme, or programmes.

Indeed, there has already been one casualty of the Bush administration's fixation on the Six-Party Talks and its reluctance to persist with alternative multilateral frameworks for diplomacy to resolve the North Korean nuclear issue, and that is KEDO. It is possible to argue that KEDO embodies the characteristics of concert type multilateral cooperation more strongly than the Six-Party Talks do. Although KEDO did not include Chinese and Russian participation, and these powers felt aggrieved that they were eventually excluded from this US-inspired framework,[40] the concept itself of a multilateral framework to oversee the provision of technology in order to ensure the cessation of the North Korean nuclear programme did receive their tacit support. Moreover, the presence in KEDO, alongside Japan and South Korea, of a range of other states and interstate organizations (although of varying sizes and contributions, ranging from New Zealand to the EU), and with a set of institutions and rules to govern their cooperation, provided a useful, if not decisive, counterbalance to US influence. The Bush administration's decision to curtail the activities of KEDO has thus spelled the *de facto* end of one platform that might have been used to draw in more states for cooperation and to construct a concert-of-powers-type approach to North Korea.

The TCOG, the PSI and other forms of multilateralism

The other forms of multilateralism that have existed as means to address the North Korean nuclear issue also do not seem likely to produce qualitatively different or more effective frameworks. The TCOG falls into the category of guided dialogue cooperation, involving as it does the USA and its alliance partners in relatively close diplomatic discussions. The TCOG has been a US-led exercise from its inception under the Clinton administration, designed to coordinate the sequencing of each of the various bilateral US, Japanese and South Korean initiatives towards North Korea, and has functioned relatively effectively in this regard. The governments of Japan and South Korea also felt that they had a stake in the TCOG because, even though Washington set the agenda, they were able to feed their own opinions into US strategy.[41] However, under the Bush administration the TCOG's functions have been altered with the result that it has gravitated more towards the hegemonic quadrant of the multilateral typologies.

The Bush administration in its early stages, and following internal policy divisions over the role of the TCOG, maintained the framework, but then increasingly utilized it as a means to convey information about its own bilateral policy in the expectation that Japan and South Korea would follow, rather than for genuine consultation with its bilateral allies. The result was that Japanese policy makers, and in particular South Korean policy makers, became frustrated at how little influence the trilateral dialogue really had upon US policy.[41] Moreover, the increasing tensions during 2001 in Japanese–South Korean relations over the history issue, and the fact that their policy approaches towards engagement differed from those of the USA, did not assist the functioning of the TCOG.

Since the middle stages of the Bush administration, the TCOG has recovered its stability and moved to a less public format, concentrating increasingly on formulating a joint approach to the Six-Party Talks and thus creating a *'de facto*, allied caucus' within the multilateral dialogue framework.[42] In this sense, although the governments of Japan and South Korea have clearly not been entirely willing to submit to Washington's bidding in the TCOG and have pursued their own distinct bilateral policies towards North Korea, the TCOG as a multilateral framework, rather than serving to bind US policy, has functioned to augment US influence in the format of the Six-Party Talks.

Meanwhile, it is not only the TCOG as a multilateral framework that has worked to empower rather than constrain the particular US policy approach towards North Korea. Since the events of 11 September 2001, Washington in hegemonic fashion has expressed renewed interest in the ARF and adjusted its agenda to focus on transnational terrorism, but it has also pushed for the endorsement of its Six-Party Talks formula within ARF discussions and statements since 2003.[44] As for the PSI, this is a clear exercise in hegemonic multilateralism. It is in fact nothing more than an ad hoc 'coalition of the willing' involving a selection of regional states (Japan, Australia and Singapore) under US leadership and serving largely US-dominated objectives.

Hegemonic multilateralism, the North Korean security issue and North-East Asian security

From the above it is apparent that the quantitative growth in multilateralism in North-East Asia resulting from the North Korean security issue has not been accompanied as yet by any significant qualitative change in approaches to the issue itself. The Six-Party Talks, with the exception of the very latest round, have veered more towards a form of US-directed hegemonic multilateralism, the TCOG has not functioned to any great extent to influence US policy, and the PSI is essentially a coalition of the willing. The fact that most extant forms of multilateralism are hegemonic in nature raises further questions about their efficacy for addressing the North Korean issue and their adaptation for other purposes in North-East Asian security.

The Six-Party Talks are unlikely to succeed fully as long as the US government retains its inclination to thrust forward its own and unchanging agenda regarding North Korea, but to do this with a veneer of multilateral legitimacy, and without sufficient consultation with, and in some cases in contravention of the interests of, the other major powers. North Korea clearly will not 'buy' this type of multilateral format, especially if Washington fails to build on the trend of the last round of talks and does not significantly shift its negotiating position. The other format of the TCOG may enhance US influence in the Six-Party Talks, but is not likely to enhance the influence of the Japanese and South Korean allies over the USA. The PSI may be a useful coalition for interdicting North Korean WMD exports, but as long as it remains a group of core US allies then it is unlikely to further multilateralize to include other states such as China or the non-aligned ASEAN states and provide a more effective means to address proliferation.[45]

The conclusion is thus that the recent developments in multilateralism have produced no great qualitative or effective change in approaches to dealing with North Korea – in fact, as in the case of the Six-Party Talks, in their current form they are arguably inappropriate and diversionary mechanisms that may hinder the process of negotiating with it.

All this raises doubts about the prospects of a platform such as the Six-Party Talks being used to construct a broader security mechanism in North-East Asia. Chinese and Russian policy makers are clearly not interested in signing on to frameworks that are largely dominated by the USA and that may be incompatible with their interests. Even South Korean and Japanese policy makers have shown discontent with the US attempts to engineer multilateral frameworks such as the TCOG to serve primarily its own policy.[46]

Japan's diplomatic and security policy and multilateralism

The Japanese role in bringing about qualitative change in addressing the North Korean security issue and in supporting North-East Asian security through multilateralism, as well diversifying its own diplomatic and security policy towards North Korea, appears equally doubtful. The Japanese government, as noted previously, has played an important role in participating in the quantitative expansion of multilateral frameworks, but because these frameworks are predominantly hegemonic in nature, the main Japanese input has been to reinforce US-led approaches towards North Korea.

Tokyo, seeking its own direct voice in Korean Peninsula affairs, has backed the US formula of the Six-Party Talks, and functioned largely to support US influence within the various frameworks as part of the US–Japanese–South Korean trilateral caucus. In the meantime, although it fought a limited rearguard resistance against the US stoppage of heavy fuel oil deliveries in November 2002 and the suspension of the KEDO project to supply North Korea with a light-water reactor (LWR) in early 2003, Tokyo has proved powerless to utilize the TCOG framework as a multilateral means to prevent the *de facto* end of the KEDO multi-lateral framework (Tokyo, after initial hesitation, having arguably become a strong convert to KEDO as serving its essential security needs). In other instances the TCOG has provided Japanese policy makers with only occasional opportunities to impose on their US counterparts their preferred policy options with regard to North Korea. The governments of Japan and South Korea, despite failing to convince Washington not to wind up the LWR project, did successfully combine at the January 2003 TCOG to nudge the USA towards acknowledging that even though it would not offer an explicit quid pro quo of concessions it would still consider dialogue with North Korea over its nuclear programme. In many other instances, though, as outlined above, the TCOG has not functioned to constrain the USA or to push it towards the Japanese line of enhanced emphasis on engagement as well as containment.

Similarly, the Japanese participation in the PSI project has served to strengthen the US ability to mobilize coalitions against North Korea. Japanese policy makers have played the issue carefully, viewing the PSI as a means to enhance the options of containment, but showing some reticence at first in hosting exercises in 2004 for fear that this would endanger Koizumi's ongoing bilateral diplomacy with North Korea, as well as inviting criticism from other East Asian states. Nevertheless, by committing itself to the PSI, Tokyo has further encouraged Washington in its hardline approach towards North Korea and created the expectation that Japan will participate in containment. Hence, multilateralism in this instance may only serve to lock Japan further into the US approach towards North Korea.

The Japanese participation in the enhanced number of multilateral frameworks may therefore not have enhanced Tokyo's diplomatic and security options. The Japanese participation, rather than boosting frameworks that might act as a counterweight to US influence, is actually augmenting its ally's influence. The Japanese government, certainly, can utilize the Six-Party Talks as a means for more direct dialogue with North Korea over contentious bilateral issues, such as the abductions, and can even use the format as a means to berate North Korea. However, the Six-Party Talks, given that they centre around US policy aims, are no substitute for progress in the Japan–North Korea normalization talks. The latter have continued on their faltering track since Koizumi's 2004 summit meeting in Pyongyang, are currently on a downward trajectory, and are unlikely to pull out of this until Japanese domestic opinion on the abductions issue is assuaged. The result is that Japan is deprived of functioning bilateral channels to respond to the North Korean security issue but cannot look to multilateral channels to provide any relief from this. Even if Japanese policy makers look to achieve a flexible balance between policies of engagement and containment, they are now on bilateral and multilateral paths that are converging towards containment, thereby undermining Japan's preferred default strategy, as devised by Prime Minister Koizumi, and as outlined in the beginning of this chapter.

Finally, it is also apparent that Japan's presence in the Six-Party Talks has at times made an already difficult format even less likely to succeed and to transform itself into a new approach. Japan's need to raise the abductions issue in the talks in order to satisfy domestic political pressures has clearly provided a pretext for North Korea to impede progress in the talks. At the same time it is clear that the abductions issue has genuinely been seen in China as a not entirely helpful distraction within the talks. Hence, Tokyo is involved in a dynamic that means that it not only supports the US line in the talks, but actually creates obstacles to attempts by other powers, and especially China, to create forward momentum that might help the talks to progress beyond the hegemonic domination of the USA.

In sum, therefore, the Japanese support for hegemonic forms of multilateralism under the strong aegis of the USA has a mixed record of assisting Tokyo's own diplomatic interests *vis-à-vis* North Korea: it creates some avenues for dealing with North Korea, but these are limited, and ultimately the current forms of multilateralism serve to bind Japan to the US position, hinder attempts at balanced policies of engagement and containment, and stunt the prospects of multilateral frameworks evolving into qualitatively different forms of cooperation.

In the meantime, the irony is that, despite an avowed Japanese interest in multilateralism to address the North Korea security issue, its security policy in general is becoming more wedded than ever to bilateral means. The upgrading of military capabilities, the interoperability of the US–Japan alliance, and the adoption of BMD, all in large part in reaction to the perceived North Korean threat, are making for Japan's increasingly inextricable integration into the US bilateral alliance system in North-East Asia.[47]

Conclusion: the future of multilateralism and North Korea

The Korean Peninsula is not seeing the growth of qualitatively different approaches brought about by the switch to multilateralism, but rather the perpetuation of hegemonic-inspired multilateral frameworks, that do not offer sufficient benefits to many of the crucial participants. The Six-Party Talks do not as yet match the aspirations of the participants and thus are unlikely to succeed in their own objectives or to evolve to meet the same or different security challenges. In fact, they may be a diversion – or, even worse, a cul-de-sac or dead end – which policy actors are unable to reverse out of because of their investment of face and credibility in attempts to find a resolution to the nuclear crisis. Other multi-lateral formats merely reinforce the US dominance over the security agenda, and thus are unlikely to provide a means to broker new forms of addressing the North Korean issue.

Likewise, the Japanese participation in multilateral frameworks has brought only limited diplomatic benefits. It has enhanced Japan's influence by providing Tokyo with a place at the negotiating table, but once it is actually there it forms part of the same US-led coalition and hinders the process of taking the talks forward. The lack of functioning bilateral and multilateral routes to engage North Korea is increasingly forcing Tokyo back on its containment options and contributing to the lack of flexibility in ensuring its security interests.

Does this all mean, therefore, that multilateral approaches towards North Korea are futile and doomed to failure? Nicholas Eberstadt, for instance, has argued that the Six-Party Talks are similar to forms of inter-war conference diplomacy which ultimately failed because of idealist hopes that concerned states could negotiate with intransigent and revisionist powers.[48] The degree to which nego-tiation, multilateral or bilateral, can succeed with North Korea is an imponder-able, largely depending on the interpretation of the evidence of past North Korean behaviour, or (in the case of some policy makers) an ideological and normative view of the North Korean regime. If it is assumed – as this chapter assumes, on the basis of past evidence[49] – that negotiation with North Korea can succeed, then the question to be posed is not whether negotiations should be attempted, but whether the multilateral format is the correct one.

As noted above, the hegemonic cooperation approach camouflaged by the seem-ing concert-type multilateral approach of the Six-Party Talks is not the appropriate format. Arguably, an adjusted format that involves a genuine concert-type approach and genuine negotiations is more appropriate, and it may also be the case that the current fixation on multilateralism as the key to resolving the North Korean nuclear issue needs to be bypassed in certain instances in favour of a return to bilateral talks.

It can be envisaged that US–North Korean bilateral talks, which Pyongyang has always called for, might be a strong starting point for achieving genuine negotiations, reassurances and a 'grand bargain' for North Korea, and progress on the nuclear issue.[50] At the same time, these bilateral talks could be supported by a coordinated multilateral, concert-type cooperation forum that would feed into the bilateral negotiating positions of both sides and endorse the decisions of the bilateral talks regarding security assurances and economic assistance, thereby preventing defections from agreements. This formula could even be achieved within a re-jigged current format of the Six-Party Talks as a face-saving measure, but the crucial point is not just bilateral contacts between the governments of USA and North Korea but also genuine negotiations on both sides. In this way, rather than the present obsession with the form of the talks, real substance could be given to the talks, and real hope to the promise of a more multilateral security architecture in North-East Asia. Washington in the fourth round of the Six-Party Talks and in the Joint Statement of September 2005 may finally be inching towards this position, but how far it will fully shift in this direction is a crucial question yet to be answered in future negotiations.

Notes

1 Nautilus Institute, 'Special report, February 14th, 2005: DPRK "manufactured" nuclear weapons, to "suspend" 6-way talks for "indefinite period", Korean Central Broadcasting Station statement', available HTTP: <http://www.nautilus.org/napsnet/sr/2005/0513A_KCBS.html>.

2 Japanese Ministry of Foreign Affairs, 'Joint statement of the fourth round of the Six-Party Talks', 19 September 2005, available HTTP: <http://www.mofa.go.jp/region/asia-paci/n_korea/6party/joint0509.html>.

3 International Crisis Group, *North Korea: Where Next for the Nuclear Talks?* Seoul and Brussels: International Crisis Group, 2004; and Institute for Foreign Policy Analysis, *Building Multi-Party Capacity for a WMD-Free Korea: An IFPA Workshop Report*, June 2005, available HTTP: <http://www.nautilus.org/napsnet/sr/2005/0558IFPA.pdf>.

4 Charles Krauthammer, 'The unipolar moment', *Foreign Affairs*, 70/1, 1990/1, pp. 11–33.

5 Don Oberdorfer, *The Two Koreas: A Contemporary History*, London: Warner Books, 1997, pp. 385–6.

6 US Department of State, 'Regional implications of the changing nuclear equation on the Korean Peninsula', Testimony by James A. Kelly, Assistant Secretary of State for East Asian and Pacific Affairs, before the Senate Foreign Relations Committee, Washington, DC, 12 March 2003, p. 70, available HTTP: <http://www.state.gov/p/eap/rls/rm/2003/18661.htm>.

7 Ibid.

8 Peter van Ness, *The North Korean Nuclear Crisis: Four-plus-two – An Idea Whose Time Has Come*, Research School of Pacific and Asian Studies, Australian National University, 2003, p. 17; and Peter van Ness, 'The North Korean nuclear crisis: Four-plus-two – An idea whose time has come', in Mel Gurtov and Peter van Ness (eds), *Confronting the Bush Doctrine: Critical Views from the Asia–Pacific*, London: Routledge, 2005, pp. 242–59.

9 Francis Fukuyama, 'Re-envisioning Asia', *Foreign Affairs*, 84/1, 2005, pp. 75–88; and James L. Schoff, Charles M. Perry and Jacquelyn K. Davies, *Building Six-Party Capacity for a WMD-Free Korea*, Herndon, Va.: Brassey's Inc., 2005.

10 Japanese Ministry of Foreign Affairs, 'Joint statement on North Korea', 19 February 2005, available HTTP: <http://www.mofa.go.jp/region/n-america/us/fmv0502/n_korea.html>.

11 Japanese Ministry of Foreign Affairs, *Diplomatic Bluebook 2003*, Tokyo: Ministry of Foreign Affairs, 2003; and Kuniko Ashizawa, 'Japan's approach toward Asian regional security: From "hub-and-spoke" bilateralism to "multi-tiered"', *Pacific Review*, 16/3, 2003, pp. 361–82.

12 Christopher W. Hughes, *Japan's Economic Power and Security: Japan and North Korea*, London: Routledge, 1999; and Kenji Hiramatsu, 'Sori hocho niccho Pyonyangu sengen shomei e no michi', *Gaiko Foramu*, 173, 2002, p. 23.

13 Richard J. Samuels, 'Payback time: Japan–North Korea economic relations', in Choong-Yong Ahn, Nicholas Eberstadt and Young-Sun Lee (eds), *A New International Engagement Framework for North Korea? Contending Perspectives*, Washington, DC: Korea Economic Institute of America, 2004, pp. 324–8; and Michael H. Armacost,

'Japan: Tilting closer to Washington', in Richard J. Ellings and Aaron L. Friedberg (eds), *Strategic Asia 2003–04: Fragility and Crisis*, Washington, DC: National Bureau of Asian Research, 2003, pp. 87–91.

14 Katsuyuki Yakushiji, *Gaimusho: Gaikoryoku kyoka e no michi*, Tokyo: Iwanami Shoten, 2003, pp. 17–18; and Mike M. Mochizuki, 'Japan: Between alliance and autonomy', in Ashley J. Tellis and Michael Wills (eds), *Strategic Asia 2004–05: Confronting Terrorism in the Pursuit of Power*, Washington, DC: National Bureau of Asian Research, 2004, pp. 118–20.

15 Christopher W. Hughes, 'Japan and North Korea relations from the North–South summit to the Koizumi–Kim summit', *Asia–Pacific Review*, 9/2, 2002, pp. 61–78.

16 Christopher W. Hughes, *Japan's Re-emergence as a 'Normal' Military Power*, Adelphi Paper 368-9, Oxford: Oxford University Press for the International Institute for Strategic Studies (IISS), 2004; Christopher W. Hughes, 'Japan: Japanese military modernization in search of a "normal" military role', in Ashley J. Tellis and Michael Wills (eds), *Strategic Asia 2005–06: Military Modernization in an Era of Uncertainty*, Washington, DC: National Bureau of Asian Research, 2005, pp. 102–34; or Christopher W. Hughes, 'Japan–North Korea relations and the political economy of sanctions', unpublished paper presented at the JSPS–University of Hokkaido-University of Tokyo workshop on The Political Economy of Remittances in Northeast Asia, Tokyo, 15 January 2005.

17 Hughes, 'Japan–North Korea relations and the political economy of sanctions'.

18 Japanese Ministry of Foreign Affairs, 'Joint statement on the fourth round of the Six-Party Talks'.

19 Robert Keohane, 'Multilateralism: An agenda for research', *International Journal*, 45/4, 1990, p. 731.

20 John Ruggie, 'Multilateralism: The anatomy of an institution', *International Organization*, 46/3, 1992, p. 556.

21 Jörn Dosch, 'Asia–Pacific multilateralism and the role of the United States', in Jörn Dosch and Manfred Mols (eds), *International Relations in the Asia–Pacific: New Patterns of Power, Interest and Cooperation*, New York: LIT and St Martin's Press, 2001, pp. 87–110.

22 Dosch, 'Asia–Pacific multilateralism', p. 91; and David Kang, 'Hierarchy and stability in Asian international relations', in G. John Ikenberry and Michael Mastanduno (eds), *International Relations Theory and the Asia–Pacific*, New York: Columbia University Press, 2003, p. 166.

23 Steve Weber, 'Shaping the postwar balance of power: Multilateralism in NATO', *International Organization*, 46/3, 1992, pp. 633–80.

24 Richard B. Elrod, 'The Concert of Europe: a fresh look at an international system', *International Organization*, 28/2, 1976, pp. 159–74.

25 Amitav Acharya, 'A Concert of Asia?', *Survival*, 41/3, 1999, pp. 84–101.

26 US Department of State, 'North Korea's legacy of missed opportunities', Remarks by Mitchell B. Reiss, Director of Policy Planning, to the Heritage Foundation, Washington, DC, 12 March 2004, available HTTP: <http://www.state.gov/s/p/rem/30363.htm>.

27 James L. Schoff, *First Interim Report: The Evolution of the TCOG as a Diplomatic Tool*, Washington, DC: Institute for Foreign Policy Analysis, 2004, p. 20.

28 William Dobson, 'Failure to communicate: administration hawks raise the bar in talks over North Korea', *Newsweek*, 12 January 2004, p. 22.

29 International Institute for Strategic Studies, *North Korea's Weapons Programmes: A Net Assessment*, Basingstoke: IISS/Palgrave Macmillan, 2004, p. 20.

30 Peter Hayes, 'Multilateral mantra and North Korea', Nautilus Institute, 20 February 2004, available HTTP: <http://www.nautilus.org/DPRKBriefingBook/multilateralTalks/PHMultilateralMantra.html>.

31 Adam Ward, 'China and America: Trouble ahead?', *Survival*, 45/3, 2003, p. 49.

32 Clay Moltz, 'Russian policy on the North Korea nuclear crisis', April 2003, available HTTP: <http://www.nautilus.org/DPRKBriefingBook/russia/ruspol.htm>.

33 Alexander Zhebin, 'The Bush Doctrine, Russia and Korea', in Gurtov and van Ness (eds), *Confronting the Bush Doctrine: Critical Views from the Asia–Pacific*, pp. 143–7; and Alexandre Y. Mansourov, 'Russian–North Korean relations and the prospects for multilateral conflict resolution on the Korean Peninsula', in Choong-Yong Ahn, Nicholas Eberstadt and Young-Sun Lee (eds), *A New International Engagement Framework for North Korea? Contending Perspectives*, Washington, DC: Korea Economic Institute of America, 2004, p. 363.

34 B. C. Koh, 'Six Party Talks: Round three', 2004, available HTTP: <http://www.nautilus.org/fora/security/0426A_Koh.html>.

35 Hajime Izumi, 'Forward motion in talks with Pyongyang', *Japan Echo*, 31/3, 2004, pp. 34–5.

36 Peter Hayes, 'Special report: Bush's bipolar disorder and the looming failure of multilateral talks with North Korea', 2003, available HTTP: <http://www.nautilus.org/DPRKBriefingBook/multilateralTalks/Hayes_10.html>; and Hayes, 'Multilateral mantra and North Korea'.

37 Mansourov, 'Russian–North Korean relations'.

38 Krauthammer, 'The unipolar moment'.

39 Aidan Foster-Carter, 'The Six-Party failure', PFO 05-16A, 17 February 2005, available HTTP: <http://www.nautilus.org/fora/security/0516A_Carter.html>.

40 Alexander Zhebin, 'A political history of Soviet–North Korea nuclear cooperation', in James Clay Moltz and Alexandre Y. Mansourov (eds), *The North Korean Nuclear Program: Security, Strategy, and New Perspectives from Russia*, London: Routledge, 2000, p. 34; Evgeniy P. Bazhanov, 'Russian views of the Agreed Framework and Four-Party Talks', in Moltz and Mansourov (eds), *The North Korean Nuclear Program*, pp. 225–6; and Joel S. Wit, Daniel B. Poneman and Robert L. Gallucci, *Going Critical: The First North Korean Nuclear Crisis*, Washington, DC: Brookings Institution Press, 2004, p. 343.

41 Schoff, *First Interim Report*, pp. 7–10.

42 Ibid., p. 14.

43 Ibid., p. 20.

44 ASEAN, 'Chairman's Statement, The tenth Meeting of ASEAN Regional Forum, Phnom Penh, 18 June 2003', available HTTP: <http://www.aseansec.org/14845.htm>; and ASEAN, 'Chairman's statement, the eleventh Meeting of ASEAN Regional Forum, Jakarta, 2 July 2004', available HTTP: <http://www.aseansec.org/16245.htm>.

45 Mark J. Valencia, *The Proliferation Security Initiative: Making Waves in Asia*, Adelphi Paper 376, London: Routledge/IISS, 2005, pp. 71–3.

46 Schoff, *First Interim Report*.

47 Hughes, *Japan's Re-emergence as a 'Normal' Military Power*.

48 Nicholas Eberstadt, 'Conference diplomacy, all over again', 6 July 2004, available HTTP: <http://www.nautilus.org/fora/security/0425B_Eberstadt.html>.

49 Hughes, *Japan's Economic Power and Security*.

50 Michael O'Hanlon and Mike Mochizuki, *Crisis on the Korean Peninsula: How to Deal with a Nuclear North Korea*, New York: McGraw Hill, 2003, pp. 7–8.

Index

Notes are indicated by the letter n.

For Product Safety Concerns and Information please contact our EU
representative GPSR@taylorandfrancis.com
Taylor & Francis Verlag GmbH, Kaufingerstraße 24, 80331 München, Germany